ALWAYS CHANGE
A LOSING GAME

To contact Dr. Posen for speaking engagements or seminars, please call or write:

David B. Posen, MD
1235 Trafalgar Road
Suite 406
Oakville, ON • L6H 3P1 • Canada

Telephone: (905) 844-0744
Toll-free: (1-800) 806-2307
Fax: (905) 844-4540
E-mail: david@davidposen.com
Web site: www.davidposen.com
Twitter: @drdavidposen

4th Edition

ALWAYS CHANGE A LOSING GAME

Winning Strategies for Work, Home and Health

DAVID POSEN, MD

FIREFLY BOOKS

A FIREFLY BOOK

Published by Firefly Books Ltd. 2013

First printing

Publisher Cataloging-in-Publication Data (U.S.)
Posen, David B.
    Always change a losing game : winning strategies for work, home and health /
David B. Posen, MD.
4th ed.
[304] p. : Includes index.
Summary: The ultimate step-by-step guide to make positive personal changes, such as conquering compulsive eating, addiction to caffeine or being stuck in an unhappy relationship.
ISBN-13: 978-1-77085-179-5 (pbk.)
1. Change (Psychology). 2. Self-actualization (Psychology). I. Title.
158.1 dc23   BF637.C4P674 2013

Library and Archives Canada Cataloguing in Publication
Posen, David B.
    Always change a losing game : winning strategies for work, home and health /
David B. Posen. — 4th ed.
Includes index.
ISBN 978-1-77085-179-5
1. Change (Psychology). 2. Self-actualization (Psychology).
I. Title.
BF637.C4P67 2013   158.1   C2013-901225-7

Published in the United States by
Firefly Books (U.S.) Inc.
P.O. Box 1338, Ellicott Station
Buffalo, New York 14205

Published in Canada by
Firefly Books Ltd.
50 Staples Avenue, Unit 1
Richmond Hill, Ontario L4B 0A7

Cover: Gareth Lind/LINDdesign
Interior design and layout: Interrobang Graphic Design Inc.

Printed in Canada

The publisher greatly acknowledges the financial support for our publishing program by the Government of Canada through the Canada Book Fund as administered by the Department of Canadian Heritage.

To my beloved father, Harry Posen,
who taught us about values and integrity
by quiet example

and

To my remarkable mother, Ida Yudashkin Posen,
a woman well ahead of her time
but who died much too soon.

Contents

Acknowledgments

THE PREPARATION OF THIS BOOK WAS A LONG and collaborative process during which many people touched my life in significant ways. I wish to thank:

Shirley Molot for first (and repeatedly) urging me to write a book;

Malcolm Lester for giving me early guidance and frequent direction;

Rick Winchell for helping me with my proposal and media training;

Dr. Jill Harkaway for giving me early encouragement and, later, a much-needed final kick;

Drs. Peter Norlin and Shelley Posen for reading early draft chapters and giving valuable, timely feedback;

Tony McLean and Dr. Andy Wilson for wading through several early drafts;

Dr. Terry Riley, Joanne Riley and Dr. Robbie Campbell for reviewing the full manuscript and giving helpful suggestions;

Judy Knapp, my receptionist, for reading every word of every draft and being a constant cheering section at every step along the way;

Beverley Slopen, my agent, for her teaching and guidance and for having faith in me and my project from our very first meeting;

Jennifer Glossop, my editor, for finding the book carefully hidden in my massive manuscript and for patiently, always cheerfully, helping me extract it;

Stephen Prudhomme and Bruce Squires at the CMA Publications Department for showing interest and confidence in the book and for sending it, with their endorsement, to Key Porter;

Dr. Matthew Budd, my mentor in the field of stress reduction, for directing my learning during the early formative years;

Drs. Paul Watzlawick and Bob Shaw, whose writing and teaching were invaluable to me in my early training;

Friends and colleagues too numerous to mention by name, whose stories and insights appear throughout the book;

Steve Posen, my brother, lifelong teacher and dearest friend, for generating the title of this book and countless other pieces of wisdom;

Karen Davidman, my twin sister and soulmate, whose constant support and enthusiasm for all my endeavors have meant so much to me;

My wonderful wife Susan and our children Jaime and Andrew for their endless patience during many late suppers and lost Saturdays, for their excitement at the completion of each stage of the book and for the joy with which they have filled my life;

And my patients for their trust and for sharing their lives and struggles with me, from which I learned and was enriched immeasurably.

Preface

*A*LWAYS *CHANGE A LOSING GAME* began as a labor of love, a chance to share ideas I'd developed and to tell stories that my patients and audiences had found helpful. It's come a long way since then. It is now in its 11th printing, has sold on four continents and has been translated into other languages.

The success of any book depends on many things. In this case, the fact that stress is such a widespread and pervasive problem is one of them. If anything, the book is more relevant and necessary than ever. Sadly, people today are really struggling and looking for answers. They're feeling a lack of control. The book gives hope and encouragement because it focuses on all the things we *can* control—primarily the way we think, the way we behave and the lifestyle choices we make. It illustrates my belief that "we have more control than we think."

I've received wonderful feedback about this book over the years—often from total strangers. The most common phrase I've heard is: "Your book changed my life!" An author can't ask for more than that. As a result, it became a word-of-mouth book, with people recommending it, lending it to friends and giving it as a gift. Health care professionals (doctors and therapists) played a huge role by enthusiastically suggesting it to clients, and it has found its way onto reading lists at universities, in hospitals and in other courses.

The book was purposefully written in everyday language to make it both easy to read and reassuring in tone. People tell me it's warm, friendly and non-threatening. Many have said: "You write just like you talk" and "I could hear your voice as I was reading."

I've always enjoyed telling stories and I'm told the stories *make* this book. Readers relate to the information and understand the concepts better because they're illustrated by real examples. Many have said: "I saw myself on practically every page." One reason the anecdotes resonate is that they're about ordinary people and everyday situations. Success stories about individuals who became CEOs and champions are inspiring but often hard to identify with. My examples are about patients and folks I know (including myself) who conquered more mundane challenges. Readers have been able to connect and say, "Hey, *I* can do *that*!" Then they've applied the suggestions and found that they work.

Many people framed their comments with the metaphor of the title: "I realized I was playing a lot of losing games" or "I'm playing a losing game and I want to fix it." The connection to games and sports appeals to a lot of people. It also provides a fresh approach for many therapists— one of whom was working with convicted felons from the court system who asked if she could use my model with her clients because "I've tried everything else and nothing really hooks them. They'll be able to relate to *this*."

The book found a wide audience because stress is not its only focus. It deals with health, relationships, problem solving, self-esteem and productivity among other topics. And it explains *how* to make changes in your life when what you're doing isn't working out.

I thank you, the reader, for choosing to pick up this book and hope it will help to change *your* life.

Introduction
Pre-Game Warm-Up

THIS BOOK IS ABOUT MAKING CHANGES. In it I hope to show you that change is necessary, beneficial and easier than you think. It is not something to be afraid of.

Years ago, when I played tennis, I would stand at the baseline and hit the ball as hard as I could. I lost a lot of games that way. One day my brother suggested I play the net and take the offensive. I was reluctant to do that since volleying wasn't one of my strengths. That's when he pointed out that, since I wasn't winning anyway, I really didn't have much more to lose.

"Always change a losing game," he said.

That sounded reasonable so I gave it a try. Remarkably, my play improved.

I soon realized that this wisdom also applies to everyday life. How often had I continued to do things that weren't working (like spinning my tires when I was stuck in snow and just sinking deeper into the drifts)? How many times had I watched my patients and friends fail at diets or mismanage money, even though they were "replaying" previous behavior? Using the sports analogy as a touchstone, I began to change my own

Patient: Doctor, it hurts when I do that.
Doctor: Then stop doing that.
HENNY YOUNGMAN

"game" (including a career switch at age forty-two) and to suggest that my patients do the same. It got great results. People started to take control of their lives, to feel better about themselves and to relieve stress by changing basic aspects of their behavior and thinking.

"Always change a losing game" became my motto for success. We *all* play losing games at times. A losing game is simply a way of acting or thinking that is not working or is costing more than it's worth (like using

$5.00 worth of gas to save $3.00 on a purchase across town). Losing games like procrastination or eating poorly are very common. When my patients play losing games, I urge them to see that the logic from sports applies to everyday situations and can bring the same positive results.

Please note that, by comparing daily events to sports, I do not intend to trivialize life. Nor am I trying to exalt games and sports by suggesting they are as important as our lives. However, the principles that apply in sports often apply to life—and the lessons are easier to see and less threatening to acknowledge in that context.

Take the following example, where a sports principle helped a patient with a business problem. He was a "take charge" boss who barked orders at his staff and got grumbling and poor performance as a result. I suggested a lighter tone might work better to motivate his employees and improve their productivity.

To illustrate this suggestion I compared his management style to hitting a golf ball. When I first took up golf, I figured the best way to get power was to swing as hard as I could. I soon learned my logic was flawed. I hit the ball erratically, often topping it or slicing into the trees. The poor shots were as infuriating as they were puzzling. A friend suggested I swing a little slower and not try to "muscle" the ball. Lo and behold, the ball went straight and pretty far. I not only replaced a losing game with a winning one, I learned another important lesson: often in sports, as in life, less is more. Force doesn't always win.

My patient got the message and he applied it immediately. By softening his approach at work, being more courteous and giving praise when warranted, he found the mood in the office improved immeasurably—and so did the output and the bottom line. A change produced better results.

There are different ways for change to occur. Take the 1977 Grey Cup football game. The field at Montreal's Olympic Stadium was so icy that neither team could get their footing. In the third quarter, the Montreal Alouettes took command of the game and won convincingly. Their secret was revealed after the game. At half-time they had taken all their players' shoes and inserted dozens of staples in the soles. These gave them the traction they needed to overwhelm the Edmonton Eskimos, who were still slipping and sliding all over the field. In this case the team won by *doing* something different.

Winning can also result from *thinking* differently. In 1954, Roger Bannister ran the first four-minute mile in history. Almost immediately dozens of other runners broke the four-minute barrier, not because they could suddenly run faster but because they changed their *attitude* about how fast humans could run. By changing their beliefs about what was possible, runners were able to break through a psychological barrier that had stood for generations.

Change and Risking

At times, "changing a losing game" requires vision and risk taking. A dramatic example from recent world history involves Anwar Sadat, former president of Egypt. When a decade of fighting with Israel failed to regain Egyptian sovereignty over the Sinai Desert, Sadat reversed his strategy of war and made a conciliatory overture that stunned the world. His historic trip to Jerusalem in 1977 led to a peace treaty with Israel and the return of the Sinai to his control. His adversarial strategy was a "losing game." So he changed his approach and won back through negotiation what force had failed to achieve.

Another kind of risk taking involves intimate relationships and expressing feelings. A middle-aged woman told me how insecure she felt about her mother's affection and approval. She never felt close to her mother, although she had a "fantastic" relationship with her father. In fact, she felt neglected and rejected. To make matters worse, her mother had always favored her younger brother. Throughout the years, she had sought her mother's favor by being a model daughter and a pleaser. But she never got the response she was seeking.

In our discussion, I wondered if the close ties with her father had caused her mother to feel left out. It could even explain why she had gravitated toward the younger brother. Maybe, I suggested, her mother needed *her* approval more than the reverse. The daughter had always been reserved with her mother, not showing affection for fear of being rejected. People commonly protect themselves in this way. I asked if she'd ever told her mother she loved her, and she said no.

"*Do* you love your mother?" I asked.

"Of course I do," she replied.

"Then why don't you tell her?" I suggested. "Not to get anything back, but because it's true and it would be nice for her to hear."

The result was dramatic. Her mother, who was then in her seventies, hugged her and said: "I love you too. But I don't know how to say it." This moment opened a whole new chapter in their relationship. And the key was to give up a strategy that wasn't working and simply speak the truth. But to do that, the younger woman had to let down her defenses and take the chance of being hurt—with no guarantee of a good outcome. That is what risk taking is about.

The daughter's new approach included several instructive elements. First, she stopped behaving in a passive way and took the initiative to redefine the relationship. Second, she took a positive approach. She didn't berate her mother or complain. And third, she chose to give what she wanted to receive. And when it comes to love, that's an excellent formula.

What Is a "Winning Game"?

When I discussed this book with a friend, she asked me what I meant by a "winning game." Was I advocating the defeat of competitors? Did I suggest getting the best of someone in a business deal? Or looking good by making others look bad? She was concerned about the connotations of the word *winning*.

Even in sports, winning can be defined in different ways. The conventional concept is winning on the scoreboard—getting more points than your opponent. But there are other ways to define it. Achieving your own personal best is often seen as a victory, even for professional athletes. Harvey Haddix made baseball history by pitching a no-hitter for twelve innings—but his team lost the game. A runner might lose a race but still run the fastest time in her career. Surely she's entitled to feel she was a winner that day. It all depends on the criteria you use. Just getting exercise and enjoying the fresh air is fully satisfying to a lot of weekend athletes who aren't out to prove anything to anyone. If you define winning in terms like these, it makes your achievements more pleasing—and more realistic.

In a sense, winning is whatever you say it is or allow it to be. A man I know became the manager of a small company in a very competitive industry. The outgoing manager threatened to take his whole staff with him to the firm he was about to join. My friend said to himself: "If I keep even *one* of the senior people, I will feel I've won." In the end, many staffers left—but he kept four of the best people. By defining his own terms for winning, he was able to feel good about the outcome, even though several employees jumped to the rival company.

Winning does not have to mean having the most money or the biggest house or the most powerful position. It shouldn't be necessary for someone to lose in order for you to win. Winning is deciding what's important to you and living in accordance with those standards. Your goal can be a life that is balanced, enjoyable and satisfying. It can be good health, warm friendships and self-respect. It might include setting and achieving goals, doing things for others, feeling in control of your life and feeling good about yourself. Not bad things to strive for.

I learned a lot about winning years ago from a story my brother told me about a policeman he met in a New York City restaurant. The policeman was a neighborhood patrolman, a uniformed officer walking the beat, who had been with the force for fourteen years.

My brother expressed surprise. "Don't you get promotions?" he asked.

"Oh, I've had lots of offers, but I've turned them all down," the policeman replied. "I enjoy my job a lot. I've been in this neighborhood for years. I've seen people die and babies born. I'm a part of the fabric of this community. If I took a promotion, I'd have a desk job, away from the people I care about. I'd push around a lot of paper and have a lot more responsibility and aggravation. This way I go home at night and forget about work. I enjoy my family, my library of books, my record collection. I'm perfectly content to walk the beat until I retire."

I heard that story more than thirty years ago and never forgot it. Here was a man who knew what was important to him and who lived his values. Many people might define him as a loser, a man with limited goals and no ambition. I've always seen him as a winner because, in his own frame of reference (the only one that matters), he was happy in his work and satisfied with his life. In today's world, people with his peace of mind are to be envied.

Are You Playing Any Losing Games?

In sports, if you're losing, you must figure out why and change your tactics. Yet as clear as this principle is in the realm of athletics, people rarely apply the same logic to the domains of work and relationships. We all do things that are self-defeating or counterproductive.

Here is a checklist of common examples. Take a moment to see where you stand. And if a rueful smile of self-recognition crosses your face, be assured you are not alone.

- Do you get less sleep than you need—and walk around chronically tired as a result?

- Do you periodically go on diets that don't work or whose benefits don't last?

- Do you own all the labor-saving devices yet find yourself with less free time than you had ten years ago?

- Do you criticize and insult yourself, calling yourself names like "jerk" and "klutz"?

- Do you take better care of your house (or car) than you do of yourself?

- Do you feel guilty when you do things for yourself or take some leisure time?

- Do you buy things you know you can't afford?

- Do you skip breakfast and/or lunch—and then eat a huge supper because you're so hungry? Or snack on junk food to tide you over until suppertime?

- Do you ruminate about events from the past, replaying them in your mind—and upsetting yourself all over again?

- Do you worry a lot about things that never come to pass?

- Do you keep putting off vacations because you're too busy at work to get away?

- Do you often find yourself driving with your gas gauge at "empty" and sweating about whether you'll find a gas station before you run out?

- Do you file your income tax hours before the deadline—year after year after year?

- Do you drink caffeine to give you a boost and then need tranquilizers or alcohol to calm you down?

- Do you work long hours even though much of your time is unproductive?

- Do you say yes to people when you want to say no—and then kick yourself afterward?

- Do you say you place a high value on your family—but spend very little time with them?

- Do you work hard to achieve things—but find no lasting satisfaction from your accomplishments?

- Do you spend more time wondering "What will people think?" than asking "What do I think?" and "How do I feel?"

- Do you do more for others than for yourself? Do you frequently feel resentful about this?

- Do you keep dreaming about how you'd like your life to be—but do nothing to change it?

- Do you feel you're working harder but still falling behind financially?

- Do you work at a job you dislike or find unsatisfying and unfulfilling?

- Do you yell at your children a lot—and then berate yourself afterward, feeling guilty and remorseful?

- Do you put up with abusive relationships because you feel you don't deserve anything better? Or that you have no alternative (or nowhere else to go)?

- Is your job the only thing that seems to give your life purpose and meaning?

If you answered yes to even a third of these questions, welcome to the ranks of human frailty. Recognition of a problem is the first major step toward corrective change. And change is what this book is all about.

When I talk about change I am referring to the whole range of human experience. In my teaching and work with patients, I address four areas in which change can produce benefits:

- the way people think,

- the way they behave,

- the lifestyle habits they adopt and

- the situations they get into or put up with.

I will be discussing all of these domains in the chapters ahead. The examples I use are representative: some involve minor issues (like not eating foods that give you heartburn) while others pertain to major elements of life (like quitting a job or moving to a new town). However, the principles that apply to mundane events also apply to the most significant aspects of our lives.

The ideas and stories in this book are the result of many years of medical practice, counseling and teaching, and they reflect what my patients and seminar participants have found useful. It is my hope that you, the reader, will find them equally effective in your life.

CHAPTER ONE

Change

ANYONE WHO'S EVER TRIED TO RELEARN their tennis serve or alter their golf swing knows that change can be frustrating and difficult. You have to give up what's comfortable to do something that's awkward and unfamiliar. However, there is usually a payoff if you persist.

If you change nothing, nothing changes.
UNKNOWN

Whether it's getting used to a new pair of shoes or a hotel bed when you're traveling, change and adjustment to new circumstances are part of everyone's life experience. Most of the time, these transitions are made with ease and minimal attention. Why is it, then, that the idea of change spooks people or fills them with fear and trepidation? Change often improves things and should be embraced. But many people are cautious and see change as a threat or something to be avoided. I encourage a more welcoming attitude toward change—especially because it is the key to overcoming the losing games in which so many people are stuck.

Change Implies Choice—and You Always Have a Choice

People often say things like "There's nothing else I can do" or "I don't have any choice" when changes are suggested to them. Or they greet every suggestion with a reason that it won't work—and then conclude that they're stuck with the status quo. (A friend of mine calls this "having a *problem* for every *solution*.") The first thing to note is that you always have a choice in what you do and how you think. Everything you do is a choice. Even not choosing is a choice.

Life is like a blank computer screen that you write on every day. From the time you wake up each morning, you decide what will happen.

You decide when your alarm will ring and whether you'll get out of bed right away or roll over for another quick snooze. You decide whether to shower, brush your teeth or eat breakfast—and in what order. You choose your own clothes and decide when to leave for work or to start work if you work from home—or whether to even go to work. (Of course, all your choices have consequences. If you choose not to go to work, you may lose your pay for the day or anger your boss, but you *do* have that choice.) If you don't work outside your home, you have other choices: do you stay home and do housework, run errands, go shopping, entertain your kids, etc.? These choices continue all day long. Every activity in your day is there because you put it there at some point along the way.

This story illustrates an evolving awareness of choice and its importance. A middle-aged woman in a less-than-happy marriage complained to me about her husband. But although she blamed most of her problems on him, she had never confronted him about his controlling behavior. Nor had she ever done anything to make her personal life more interesting and satisfying. Eventually she began to realize that she had a choice: "I can't change the present situation with my husband unless *I'm* prepared to change. If I don't change *my* behavior, it's not going to get any easier for me." She told him how she was feeling and pointed out when he was being bossy. She planned activities with friends and joined a fitness club. As she became less dependent on him, her mood improved. Her husband became less critical and more attentive, and slowly the tension between them eased—and they started to enjoy each other again.

People often acknowledge they have a choice in the phrases they use. A young man had held a deep secret for over twenty years: he had failed third grade. After we discussed it for a while, he made an important statement: "I don't know whether I should care about it or not." By his own admission he had a *choice* about how (or even *whether*) to care about it. Other statements we make show that we have a choice. "I can't believe the number of things I let bother me"; "I let his comments get to me"; and "It's a matter of what I make important to myself" are all subtle examples.

Sometimes the choice is not in what you do but how you choose to feel about it. A mother lost a day's pay when she stayed home with her sick child. She said, philosophically: "I can either tie myself up in knots or roll with it. I can't change the situation, but I *can* change how I react to it."

Four Important Principles

1. **Any behavior you persist in doing, after you become aware of it, is a conscious choice.** If you're unaware that you're cracking your knuckles, you don't really have control. But once you become aware of what you're doing—and you continue to do it—you are making a conscious choice (even if you only choose *not* to control your behavior). The same applies to people who swear a lot, have overloaded schedules, feel oppressed by guilt, drink too much, yell at other people, wallow in self-pity, etc. You always have a choice.

2. **At times you don't see your choices clearly because of restrictions you put on yourself.** A business executive took a new job and realized, within months, that he disliked the position. But he was reluctant to quit because it would look bad on his CV to leave a job too soon. He saw no option but to stick it out for a respectable length of time. He perceived that he had no choice. Then one day, after a year of misery, he announced: "I can leave now without impairing my career. I won't look like a job hopper." Technically he'd had a choice all along. But he'd felt trapped because of constraints he'd put on himself.

3. **Sometimes people don't feel they have a choice because they don't *like* any of their choices.** As a family doctor, I had the sad experience of counseling several teenage girls with unwanted pregnancies. When we discussed their options, one of the first things I told them was that they had no good choices to pick from. Having an abortion, giving the baby up for adoption or keeping the baby and raising it were all difficult routes to take, physically and emotionally. Rather than look for a "good" choice, their task was to select the least bad option. I didn't say this to be unkind. I just felt it was more helpful for them to think realistically.

4. **Sometimes people get off track because they're looking for the ideal solution.** A professional woman felt she could no longer cope with her high-pressure job. We explored many options, from revising her current job to seeking other employment. She rejected each option until she was back to square one—which she also ruled out as untenable. She made the mistake of looking for the perfect choice, one with no drawbacks. She even said: "I can't accept that I can't have it all."

Unfortunately, in the real world there is no such thing as the perfect house, the ideal job or the flawless mate or partner. People who look for the perfect choice paralyze themselves by ruling out all the alternatives and leaving themselves with nothing.

There are always choices, even when you don't like them. Weigh the options. Recognize the advantages as well as the drawbacks. Then choose the best (or the least bad) of all the alternatives available. Accept that every choice will involve trade-offs, some of which might be unpleasant. By acknowledging your choices, you can exert some control over your life and not live as if you are powerless.

Change Involves Risk—But Only as Much as You Want

When have you ever gotten something in life by doing nothing? Even winning a lottery requires that you buy a ticket. Only in fairy tales does Prince Charming find the fair maiden. In the real world, she has to get out there and meet people. Phrases like "there are no free lunches" and "you can't win if you don't play" are clichés, but they ring true. People who play it safe will have lives that are predictable, familiar and secure. But they will also be without excitement, vitality, growth and development. And if you're stuck in an unpleasant situation, it will remain so. The bad news is that change often involves some element of risk. The good news is that change brings great benefits and you can decide how *much* risk you're willing to accept.

You can't steal second base and keep one foot on first.
ANONYMOUS

I learned about the pros and cons of risk taking (and of *not* risking) when I was a teenager in the 1950s. Those were the agonizing years of having to ask girls out on dates. Face-to-face invitations were almost unthinkable. At least the telephone provided some protection from the greatest fear of all—rejection. How I envied my twin sister who had only to wait for the phone to ring. She didn't have to take the initiative or put herself in jeopardy. In fact, there was a social stigma against girls calling boys for dates. So boys had to do all the work and take all the chances. Why did we put ourselves through this wringer?

The reason, aside from societal custom, was that there was a payoff for taking those risks. You got to go out on dates with a girl of your choice, at a time of your choosing, and to do what you wanted. I'd get to call Barbara and invite her to a movie on Saturday night. My sister, who had to risk nothing, paid a price for that. She might not get invited out at all. Or she might get called by Melvin (when she really wanted to go out with Frank) to go for a milkshake (she preferred a pizza) on a Friday night (when she favored Saturday). Or even worse, she'd accept an invitation from Murray to go to some obscure play only to have Harvey Heartthrob call the next day to invite her to a dance.

What constitutes a risk is very subjective. For some people, buying a house is a huge gamble. Others feel that way about applying for a job. For a shy person, inviting someone to lunch seems fraught with peril, while those who fear flying find airplanes the ultimate form of danger.

What you decide to risk is up to you. It might be physical safety, as with skydiving. Or it could be money, as in a chancy investment. If you bet on a horse race, do you bet two dollars or two hundred dollars? It depends on your comfort level. When you give a speech in front of a large audience, do you use notes or trust your memory? These are choices you get to make.

What do you lose by playing it safe? It depends on how bad your current situation is. One woman was in a totally unpleasant relationship with an alcoholic but took five years to get up the courage to leave. Another hated her job but stuck it out for three years before getting up the gumption to quit. Both women decided the known present was better than the uncertain future. And in both cases they stayed stuck and unhappy for a long time. A young man referred to himself as "a fairly conservative guy. I'm not willing to take many chances. I'm just sort of tiptoeing through life. I could stand more variety and enjoyment." For him, the cost of playing it safe was boredom.

If you aren't making some mistakes, you're probably playing it too safe. A skier who never falls isn't pushing himself enough. If you don't fail occasionally, you're not stretching yourself, not growing as much as you could. Read the life stories of successful people and you'll always find they failed many times on their way to the top of their field.

Abraham Lincoln, Thomas Edison and Helen Keller struggled but continued to strive and challenge themselves—with stunning results.

What are the benefits of taking chances and leaving the security blanket? The satisfaction of meeting a challenge or overcoming adversity; improvement in your life circumstances; increased happiness and fulfillment; adventure, exhilaration, personal growth, financial success, even triumphant fame and fortune are all possible for those who choose risk taking over the status quo.

Taking a risk in one area can give you courage to do the same in other realms. A patient of mine who is a high school teacher was asked to teach a new subject. Her first reaction was to decline. But gradually she talked herself into it. "If I don't do it, I'll never know if I'm able to—I'll always think I can't do it. It might even help me get organized." Her willingness to take this risk had a ripple effect. She returned a month later from her holiday and reported two major breakthroughs. First, she'd gone white-water rafting, something that had always scared her. Two weeks later, she took a motor trip to the Midwest, a totally new experience. The benefits of these risks were written all over her glowing face. She summed it up by saying: "Now I know I could do that again and be on my own. I was really comfortable with myself."

In Ron Howard's film *Parenthood*, there is a scene in which the grandmother, a woman in her eighties, presents her philosophy of life. "When I was nineteen, Grandpa took me on a rollercoaster. Up, down . . . up, down . . . Oh what a ride! I always wanted to go again. You know, it was just interesting to me that a *ride* could make me so . . . so *frightened*, so *scared*, so sick, so . . . so excited and . . . and so *thrilled*, all together. Some didn't like it. They went on the merry-go-round. That just goes around. Nothing. *I* like the *rollercoaster*. You get more *out* of it." This wonderful outlook can be applied to life decisions generally. The ones that carry some risk also carry opportunity and the possibility of reward. And in the meantime, risk taking makes life more colorful and dynamic and interesting—pretty good rewards in themselves.

Change Involves Trade-Offs

Wherever there is a choice, trade-offs are inevitable. In order to get something, you usually have to give up something else. In sports, trade-offs are an integral part of the game. Many pitchers can throw a baseball more than ninety miles per hour but can't get the ball over the plate. They have to take a little off their speed to get better control. In essence, they are trading speed for accuracy—a necessary trade-off if they want to succeed. In hockey, a team that's losing will sacrifice some defense to increase their scoring potential. Hockey goalies are often pulled in the final minute in favor of an extra attacker. This is an example of trading defense for offense. Trade-offs are an accepted part of most sports.

The same principle applies in life. Even the most common trans-actions involve choices and trade-offs. Benefits are weighed against costs. That's how you know if something is a good deal or not. When you buy a coat, you look at the garment and decide if it's good value for the price. If you think it's worth it, you buy; if not, you don't. I decided to go to university for seven years after high school in exchange for my medical degree. That was a good trade-off to me. But I declined to enter a residency program because the additional five years of training did not feel like a worthwhile expenditure of time for the benefit that would result.

If you think education is expensive, try ignorance.
DEREK BOK

When contemplating change, recognize that trade-offs are inevitable. If you decide to get more sleep, you'll have to skip some late-night television. To get out of debt, you'll have to forgo some of your pleasures. Many people resist change because they don't like the trade-offs. For example, countless folks agree to do things because they don't want to offend others or cause conflict. Saying no involves trade-offs they're unwilling to make, like feeling guilty or risking disapproval. However, the flip side often goes unnoticed: saying yes also has drawbacks—which might be even worse than the costs of saying no—like feeling resentful or manipulated or powerless. Whichever decision is made, there are consequences. There is no such thing as a choice or decision that doesn't involve trade-offs. So don't avoid change just because there are trade-offs. The key is to be aware of the costs and the payoffs and then make the best deal you can.

Just as change involves trade-offs, continuing your present behavior *also* involves trade-offs. How many individuals stay in jobs they dislike for fear of being unemployed or having to hunt for a new job? How many gorge themselves with rich food every Christmas even though it always leads to indigestion and insomnia?

My favorite example of a poor trade-off is smoking. Smokers often resist quitting because they'll feel irritable or gain weight. Many have stopped smoking only to find themselves chewing people's heads off, pacing and fidgeting or going on eating binges. So what do many of them do to relieve the anxiety symptoms or overweight? They turn back to nicotine. And by and large it works. It certainly calms them down (the payoff) but with all the ill effects they conveniently overlook (the cost). In order to appreciate the trade-offs this return to smoking entails, let's turn the scenario around and picture an anxious patient visiting his doctor looking for relief.

Patient: Hi, Doc. I've got a real problem with my nerves. I'm tense and jittery all the time. Can you give me something to calm me down?

Doctor: Sure, there's a new product out that people just swear by.

Patient: Great. How quickly does it work?

Doctor: Seems to work right away.

Patient: Wow, can you give me a prescription?

Doctor: No problem.

Patient: By the way, Doc, how does it work?

Doctor: Well, it's a bit unusual. It comes in the form of a dried tobacco leaf that's rolled up and wrapped in paper. You put it in your mouth, light it with a match and then suck on it. The smoke from the burning leaves goes into your lungs and enters the bloodstream. It acts on the brain to make you feel calm.

Patient: Sounds pretty weird to me. How often do you have to take it?

Doctor: The dosage is twenty times a day, ten puffs each time.

Patient: You're kidding! I won't have time to do anything else if I take this medicine. Is it expensive?

Doctor: Between eight and nine dollars a day.

Patient: Doc, that comes to over $3,000 a year. This sounds crazy. By the way, are there any side effects I should know about?

Doctor: I was hoping you wouldn't ask. I have to tell you that there are over two thousand chemicals in the tobacco smoke. At first it'll probably make you feel dizzy and cause you to cough or choke, but you'll get used to it. It will irritate the mucous membranes lining your nose, mouth, throat and respiratory tract, so you'll be more prone to coughs and colds. Sinusitis and bronchitis are more likely too. Eventually your risk of chronic bronchitis and emphysema will be much higher, but that'll take years to develop. The risk of heart disease, heart attacks, strokes and hardening of the arteries throughout your body is significantly higher. And unfortunately it also causes a lot of cancers. Mouth, throat, lung and bladder cancers are all much higher in people who smoke this drug. But remember, it *will* make you feel more calm. Which is what you asked me for in the first place.

Patient: Doc, I don't want that new drug. And I don't want you for my doctor anymore either. You'll be hearing from my lawyer!

If this conversation sounds contrived, consider what smokers are doing every time they light up. They're weighing the benefits of a nicotine hit against the costs to their health and their pocketbook. And they're making a very poor trade-off to my way of thinking.

Some forms of eating involve questionable trade-offs. It requires an hour of walking to burn off the calories in a piece of cake. Even a slow eater can't make the pleasure of that cake last much more than five or ten minutes. But the calories stay in your body for hours or days, depending on your activity level. The question is whether the pleasure of eating high calorie foods is worth the weight gain (and emotional upset) that results.

Change Involves Letting Go of the Past

One of the most difficult skills to learn in sports is how to forget what happened a minute ago and to concentrate only on what's happening right now. A batter in baseball has to focus on every pitch and has about a second to decide whether to swing. If his mind is on the last pitch (which he may have swung at and missed), he will be unable to give his full attention to the ball that's coming at him right now. The same applies to tennis players and golfers who get down on themselves after a lousy shot—and promptly muff the next shot as well.

Living in the moment is a life skill as well as a sports skill, and one worth learning. Letting go of past thinking and behavior patterns is mandatory if you're going to make changes in your life. People usually end up in losing games because their old strategies aren't working anymore—if they ever did. Their losing games are often tied to stories they tell themselves (like "I behave this way because my family moved around a lot" or "I do this because I was an only child") or to the guilt, regrets and resentments that run so many people's lives. One woman could not get her life in order because of low self-esteem. She'd been telling herself since childhood that her mother favored her sister, that her sister was better than she, that she was never good enough. She finally realized this story was getting tiresome and irrelevant. Finally she decided: "I can't change what happened. I don't want to go back to being sad anymore. I have to live in the present and deal with that."

People often cling to the past like a security blanket. They fear letting go of old habits because they are familiar and comfortable—even if they are also dysfunctional (the devil you know is better than the devil you don't know). Some folks are simply rigid. Others harbor grudges or won't let go of bad memories. On the other side of the coin are persons who glorify the past and prefer living there to existing in the present. Nostalgia buffs long for the good old days when towns were smaller, neighbors friendlier, air cleaner, music better, athletes pure and innocent, etc. Nothing in today's world measures up for these individuals, so they spend their days complaining about what is and gazing longingly at a bygone era.

There's nothing wrong with remembering the past for its warm memories and special people. It's just when you get stuck in the past that it becomes a problem, a losing game. It is not your destiny to simply repeat the past over and over. And if your past has been upsetting or painful, my advice is this: don't regret the past; just learn from it. Then move on and make each day a new opportunity to rewrite your own personal history.

The Future Can Determine the Present

Conventional wisdom tells us that the past determines the present. In other words, everything that is happening now (where you live, who you know, what job you do, how you behave) is a result of previous events. This linear view is how people tell stories, study history and explain current situations. Classical psychiatry was built on the premise that exploring the past provides clues as to why persons behave or think as they do now.

If you can dream it, you can do it.

WALT DISNEY

While it appears logical that the present is shaped by the past, it's not always helpful to think in those terms. After all, since the past has already happened, it cannot be changed. So if the past governs the present, it follows that the present cannot be altered either. Letting the past determine the present is like driving a car in which the entire windshield is replaced by a rear-view mirror. I learned this powerful analogy from Dr. Matthew Budd of Harvard University. Can you imagine steering your car without being able to see ahead of you? Where all you can see is where you've been? Living your life looking backward doesn't make much more sense. Granted, looking back can be a source of guidance, a gathering of experiences from which to learn. But even those lessons should not be relied on exclusively.

A much more useful concept is to see how the *future* can determine the present. Of course, on first reading, this seems absurd. How can something that hasn't happened yet influence what is happening now? The answer is this: the future here refers not to the *factual* future (which cannot be known with certainty) but to the *predicted* or *desired* future—which then acts as a guide to decisions and behavior in the present. The benefits of this premise are considerable because it allows you to write any script you want. Suddenly, constraints are removed, and freedom of choice becomes possible. If you want to make changes, it's a compelling model to explore.

To illustrate this premise, I offer the story of one Archibald Alexander Leach, born in Bristol, England, in 1904. He grew up in a poor family and lived in a tough neighborhood. Nothing in his background would have suggested or prepared him for the life he was to lead. At an early age, he studied people he admired and began to emulate them. He copied their behavior, their speech, their style. He practiced being like them, affecting their cultured and elegant manners. He got so good at it that he truly became like them. As he put it: "I pretended to be somebody I wanted to be until finally I became that person. Or he became me." In time, he became the very model of urbane sophistication, known the world over for his refinement and charm. In 1931, he went to Hollywood and changed his name to Cary Grant. People probably thought he was a well-bred son of nobility (the past shaping the present). In fact, he had simply decided what he wanted to be and created that reality. The future (his vision or goal—based on a picture in his mind) had produced the present (how he chose to behave until it became his natural behavior).

The American Dream—that you can be successful and achieve anything you want, based on hard work and not on where you come from—is another illustration of the future determining the present. David Halberstam discussed this in his book *The Next Century*. He says of the early 1900s: "In Europe, no matter what your skills and intelligence, you were a prisoner of the past, likely to be what your parents and grandparents had been, a member of the same class, and no better educated. In America, by contrast, the past meant nothing. Here you could reinvent yourself and be whoever you wanted to be. . . . By the mid-fifties, ordinary people had a sense that their lives were going to be better than those of their parents . . . a new sense of optimism that the future was going to be better than the past."

It is liberating and exciting to know that your present does not have to be simply a continuation of your past. It may not even require much effort for the future to start influencing the present. Just a change in mind-set can begin the process. I read a story about a ski instructor who had a class of intermediate skiers on a hill. He told them to ski in their usual way while he videotaped each of them. He then took them back up the hill and gave them only one instruction: "Now, ski the way you'd *like* to ski by the end of the course." He videotaped their second run. Then he compared the two films. In most cases, the students all skied significantly better the second time. And yet they hadn't even started the lessons yet. They hadn't received any instruction, nor had they practiced. The improvement was based on only one thing: a vision in their mind's eye of what they wanted to look like. They took that picture of a desired *future* result and converted it subconsciously into an improved performance in the *present*.

The present does *not* have to be a continuation of the past. Whenever I hear a patient say "I'm always late" or "I'm impulsive" or similar self-descriptions, I always stop them. I tell them that's only a report on how they've been in the past. It's not their *destiny*. It would be more helpful—and more accurate—to say: "Up until now I have behaved in such and such a way. And I can change that whenever I wish."

Insight Does Not Produce Change, and Insight Is Not Necessary for Change to Occur

One of the myths about change is that you have to understand *why* you do something before you can change the behavior. Many people see insight as a prerequisite for change. They assume that once they know why they behave as they do, change will follow. There are two assumptions operating here: that change cannot occur without insight, and that insight can, on its own, lead to change. Both these premises are untrue. Worse than that, the search for *why* often delays or even prevents change. In many cases it is a convenient stalling tactic, putting off the inevitable moment when action must finally be taken.

There is a delightful story about a thirty-year-old man who is a bed-wetter. He decides to go for counseling to deal with his problem. Five years later, he runs into an old friend who, among other things, asks him about his enuresis (as it is called).

"Oh, I'm making good progress," he replies.

"Really? You mean you've stopped wetting your bed at night?"

"Well, no, not exactly."

"Then what do you mean you're making progress? You've been in therapy for five years!"

"Yes, it's true I'm still wetting the bed. But at least now I know *why*!"

It is usually more productive to work on changing the behavior than on understanding its origins.

The notion that insight is required for change is based on the premise that the past determines the present. Knowing why you behave in a certain way implies that something from the past is operating on the present, and if you can just understand what that is, you can change your current behavior. However, as I explained earlier, the past does *not* have to determine the present. And therefore, insight alone does not produce change. In fact, since the future can govern the present, you can change what you are doing with no reference to the past at all.

I heard two prominent psychotherapists make this point. One said: "In thirty years of doing therapy, I never once saw a patient change on the basis of insight alone." The other was asked, in an interview, how he felt about insight. He replied: "I don't mind if the client has insight. As long as it doesn't interfere with the therapy!"

Let me make an important distinction here. There are two kinds of insight. One refers to awareness of *what* you are doing, of patterns in your behavior, etc. This kind of insight is very important. You cannot change or deal with something without being aware of it first. You might, for example, be a slow worker because of your perfectionism. It would be very helpful to know that. The other kind of insight refers to understanding *why* you do it, the reasons or causes for your behavior (for example, the reason you are a Perfectionist). This insight involves figuring out when you first started to do it, what the circumstances were, who was influencing you, etc. This information is far less relevant and may be of no importance whatever.

I have encountered many patients with insight and understanding who are still stuck in their behavior patterns. Here is a sampling of quotes from these folks:

"I'm tired of introspection. I want to get *on* with my life."

"I know a lot of this stuff. I'm not a stupid person. I just don't *act* on it."

"I know that stuff. I *teach* it. But what I *know* and what I *do* are so different."

"I've got the theory but I can't put it into practice."

"We don't need to analyze the thing to death—we need to *do* something."

Insight without action achieves nothing. It's like knowing how to read but never picking up a book. A hard-working young man never allowed himself to have leisure time. He traced his work ethic back to his father's teachings. His dad was a Workaholic who disdained time off and taught his children that leisure was wasteful and frivolous. He understood the origins of his behavior (and even disagreed with his father's strong views about leisure). But recognizing *why* he behaved this way did not lead him to change. Understanding takes you only so far. Eventually you have to *do* something about it. Taking action is what produces change.

The search for information or insight is often just a way of procrastinating. Governments are famous for this. If they don't want to take action on an issue for political reasons, what do they do? They order yet another study of the problem (an inquiry, a royal commission or what have you). When the study is completed, it is filed on a shelf with all the other reports that are gathering dust at taxpayers' expense. However, the deliberation serves a useful purpose. It gives the illusion of taking action. A lot of people do the same thing when they substitute the question "why?" for the action-oriented questions: "What am I going to do? And when?"

Robert Shaw, a psychiatrist in Berkeley, California, puts it this way: "The question we ask people is not 'How did you get the way you are?' but 'What would you like to happen now?'" This approach leads to meaningful change. Just as you don't need to know how a car or a computer works to operate one, similarly, you don't have to know how you got a certain way in order to change.

Here is a story of significant change that occurred with no insight at all. It is about a confirmed, dyed-in-the-wool collector of things. From childhood, he saved everything: letters, baseball cards, theater programs, magazines, souvenirs, etc. As he got older, the boxes containing these treasures grew increasingly numerous. Storage became a problem. His memorabilia traveled from his parents' house to his brother's cellar and finally to the basement lockers of several apartment buildings. Then he got married and moved into a new house. As he was packing his worldly possessions, his wife eyed the stacks of cartons and asked: "You're not going to move all that stuff to the new house, are you?" His moment of truth had arrived. He couldn't explain to her why he wanted to keep all this material. He was even having trouble explaining it to himself. He had never looked at any of it in all the years he'd been saving it.

Finally, he bit the bullet. In the next week he threw out seventeen garbage bags of material—valued possessions that had suddenly become disposable. The first few bags were tough to pitch. But then it got easier.

By the tenth bag, it was positively liberating. The spell had been broken. His *things* no longer had such a hold on him. More important, he stopped accumulating similar articles, except for the odd collector's item.

The most fascinating part of his whole decluttering process is that he had no idea why he collected all that stuff in the first place. Was it to hold onto the past? Was it a security blanket? Was it to have a memorabilia library some day? He hadn't a clue. But he was able to throw out great quantities of these possessions *without knowing why he had saved them*.

I don't mean to suggest that seeking insight is never a valid pursuit. In some cases it can be a helpful adjunct to change. It might also be very important to the recovery of self-esteem, especially in cases of traumatic childhood experiences like sexual abuse or rages of an alcoholic parent. But overall it is not essential to know why you behave as you do in order to change it. And the search for an explanation can actually be detrimental if it delays taking action to deal with the problem.

Change in Thinking—Change in Behavior: Which Comes First?

Changes in how you think and how you act usually go hand in hand, each complementing and supporting the other. But there's no rule about which has to come first. If you want to change, you can first modify your actions, letting your thinking change as a result of the new experience. Or you can alter your attitude and let that lead you to behave differently.

It intrigues me to note how many people don't take regular holidays—even when their company pays for the time off. This reluctance to get away is rationalized with statements like "Holidays are luxuries" or "Vacations are frivolous." Even when I urge patients to take periodic breaks, many resist my suggestion. Sometimes I can convince them by offering a new way of thinking. My credo is that "holidays are a necessity," a requirement for mental health and good performance at work. If they accept this different point of view, many people then give themselves permission to take their first vacation in years. In summary, a change in thinking produces a change in behavior.

Sometimes the opposite occurs. One man proudly told me he hadn't taken so much as a day off in three years. When I prevailed on him with logic to take a break, he disdained the idea. But finally, and only as an experiment, he reluctantly agreed to take the odd day off—and liked what happened. He reported: "My attitude is different (at work and at home) when I take time off. I'm more tolerant of others, less snappish, more easy-going." Finally he announced he was planning a ten-day holiday. "I never saw the value of vacations till now." In this case, an arbitrary change in behavior resulted in a change of thinking.

Ingrained behavior can be hard to change. In such cases, a shift in thinking will enhance the process. Take the man who admitted he had a drinking problem but was reluctant to stop. He felt strongly that he needed alcohol to have fun socially, that it relaxed him and made it easier to talk to people. He was about to go away for a weekend bash with friends, an annual event in which alcohol was the main focus. I suggested he consider going and not drinking, a prospect that held no appeal whatsoever. But when I proposed he not go at all, something shifted in his mind. The idea of missing the traditional binge in the woods upset him. In struggling with his choices, he said (as if to convince me—and himself—that he should be allowed to go): "I honestly believe I can go and enjoy myself without having a drink." This was a complete about-face from his previous statement: "I can't have fun without alcohol."

Armed with this new mind-set, he went on the weekend bender and never had a drink. Better yet, he had a great time. "I had a ball. I was the same old clown I ever was. In fact one of the guys said I was *more* fun." This story is not just about abstaining from booze. It's about making a difficult change by mobilizing a different attitude to support the new action. Some people need a "rationale" to justify a change in behavior. If you're having difficulty changing the way you behave, a change in thinking might help you to break the impasse.

Adjusting to Change—Getting Used to the New You

Change is not without fallout. Fat people who lose a lot of weight talk about the psychological adjustment involved. They tell stories about walking into clothing stores and going immediately to the large-size racks, even though they no longer need such big clothes. There seems to be a discrepancy between their physical self (which they see in the mirror) and their *image* of self (seen in their mind's eye). Some say people look at them differently once they're thinner and that makes them feel uncomfortable.

What is happening here? These obese people have struggled and sacrificed to get their weight down. Now that they've reached their goal, they don't seem to believe or accept that they finally made it. That's how it often is with change. You've been who you were for so long that you've gotten used to that person. When you change, there is a period of adjustment as you get used to the new you—how you look, how you feel, what you can do that you couldn't do before, how other people react, etc. For some folks it's like being transported into someone else's body—or life! This transition is called "self-concept dislocation" and can last for months (as many as eighteen) and occasionally for years. People going through change need to be aware of this phenomenon and not be frightened or confused by it.

A self-made multimillionaire admitted to me that he is totally pre-occupied with money. The way he frets and stews about it, you'd think he was about to have his furniture repossessed. One day I asked him about it and he replied: "I'm a poor boy who still thinks poor." He has never gotten used to the fact that he is worth millions, even though he's been well off for years. His life began during the Great Depression in the 1930s, and like so many others who went through that searing experience, he's never felt secure about his wealth. There is a difference here between intellectual and emotional insight. Even when a person knows something is objectively true, he may not have absorbed the real impact of it. Emotional insight occurs when he accepts that it's *really* true. This strange dichotomy operates through all the self-concept dislocation stories.

I experienced such a dislocation on the first day of my internship. I was on call that evening on the Pediatrics ward. One of the nurses ran up to tell me that one of the babies was having a seizure. I'd never seen a baby having a convulsion, so I replied (with some sense of alarm): "You'd better call one of the doctors." She looked at me kindly and, with a slight smile, said: "Dr. Posen, you *are* a doctor." I just hadn't integrated that concept yet.

Stages in the Process of Change

Some years ago I heard a description of the five stages in learning a new skill. This model can help you monitor where you are in the change process. It also explains some of the reasons for self-concept dislocation. The five steps are as follows:

1. Unconscious incompetence

2. Conscious incompetence

3. Learning the skill/the change itself

4. Conscious competence

5. Unconscious competence

In the first stage, unconscious incompetence, you can't do the skill but you aren't aware that you can't do it (usually because you've never tried or haven't thought about it). For example, people who don't drive may think it is easy to do. But when they try, they find it's not as simple as it looks. They are unable to operate a vehicle but they don't know it.

Conscious incompetence is the stage at which you become aware that you can't do something. Take the non-driver who gets behind the wheel of a car, expecting to drive off with ease. As the car lurches and swerves and otherwise misbehaves, he realizes he doesn't know how to drive.

Learning the skill involves taking driving lessons, practicing and developing proficiency. This stage might be awkward, slow and frustrating.

Then comes the stage of conscious competence. You can drive but you have to concentrate on what you're doing. The skills aren't imbedded solidly yet and your performance suffers if you are distracted or stop paying attention. You are competent only to the extent that you are consciously watching what you're doing.

Finally, after many months of driving, you reach the stage of unconscious competence. You drive so well and naturally that you can do it without thinking about it. You have achieved a level of ease and comfort that allows you to drive while talking to someone, listening to the radio, etc. The skill is now second nature to you.

This sequence is followed in other activities such as learning to dance, ski and ride a bicycle, all of which require concentration as you go through the learning curve but eventually reach a point of competence and comfort that flows effortlessly most of the time.

The same stages of adjustment occur when you change a behavior or situation in your life. Awareness of this sequence of events helps you realize that you may not be comfortable immediately, but you will be eventually if you are patient and persistent. If you change jobs or move to a new house, you initially feel like a duck out of water. Then you slowly adjust, things feel more familiar and the change becomes more comfortable. After a while, you are so used to the new situation that you can barely remember when it wasn't like this. You have reached the stage that is equivalent to unconscious competence.

Here is a story that illustrates the sequence as it applies to a behavioral change. It is about a very pleasant woman who was almost too nice for her own good. She was a Pleaser who avoided conflict, never recognizing her inability to speak up for herself (unconscious incompetence). She was also unaware of what it was costing her, both at work and in her marriage. When I suggested she confront some issues with her husband, she discovered she didn't know how to approach the subject with him (conscious incompetence). We discussed the principles of assertiveness and then she enrolled in an assertiveness training course (learning the skill). As she learned, she practiced the techniques, carefully deciding when to apply them, rehearsing beforehand and thinking about what she was saying during the actual confrontations (conscious competence). She got more comfortable in this role and began speaking up more. One day she announced: "I'm on an assertiveness roll lately—all over the place—and it's been good. It's feeling more natural now, not contrived. And I don't have to think and plan what I'll say—it just comes out as it should." She had now reached the stage of unconscious competence where the new behavior was a part of her and flowed with ease.

Maxwell Maltz, in his book *Psycho-Cybernetics*, says it takes three weeks to change a behavior and establish a new one. But the time required for the new pattern to feel totally comfortable is usually longer than that.

The Swinging Pendulum

In the change process, people often need time to try out different ways of behaving before they find a comfort level. I counseled a woman who spent her whole life looking after her family. She made no time for herself, feeling she didn't *deserve* leisure activities. I urged her to do something for herself every day. She began by sitting out on her deck for half an hour a day. She said that it was "lovely," but it didn't last. She fell back into her self-neglecting mode. I encouraged her again and she followed through. With vigor. She took a one-hour daily walk and spent two hours a day out on the deck, sewing, reading and relaxing. She was enjoying this self-nurturing time but felt it was "too much now." After years of doing nothing for herself, she was having trouble finding a balance that was beneficial without feeling hedonistic. The problem was that her pendulum had been stuck on the self-neglect side for so long that, when she loosened it (by giving herself permission to do things for herself), it swung over toward the self-indulgent side. Then she overreacted and pulled back too far the other way again, and so on. I reassured her that it took time to find a balance when trying out a new behavior and that eventually the pendulum would find a position of moderation and comfort.

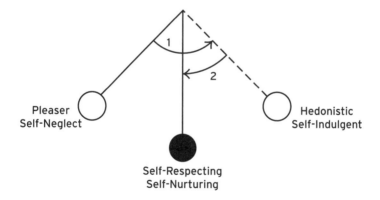

Pleaser
Self-Neglect

Hedonistic
Self-Indulgent

Self-Respecting
Self-Nurturing

The same thing happened with a young man after he decided to become more assertive. It's as if someone handed him a bucket of grenades. He began speaking up for himself all right—by telling off everyone who had tormented or bullied him in the past. It was the fantasy dream of a ninety seven-pound weakling who had suddenly filled out and become star of the boxing team—and was making up for lost time. Slowly he got it out of his system and realized he was antagonizing a lot of people with his offensive behavior. His pendulum had swung too far (from passive to aggressive). Eventually he found the right balance by which he spoke up for himself without offending others and putting them on the defensive—which is the definition and goal of assertiveness.

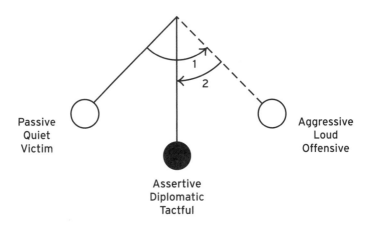

In making changes a certain amount of trial and error will be necessary. Don't be discouraged if you find yourself overdoing or underdoing it. Just work on making adjustments until the pendulum stops swinging and settles in a comfortable place. If you're aware of the tendency to swing from one extreme to the other, you won't be upset by it. Be patient and things will usually settle at the level that's best for you.

Getting to Know You: Other People's Reactions to the New You

Just as you need a transition period to get used to the new you, so other people also need time to adjust to the changes you make in yourself. Change in one person affects others in a number of ways, altering the dynamics of relationships and even the balance of power. It is important to understand and even anticipate the reaction of others as you reinvent yourself.

Take the story of a young woman who went off to her first year of college. It was a big change for her and her family when she moved to another town. Other than a brief visit at Christmas, the family wasn't reunited until June. A lot had happened. She had become more independent, responsible and mature. She now balked at some of her parents' advice. Her folks were generally pleased with the changes they saw in her but it caused some problems for them. For one thing, she didn't need them as much, which was a bit upsetting. For another, they weren't yet ready to have their little girl grow up. It redefined their relationship and even made them feel a bit older. By the end of the summer things worked themselves out.

Sometimes friends resent your changing because they have a vested interest in keeping you the way you are. They may even actively resist your efforts to change. If you've ever decided to abstain from alcohol, you will know your drinking buddies often take offense and mount a campaign to push you off the wagon and into the bar or pub. In social situations, they might push drinks at you or coax persistently; they may ridicule and mock, shouting insults and calling you names; or they might just cut you off by avoiding you. All of these gestures are not-so-subtle attempts to get you to behave the old way, the way *they* are used to and prefer.

People can react to changes in you in various ways, from support to indifference to resistance, or even hostility. If you are lucky they will be encouraging and supportive, or at least show understanding. If they are not, be patient. Give them time to work through their own feelings about the new you. But avoid the temptation to give in to their pressure and manipulation. Don't abandon changes that you feel are beneficial and necessary for yourself.

The most significant and potentially difficult reaction to change in another person occurs in committed relationships, where couples are so interdependent. Two scenarios come to mind. If one partner grows and develops (emotionally or intellectually) and the other doesn't, the relationship will be strained and may even be in jeopardy. The other scenario occurs when a passive person becomes more assertive and seeks to share power in the relationship that had been the exclusive prerogative of the other. Many strong people find this difficult to accept. They see it as an intrusion into their dominance and privilege and feel threatened by this assault on their domain. If this reaction is not addressed and Neutralized, problems will arise in the relationship.

In summary, many people pay lip service to the need for change. They're all for it until they have to take action, whereupon foot dragging and excuses take over where resolve and momentum should be. The fact is that change is difficult for a lot of people. It can be intimidating, inconvenient and hard work. It upsets the status quo that seems so comfortable and familiar. But change is possible and beneficial, and you *can* overcome the obstacles.

And it doesn't have to be difficult or threatening. It can even be fun. The formula is simple: be *aware* of what you're doing and what it's costing you; explore your *choices* and then give yourself *permission* to behave differently. Remember: you always have a choice. And the time to act is now.

CHAPTER TWO
Rules of the Game

THIS BOOK IS DIVIDED INTO THREE SECTIONS: Awareness, Choice and Permission. They correspond to the three stages in the process of change that I have defined and use in my work. I call these the "Steps for Taking Control of Your Life": *Awareness* of what you're doing and of what it's costing you; *Choice* of an alternative to your present behavior, strategy or thinking; and finally *Permission* you give yourself to implement one of your options. In other words, acknowledge when things aren't working out, develop a new plan and take action.

This brief example will demonstrate how the formula works. A secretary found her job unsatisfying and stressful but didn't know what was bothering her. She finally realized that her boss was doing a lot of chores she could do, things that she would find stimulating and enjoyable. She also recognized her underlying feeling that he looked down on her and felt she was incapable of performing complex tasks. She now had the *awareness* of what was upsetting her. Next, she explored her options and discovered many available choices: she could talk to her boss and request more work; she could take on small projects without being asked; she could sit and sulk; she could take a book to work and count herself lucky to have such a cushy job; and, of course, she could quit. She was surprised to see how much *choice* she had. The last step was to give herself *permission* to implement one of her alternatives. She decided to assert herself and have a chat with her employer. To her surprise he was delighted to turn over more work to her. He also admitted that he was a poor delegator and it was no reflection on her that he had given her so little to do.

All three steps in this formula are necessary for change to take place, and you can get stuck at any of the three stages. Some people aren't even aware that there's a problem or what it is. For example, I see many men and women in unhappy job situations who are unaware of the subtle emotional abuse they are receiving from their employers. Without an awareness of the problem, they can't begin to deal with it. Others recognize a problem but don't see any alternatives. One fifty-seven-year-old man was miserable in his job but thought he was unemployable anywhere else, so he felt stuck. He had the awareness but saw no choices for himself. Lastly, many folks see both the problem and the choices but don't take action. They are afraid of confrontation, are fearful of change itself, don't want to put forth the effort, etc. These individuals are stuck at the permission phase.

Other people can assist you through these steps. Sometimes people are unaware of a problem until someone else points it out. A woman was being subtly manipulated by a friend who was taking advantage of her. She didn't realize this until another friend drew it to her attention. The friend raised her awareness of what was happening—a form of consciousness raising. Similarly, others can help you discover your alternatives. A young student was failing one of his courses and fretting miserably but didn't know what to do about it. His teacher pulled him aside one day and laid out several options for him, none of which he had been able to see himself. He now had a range of choices about how to tackle his problem. Friends can also encourage you to take action. A doctor told me he was frequently interrupted when he was at his desk doing paperwork. The door of his office opened directly onto the waiting room, and patients thought nothing of wandering over to chat or ask questions. He was aware of the situation and knew he could close the door but felt it would be rude to do so. His nurse finally told him it was okay to close the door and gave him permission to do so (which he had been unable to give himself).

This simple formula for change is the theme and structure of this book. It has guided my patients to solve problems, improve relationships, increase their energy, reach personal goals and literally turn their lives around. The book will show you how to apply this principle to your own life with equally successful results.

I will explore four areas in which you can "change a losing game." You can change your thinking, make lifestyle changes, alter your behavior and change the situations you find stressful or unproductive. Often a combination of these four kinds of change yields the best results.

AWARENESS

CHAPTER THREE

How to Recognize a Losing Game

I N ORGANIZED SPORTS, PLAYERS KNOW WHEN they're losing. The scoreboard tells them where they stand. But what are the signals that tell you how you're doing in everyday life? How do you know when your game isn't working and needs to be changed? There are external and internal signals to watch for and monitor. External factors may be obvious (like a failing grade on an exam or a negative balance sheet in business) or more subtle (such as the quality of your work or the dynamics of your relationships). Internal signals relate to how you're feeling: physically, mentally, emotionally and spiritually. Phrases like "learning to read yourself" and "being in touch with your feelings" are just fancy ways of saying you should be aware of how you feel and how you function. Awareness is the essential first step in dealing with a losing game.

Physical Symptoms

Low back pain and stiffness have been recurring ailments of mine since the age of seventeen. Until my mid-thirties I attributed these back spasms to something I'd done, such as shoveling snow or too much tennis. One day a friend asked me what I was uptight about. I replied immediately (and defensively) that my back problem was unrelated to feeling upset, and furthermore nothing was bothering me! The wry smile I got in return caused me to look inward. Sure enough, I realized something was on my mind (and emotions). The next time my back acted up, I looked for an emotional connection and there it was again. After all those years I finally recognized the association between my physical condition and my feelings of tension. I now know that low back pain is my earliest (and most sensitive) indicator of distress, my very own "early warning system." And as I've learned to handle things better over the years, my back spasms have become less frequent.

Physical symptoms of distress are among the most common indications that something is wrong in your life, that you're "playing a losing game." Despite the long list of possible symptoms, most people have their own galaxy of signals that are particular to them. I get low back pain but rarely get headaches. Other people get frequent headaches but never chest pains, and so on. Some folks can't look at food before an exam, while others eat ravenously. Digestive problems are common, ranging from heartburn to diarrhea. Muscle tension (especially around the neck, shoulders, chest and low back) is a frequent symptom. Others include clenching your jaw, grinding your teeth, palpitations, sweating, shakiness, blushing and cold hands. Sleep disturbance is a frequent complaint and comes in three forms: trouble falling asleep, waking several times through the night and early morning wakening (say, at 4:00 or 5:00 a.m.).

The most frequently overlooked symptom is also the most common: fatigue. We all feel tired at times, and of course the cause can be anything from lack of sleep to a viral infection. But often tiredness is a signal of distress—from overload, upset, worry or similar problems.

It's extremely important to remember that any of the physical symptoms noted above can also be caused by organic illness (for example, fatigue can result from anemia, thyroid disease, diabetes, etc.), and you should not assume the cause is distress without being checked by a physician.

Other Signals

In addition to physical signals, "thought and emotion symptoms" can also alert you to something wrong in your everyday life.

Decrease in Mental Function

"Do you have trouble making decisions?"

"Well . . . yes and no."

"Any change in your memory lately? Are you forgetful at times?"

"What was the question?"

These are exchanges I sometimes have with patients that let me know their thinking is not as crisp as usual. Lack of concentration is a common problem. People report being easily distracted or having trouble keeping their mind on things. Others complain that their mind is racing or conversely that their mind goes blank at times. All these things can happen occasionally, but if they occur frequently, they probably indicate some level of distress. Confusion or disorganized thinking is another signal worth heeding. And a common complaint I hear is that people have lost their sense of humor. That's a good sign that things are amiss.

Emotional Problems

Crying spells, depression, anxiety, frustration and anger are obvious signals that something is wrong. But the signs can be more subtle. Feeling on edge or restless and being irritable and impatient (especially with your family) are examples. Apathy, losing interest in people or activities and lack of motivation are all warnings that should be heeded. Again a note of caution: organic illness can produce many of these feelings too—for example, nervousness can signal an overactive thyroid gland; depression can result from a biochemical imbalance in the brain.

Lack of Satisfaction or Fulfillment

Many people feel they're in a rut. Their job may be boring, a relationship has lost its zing or they have a general feeling of emptiness. These are indications that their game has gone off track. Everything you do does not have to be stimulating and enjoyable, but if your life is devoid of pleasure and satisfaction, you're playing a losing game of some kind.

Feelings of Insecurity or Low Self-Esteem

One of the best barometers to measure your game is how you're feeling about yourself. Self-esteem fluctuates for everyone. But if you notice your feeling of comfort and security is consistently lower in certain situations, pay attention to that message.

A young woman I know started a relationship with a charming man and was on top of the world. But after a while I noticed the glow fading from her face and she stopped bouncing into my office with the same verve. She was even making self-deprecating remarks. When I noted that she had lost her old spunk and confidence, she wasn't surprised. She told me there was something wrong with the relationship, although she couldn't put her finger on what it was. All she knew was that she felt a lot better about herself when she was with her friends than when she was with *him*. That was the tip-off. She wisely noted: "In a healthy relationship, you should feel better about yourself, not worse."

Soon she started to notice little things this man was doing to undermine her. He contradicted her at times and criticized her appearance. He ignored her when they were with other people and became generally inattentive. She confronted the man about her concerns. When nothing changed, she stopped seeing him. Her self-esteem told her that this was a losing game and it was time to bail out.

Feeling "Not in Control"

People function better when they feel they have some control in their lives. Lack of control, or of the *feeling* of being in control, is inherently stressful to most people. Think of the last time you were caught in stalled highway traffic. The delay was irritating, but the main frustration was probably that there was nothing you could do about your predicament. You couldn't turn off, abandon your car or ride the soft shoulder. You were well and truly stuck. No control—high stress.

A lot of my patients get upset over the behavior of their children, especially their teenagers. As we analyze each aggravating situation, the common theme is that these parents can't make their kids do what they want them to do. The lack of control is infuriating. "My daughter's room is a mess and she won't clean it up"; "My son never comes to the dinner table when I call him"; "My child stays out till all hours"—the variations are legion. But the thread that binds them together is the same: a feeling of not being in control.

There are situations where giving up control is an accepted part of the experience. Professional athletes have to do what the manager tells them for the sake of the team. Orchestra musicians have to obey the conductor or they'll be playing unintended solos. Apprentices have to accept orders from their superiors. Giving up control to others is sometimes inevitable; in other cases it is an acceptable trade-off for receiving a benefit.

One of the most common situations in which people feel an unacceptable loss of control is in relationships. Many marriages are power struggles or, even worse, master-servant associations in which one person has all the control and the other has none. To be in such a liaison doesn't feel good at all. Whenever you feel a loss of control in relationships (and especially if someone is running your life or abusing you), that feeling should make you examine the game you're in and ask yourself if you want to keep playing. A similar feeling of powerlessness can occur in the workplace, especially with intimidating bosses or power-tripping superiors.

Problems in Relationships

Not all signals are internal. External indicators are also important to monitor. For example, a clear indication of a losing game is conflict with other people: at home, with friends or in the workplace. Given that it takes two to tango, not every strain between you and someone else will be your fault. But if you notice this tendency with several people (like your family, your co-workers *and* your customers) the likelihood is that something's wrong at your end. If folks are getting on your nerves, if you're irritable or short-tempered, if little things are bothering you, these are danger signals. You may notice that you're having more arguments or criticizing others unduly. One man came to see me recently, shaken by the fact that he almost hit his wife during a prolonged argument. That was the moment he knew something was desperately wrong and had to be dealt with. Another clue is if people are avoiding you, not coming up to chat or suggesting you join them for lunch. Such signals should be heeded.

Changes in Behavior

My twin sister and I were in the same class through most of high school. She was the one who told me that my classmates didn't like sitting near me during exams. I was more amused than insulted when she told me why: "You jiggle your knees and tap your toes constantly. It's distracting. In fact, it drives people crazy."

Nervous habits and anxiety traits are often more obvious to other people than to you, but you can learn to recognize them. Some people get agitated and fidgety and have trouble sitting still. Others play with paper clips or fiddle with their jewelry. Nail-biting, swearing, yelling, blaming and overeating are other signs to watch for.

Decrease in Performance and Productivity

Slumps are a realistic part of life for every athlete. Baseball pitchers lose their fine control, batters go a week without a hit, hockey players stop scoring goals, tennis players miss easy shots. These lapses in performance tell the competitor that something is wrong. A dentist told me he always knows when he's ready for a holiday. He starts taking longer with each patient, he finishes later each day and he gets behind in his paperwork. If it takes you longer to get things done, if your productivity is falling or if you're less effective at what you do, take note.

Abuse or Dependence on Drugs

It's one thing to mildly increase your use of caffeine, alcohol or nicotine. It's another to cross the line and abuse these substances. A patient told me he occasionally had a drink when he arrived home from work. When office pressures increased, he drank more often until it became a daily occurrence. Then he started to mix doubles. Before long it was two stiff drinks and so on. Almost as worrisome is when people *start* to use addictive chemicals they've never touched before. One of my patients had a major heart attack in his forties—after which he took up smoking for the first time! Experimentation with drugs like marijuana and LSD often indicates an underlying problem but can also lead to other difficulties. Even prescription drugs and over-the-counter pills are subject to abuse. If you find yourself gravitating toward substance use or abuse, stop yourself long enough to look in the mirror and ask yourself what's happening. Why are you doing this? What is so wrong in your life that you are being drawn to dangerous and harmful habits to compensate or escape? You might be anxious about keeping your job, worried about money, insecure about your appeal to others, bored at work, in conflict with someone. Whatever appears to be going wrong in your life, reaching for chemicals is a danger signal and a losing game in itself.

The Human Function Curve

There are many ways to recognize when there are problems in your life. Whether the signals are internal, external or both, you can learn to detect the indicators of a losing game early and accurately. This awareness is the key first step to changing your game into a winning one. One word of caution: everyone has stress in their lives. You have to balance the need for vigilance against the tendency to overreact. Viewing these signals as a spectrum can help you keep the self-monitoring process in perspective.

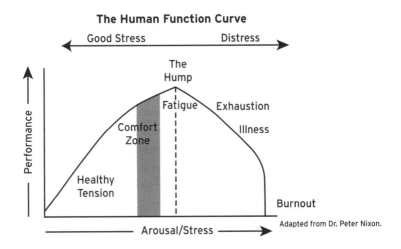

The diagram above illustrates one way to distinguish between a losing game and a winning one. I learned this diagram from Dr. Peter Nixon, a heart specialist from England, and although I've modified it slightly, I am indebted to him for introducing me to it. He calls it The Human Function Curve, and it is a graph plotting Performance against Arousal or Stress. As you can see, performance increases as arousal increases, reaching a peak at an imaginary point that he calls The Hump. But past that point, the curve starts to reverse itself and performance diminishes. Beyond the hump, the more you take on, the less well you do; and the harder you push yourself, the less productive you are. You've doubtless experienced this when studying for exams or working long hours. After a certain point you're not as efficient as you were. You make mistakes, are less decisive and don't concentrate as well. Things that take half an hour in the morning can take an hour in the late evening.

Something else happens beyond the hump. You start to experience fatigue. If you continue to endure this increased stress, you will reach a point of exhaustion. If you push yourself still farther, you will become sick. This illness can be a cold or the flu, because your resistance is down. But the illness can also be an ulcer, a heart attack, a stroke or other problem, depending on the duration and intensity of the arousal. Finally, if you ignore the signals and push yourself even more, you could reach the stage of breakdown. This stage, which is uncommon but very serious, occurs when people are totally depleted (physically, emotionally, mentally and spiritually) and unable to function. There are many warning signs before this happens though, and the process usually takes months or years.

You can see that the portion of the curve to the right of the hump has little to recommend it: decreasing performance and not feeling well. I call this the "Distress" side of the curve, and although you will drift into it at times, you need to recognize when that happens and move back to the "Good Stress" side as soon as possible.

There is also a range (from very little arousal to a moderate amount) on the left side of the curve, the "Good Stress" part. Too little stimulation is not good for you. We all need a certain amount of stress to function well. I think the optimum place to be on the curve is just to the left of the hump. I call that the Comfort Zone (which I've added to the diagram) because you can function comfortably there for long periods of time. In this zone you're operating at a very good level of performance (about 90% of maximum) but you still have some reserve before you hit the hump, and you can deal with unexpected problems or extra work without getting into the "Distress" side of the curve. You leave yourself a buffer or cushion. You could relabel this diagram to call the left side the "Winning Game" and the right side the "Losing Game."

It's important to know where you are on this curve and to monitor yourself regularly. When I ask patients to place an X at the spot on the curve where they think they are at any given time, most know without hesitation where they stand. If you're past the hump, you have to do something to reduce your level of stress so you can slide back to healthy functioning again. If you're at the point of exhaustion or ill health you will need several days or even weeks to restore yourself to the Comfort Zone. Conversely, if you find you're way off on the left side of the curve, you might benefit from some extra stimulation in the form of a new activity or project. Thus, the curve is also a guide for pacing yourself.

Missing the Important Signals

Why do people push themselves so far into the "Distress" side of the curve? Are they masochists, robots or lemmings rushing to the sea? Part of the answer lies in what happens just past the hump, when people cross the line from "Good Stress" to "Distress." As Dr. Nixon noted, you start losing your insight at this point. You become less aware of what's happening at the very time when you should be most vigilant. This loss of judgment can occur in three ways:

1. Some people don't recognize the importance of the signals when they occur. They don't realize that fatigue and decreased performance mean something—that they are early signs of distress.

2. Other people acknowledge the signals but dismiss them. "Yeah, I know I'm tired and I'm not working at my best, but this work has to get finished" and "I've got deadlines to meet" are rationalizations people use as they push on into the danger zone. We rarely ignore pain for very long. But we often ignore tiredness or treat it as a nuisance. One of Dr. Nixon's lessons is to have a healthy respect for fatigue.

3. The most dangerous way of losing insight is to subconsciously deny what is going on. It's as if fatigue is seen as weakness—and feeling weak diminishes your self-esteem. You don't want to admit you can't keep up with everyone else (and they all look as if they're doing just fine) so you press on, refusing to see what's happening to you. An incident years ago in our hospital emergency room illustrates this. It was about two in the morning and one of the doctors was obviously very tired. But when another physician said, "You look bagged. Why don't you go home? I'll see your patient for you," the weary doctor reacted defensively and indignantly replied: "I'm fine. There's nothing wrong with me. You do your work and I'll do mine!" A classic piece of denial.

In summary, there are many signals to make you aware that you're playing a losing game. The signs may be apparent in how you feel (physical, mental and emotional symptoms) or how you function (work performance, relationships and behavior). Low self-esteem, feeling "not in control" and dissatisfaction with your life are other clues worth heeding. Whether the indicators are internal or external, awareness is very important. You don't have to take your pulse every twenty minutes or do a daily "fun check" on yourself, but be sensitive to how you feel and function. Ongoing vigilance is the key to knowing when your game is getting off the track and needs a change.

CHAPTER FOUR
Common Losing Games

B EING AWARE OF *WHEN* THINGS AREN'T WORKING is an important first step in changing your losing game. The next step is to identify *what* game you're actually playing and *why* it's not working. There are two ways of losing in sports: one is when your opponent plays better than you do; the other is when you beat yourself. In the former case, all you can do is try your best and salute the winner. But in the latter situation, it's crucial to discover what *you're* doing wrong and fix it. The same is true in life. There are times when you are in circumstances beyond your control (e.g., when a relative gets sick or your company closes down). But far more often your problem results from choices *you* make and things you do or don't do.

Awareness in itself is curative.
FRITZ PERLS

A man came to see me, complaining of fatigue. I quickly learned that he wasn't getting enough sleep. Had he considered going to bed earlier? "No." Why not? "I like to unwind when I get home at night, watch a little tv, visit with my wife." He had not made the connection between staying up late and his chronic lethargy. His losing game was getting insufficient sleep and feeling tired the next day. He had been doing it for so long he'd gotten used to it.

Sometimes the losing game is not as obvious. A woman came to me with the same symptom of fatigue. Only in her case she was sleeping eight hours each night. What else was going on here? On further questioning she acknowledged drinking two cups of coffee at supper and a cup of tea at bedtime. Although the caffeine didn't interfere with the *amount* of sleep she got, it was disturbing the *quality* of her sleep in a subtle way she was unaware of. I suggested she stop drinking caffeine, and her energy level improved. She started to waken refreshed even though her total hours of sleep had not increased. Drinking caffeine near bedtime was *her* losing game.

These are just two examples of how people generate their own problems. I will survey other areas briefly in this chapter and discuss each in detail in subsequent chapters. In general, there are four categories of "losing games": how people think, the lifestyles they choose, how they behave and the situations they get into. When you recognize your own patterns, you may be surprised. People often get set in their ways and don't examine what they're doing. It's as if they live on automatic pilot, doing things unconsciously or out of habit—like the ritual of 4:00 tea in England. See which of these games you've been inadvertently playing.

Losing Games in Your Head

People create more stress for themselves by the way they think than by any other means. This happens in a variety of ways. First is the little voice in your head that chatters at you constantly. This voice is given various names like "self-talk" or "internal dialogue," and everybody has one. Much of the content of this internal conversation is neutral ("It's windy outside" or "It's almost lunchtime") or even positive ("Oh great, my favorite movie" or "Hey, I did that well").

However, some of this *self-talk* is negative and destructive. And when it is, it becomes a losing game. At times, we all berate ourselves when we make a mistake. Insults like "You jerk" and "Way to go, dummy" may seem harmless, but over time they have an undermining effect on both your performance and your self-esteem. One of my patients used to ask himself: "What is it now, Arnold?" whenever he had a problem—making him feel foolish and inept.

Here is another kind of negative self-talk. Have you ever compared yourself with someone in a way that makes you feel less good about yourself? A young business executive met an old high school friend he hadn't seen in years. When he learned that his friend was already a vice-president and earning more money than he was, he became upset and demoralized. His self-esteem took a nose-dive for about a week. He was doing something very common: making *undermining, self-defeating comparisons*. It's not a kind or helpful thing to do.

With whom do you compare yourself? Usually friends, relatives, neighbors and colleagues. You compare your money, work, social status, personal appearance, possessions, etc. If you're going bald, you notice everyone who has a full head of hair. If you're overweight, you see all the thin people out there. If you visit a friend's new house, suddenly your place looks like a cottage when you return home.

How you interpret events and situations can also be a losing game. I was recently in a restaurant when a patron berated the waiter for over-charging him on his bill. He was sure the waiter was trying to gouge a few extra dollars out of him and said so. He overlooked the possibility that it was only an honest mistake. We live in this world by making con-stant judgments and evaluations about what's going on. Many of these assumptions are "losing games" because they are subjective, negative or inaccurate.

Taking things personally is often a losing game. Have you ever en-countered a surly salesperson? He behaves rudely and you wonder: "What did *I* do?" The fact is you didn't do anything. He was just having a bad day and you happened along and got in his way. People who personalize create a lot of needless upset for themselves because most things that happen in life are not aimed at them.

Having *unrealistic expectations* of other people is a common problem. A school teacher told me of her anger and frustration with her class. They didn't always pay attention or do as they were told. She said to them: "I treat you like adults and you react like kids." The fact is she was teaching Grade 5. Her students *were* kids and it was unrealistic to treat them like adults, much less expect them to behave that way.

All-or-nothing thinking is another losing game. It involves seeing things in extremes, either black or white but never gray. The problem is that most things in life aren't that clear-cut. Sometimes this kind of thinking is misleading or unfair. Take, for example, the Academy Awards. Each winter, five actors and five actresses are nominated as best of the year. Before Oscar night, each of these professionals is a hopeful nominee, their accomplishments lauded and their stars shining bright-ly. By midnight on Awards night what have we got? Two "winners" and eight "losers." What suddenly made them losers? Aren't they still among the very best? It's as if there are only two categories and there is no room for anything in between.

Beliefs can often lead to problems. Beliefs are the assumptions we hold about how the world should be and how people should behave. We all have beliefs about everything though we are unaware of most of them. They are very powerful and literally run our lives, influencing our feelings and behavior. For example, if you believe that "work should come before pleasure," you will likely make little time for yourself. If you contend that "other people's needs should come before my own," you are apt to neglect yourself. A business executive told me with great conviction: "People always screw up. If you want something done right, you have to do it yourself." Acting on this belief, he failed to delegate and worked fourteen hours a day until he burned himself out. Even minor beliefs like "boys shouldn't wear earrings" can generate upset if your teenage son shows up for supper with a stud in his ear.

Another set of beliefs that can cause difficulty are those you hold about yourself. If you believe that "I can't talk in front of large groups" you will find public speaking more intimidating than you'd like. Any statement that begins with "I can't" or "I'm not good enough" undermines your self-confidence and generates stressful feelings. In addition, disempowering beliefs of this kind can become self-fulfilling prophecies. If you believe something about yourself, you often make it come true. If you believe "I don't mix well at big parties," you will subconsciously hold yourself back, withdraw from people, not make eye contact or smile. Then you will leave the party saying to yourself or a friend: "See, I told you I don't fit into these large gatherings"—not acknowledging that you set it up that way.

Losing Ways of Behaving

Have you ever been late for something and found yourself driving aggressively to make up time? You speed, switch lanes and run yellow lights to save precious seconds. Have you noticed that often there is another car that keeps catching up to you at red lights even though the driver is keeping to the speed limit? It confounds you that you aren't getting ahead despite all your best efforts. And what really drives you crazy is that the other motorist looks calm and relaxed, while your knuckles are white from clutching the wheel. The last straw is when the guy actually starts whistling because he's having such a nice time. At moments like these you realize that speeding doesn't get you there any faster and is much more stressful to boot. Hurrying is often a losing game—especially when it becomes a way of life.

Another losing game is to play sports or games as if your life depended on the outcome. There are many people who play bridge or Scrabble as if they're in a tournament. They're fierce competitors, fighting for every point with an awesome intensity. If they miss an opportunity or make a mistake they swear or pound the table. They groan when their opponent makes a good play. They're supposedly there for fun, but these people play to win. They can't stand losing. The result is that they often play badly and don't enjoy themselves. Even when they *win* they're playing a losing game in every other way.

People who are always in a hurry and passionately competitive are displaying two of the major characteristics of *"Type A" behavior*. A common but self-destructive way of living, this conduct upsets not only themselves but those around them as well. It may also contribute to heart disease, which makes it even more of a losing game.

Workaholism is another game with more drawbacks than benefits. Years ago I saw a young man who claimed he was working ninety hours a week. He was establishing his own business and was intent on getting rich fast. But money wasn't the only thing driving this chap. He said he got off on the pressures of his life, the excitement, the drama. There were just a few problems. First, he was so tired that he needed toxic amounts of caffeine to keep him going. Second, he had no time to enjoy his money and wasn't having any fun. Third, his wife never saw him and decided this was not her idea of a marriage, so she left him. His single-minded devotion to work, to the exclusion of everything and everyone else, was costing him in terms of health, time and relationships.

Perfectionism is a losing game because of the pressure people put on themselves to do everything just so. This tendency eats up much of their leisure time as well. A man told me how meticulous he was in everything he did. Hanging a picture was a half-hour project because he measured where to put the hook so precisely. He did dishes as if he was performing a work of art. Each fork was washed and dried one prong at a time. Chores around the house took hours, each done to a standard of perfection that even he knew was excessive. At least he finally recognized his losing game and was able to smile about it.

Then there are the *Pleasers*—they spend their lives doing things they don't want to do. They run errands, do favors, say yes when they want to say no and serve everyone else's needs but their own. Their main goals are to ingratiate themselves with others and to stay away from arguments. They may succeed in being liked and avoiding conflict, but they do so at a considerable price to themselves. Pleasers rarely feel in control of their own lives, and they can also feel angry and resentful.

In all the examples noted here, one might argue that each of these behavior patterns is beneficial at times. After all, being a hard worker and a tough competitor, paying attention to detail and doing things for others are often commendable attributes. What makes them losing games is the *degree* to which they are taken. Whereas *some* of the behavior is good, *too much* can cause problems. When your behavior becomes counterproductive, exhausts you, makes you feel not in control of your life or alienates other people, then it is a losing game. Another way of looking at it: when the behavior produces more problems than benefits, it becomes a poor trade-off—which makes it a losing game. These are all cases in which moderation is preferable and *more* does *not* mean *better*.

Losing Lifestyle Choices

Everywhere you look folks are abusing their bodies. Take the man who scrambles out of bed in the morning, rushes from the house without breakfast and lights up a cigarette as soon as he gets into his car. On the way to work he grabs a coffee, and at ten o'clock he has another coffee with a doughnut. His lunch consists of a hamburger with a side of fries, inhaled in about ten minutes because he's late for an appointment. More coffee in the afternoon keeps him awake, while more cigarettes keep his mouth and hands busy. By dinnertime he's famished, so he eats a huge supper before languishing in front of the TV for the evening, going through three or four beers (with potato chips) by the time David Letterman comes on. He finally drags his hulk up to bed after midnight but has trouble sleeping because of all he's consumed. In the morning he wakes up feeling exhausted, whereupon the scenario repeats itself. No exercise, no fresh air, inadequate sleep and poor nutrition on a background of cigarettes, coffee and beer. How's that for a losing game?

Lifestyle is more than health habits though. Leisure is another component, although many folks wouldn't know that because they don't have any. Some people cram their free time so full of activities, it's almost a relief to get back to work. Someone jokingly suggested a book for these individuals—called *Thank Goodness It's Monday*. Many professionals and business executives do something I find quite perverse: they take work home in their briefcases. This leads to two possibilities: they do the work and intrude on their leisure time, or they *don't* do the work and feel guilty or on edge. Either way it's a no-win proposition.

Poor time management is full of losing games. I used to time my trips to the airport quite precisely. If the plane was leaving at six, I'd plan to arrive at five. The drive was half an hour so I'd leave home at four-thirty. No point in wasting time by being early! However, unanticipated traffic congestion and ticket counter lineups made these trips to the airport more of an adventure than the holiday I was going on. It finally dawned on me that this was not a clever way to operate. I now depart for the airport much earlier. Leaving at the last moment and timing things down to the minute provides no margin for error or delays. Getting there early and relaxed is my new game—and it's a winner.

Money management (and mismanagement) is a domain in which losing games abound. A man told me recently about the tremendous financial pressure he felt after buying a house. The problem was that his down payment was so small that his mortgage payments were staggering. In fact, between his home and car payments, 80% of his and his wife's combined incomes were servicing those two debts. Credit card debt is another killer. Having "too much month at the end of your money" is a bad game to get into.

Losing Situations

Making the same mistake twice is a losing game. It's like the old joke about the not very bright chap who lost a thousand dollars on the Super Bowl game. Actually he lost five hundred dollars on the game itself—and another five hundred on the replay. If some of these situations weren't so serious they'd actually be funny. Long ago I talked to a woman about her unhappy marriage to an alcoholic. What surprised me was that she had been married once before—also to an alcoholic. "After going through that the first time, why did you choose to marry another alcoholic?" I inquired. "I thought I could change him," she replied. That was the same faulty logic she had used with the first man.

The two most common undermining situations are *abusive relationships* and *unpleasant jobs*. A feature they share is that people often feel trapped, miserably unhappy yet unable to get out. In destructive relationships, especially where there are children, one of the partners may feel locked in because they often have nowhere to go and no money to live on. They also feel humiliated, are embarrassed to admit failure and are afraid of living alone. Relationships can be abusive in many different ways: physical, sexual, verbal and/or emotional. Usually the self-esteem of the abused party is so low they don't feel worthy of anything better and may even blame themselves for the abuse. Dr. Susan Forward has chronicled the dynamics of many such relationships in her excellent book: *Men Who Hate Women and the Women Who Love Them*. When people live in fear and without hope, when they feel they have no control over their lives and when they have minimal self-esteem, the misery that ensues is brutalizing. And yet millions of people live in such relationships.

On the work side, I have heard that 70% of adult Americans are unhappy in their jobs. These people are exploited, overworked, underpaid, sexually harassed, verbally abused, understimulated or crashingly bored. Whatever the cause, an unsatisfactory job situation should lead people to take stock and either correct the problem or move on to some other position.

A last group of losing situations involves *values conflict*. Values are those things that are most important to you, your priorities in life, the things you hold most dear. When you don't live according to your own values, or when your values conflict with those of other people, discord and tension result. For example, I know businessmen who truly value their wives and children. But they spend most of their time and energy at work, leaving very little for family. Their dilemma is the conflict between what they want to do (spend time and energy at home) and what they feel they have to do to get ahead in their careers. Here the conflict is internal: they are not living their own values.

Often the disparity is between your values and those of others. Many couples struggle over money because one wants to save while the other wants to spend. Security is a high value for the former group, whereas the latter prefers comfort and pleasure.

I know a family where the wife wants to spend most of her time with her children and husband. But her spouse prefers to be with her and their friends, excluding the kids. These conflicts are about more than "What do you want to do tonight, Marty?" They are clashes between fundamental and deeply held beliefs and philosophies. Not resolving them creates ongoing friction and unease.

Values conflicts are also common in the workplace. A young computer specialist told me about her job problem: her company valued sales and profits while she valued customer service and human needs. She was being urged to drum up more business, even if it meant neglecting customers who were already using their product. Her priority was to service her current clients first and solicit new customers in the remaining time. The battle between these two mind-sets caused this woman considerable distress.

Just a word about *situations that are beyond your control*. As noted at the start of this chapter, you can be in a losing game through no fault of your own. You play well but lose anyway. Similarly, external events can have a direct impact on you. In this instance, the losing game is not in what happens but in how you respond. The all-too-familiar scenario of job loss offers an example. If your company is downsizing or goes out of business, you can become unemployed despite an impeccable work record. A losing game would be to react with bitterness, withdraw from activities and other people, mope and complain, sit at home and not look for work, etc. Even though it's understandable to be depressed in such circumstances, excessive negativity and inertia are not helpful ways of dealing with the upset. On the other hand, a winning response would include updating your resume, active jobseeking, upgrading skills through special courses, networking, continued social involvement, exercise and hobbies. This constructive approach would lead to optimism, resilience and the best chance of finding new employment.

In summary, you're playing a losing game when: (1) you're not getting what you want in life; (2) you're getting a payoff but the price you're paying is too high or (3) a combination of these two. It is important to be aware of the four areas in which you may be playing a losing game.

How you think, how you behave, the lifestyle choices you make and the situations you put yourself in can all generate dissatisfaction, upset or even illness. The ways in which we beat ourselves are varied but the result is the same: some form of suffering. The logical solution is to identify what you're doing wrong and to set about fixing it.

CHAPTER FIVE

Be Aware of Your Thinking

W HEN I WAS FOURTEEN I LEARNED ABOUT THE power of the mind in sports. I was playing in a tennis tournament and was leading 5-2 in the one-set match. As I moved to the baseline for the next game, a strange thought came into my head: "Boy, am I in trouble!" Where that notion came from is beyond me. My opponent had to win the next five games to take the set, I had to win only one. It probably reflected a belief I had about myself: that I "choked" in pressure situations. Maybe it was even deeper: that I wasn't good enough to win or that I didn't deserve to win. As if in a spell or caught in a terrible movie script, I tensed and clutched and sabotaged myself into a 7-5 loss of that match. I'll never forget my opponent's exclamation after the final point. He said: "I *won* the cotton-picker!" and it was all I could do to smile, shake hands and refrain from saying: "You didn't win, I lost."

You really don't know what pressure is until you play for ten dollars . . . and have only five dollars in your pocket.

LEE TREVINO
(ON THE PRESSURE OF PLAYING GOLF FOR MONEY)

What happened is that I psyched myself out. I programmed myself to lose. By setting up a negative image of my performance and the game's outcome, I created a self-fulfilling prophecy. My mind controlled my body. I started to doubt myself, became nervous and tentative, and the resulting muscle tension impeded my performance.

From Sports to Life—Negative Self-Talk

As noted in Chapter 4, we all have a little voice in our heads that talks to us. It's like our alter-ego talking to us, except no one can hear it but us. Some of these messages are repeated frequently, often for years, and have been labeled "internal tapes." When the messages are negative and counterproductive (as they frequently are), we would do well to erase the tapes—forever!

What is the content of these damaging messages? What does the voice say that is so undermining and hurtful?

Criticisms: Negative self-talk is often critical and judgmental. It's the voice that tells you you're a "klutz" when you trip on a sidewalk, or that you're a "jerk" when you make a mistake. It calls you "stupid," "nerd" and names I wouldn't want to repeat here. I've started a collection of put-down names people call themselves. Ironically many of these are one-syllable epithets, as if the internal voice is trying to conserve energy while dumping on you. Here is a partial list: goof, ditz, clod, wimp, dolt, slob, creep, slut, dork, geek, wuss, dweeb, flake and schmuck. The two-syllable insults include dummy, moron and loser, while "idiot" leads the three-syllable group. Then there are the combination names. One middle-aged woman says "sloppy bitch" when she spills something. When she makes a mistake, her voice calls her "dumb broad" or "you twit." How would you like to walk around all day with that message banging on your brain?

Bossiness: The voice in your head can be very bossy. It's like a dictatorial employer or parent telling you what to do in a persistent and domineering way. This is the voice that tells you what you have to do, what you must do and what you should do—sometimes called "The Tyranny of Should." It keeps you on a treadmill of duty and obligation and scolds you if you start to relax. When you sit down to read a book on a quiet Sunday afternoon, it's the voice that rebukes you: "What is this? You've got nothing better to do? I thought you were going to clean out the basement" or "You should be going to visit your mother." Or it undermines pleasant activities with nagging remarks like "I shouldn't be doing this" or "I should be doing my homework." You would never work for a boss who rode you as hard as the little voice in your own head.

Destructive Emotions: Your internal voice articulates stressful emotions. These feelings waste your time and energy. They include worry, regret, remorse, resentment, jealousy, hatred and self-pity. Anger, fear and guilt can be added to this list, although I keep them separate be-cause there are times when these three emotions are appropriate and helpful. Anger alerts you to things that are offensive or that feel wrong (for example, when you're being exploited or abused by others). Fear protects you from danger and cautions you in new or difficult situations. Guilt guides you when it is the voice of conscience, leading you to distinguish between right and wrong. However, when anger, fear and guilt are excessive or inappropriate to the circumstances, they can be added to the list of "destructive" emotions. Getting angry when a can opener doesn't work is not helpful. Being fearful of meeting new people is very limiting. And feeling guilty when you sit down to relax for fifteen minutes is not at all constructive.

Worry is a draining emotion. It's natural—though not very helpful—to worry before an exam or important job interview. But there are people who worry well in advance of events, and these folks really suffer. I spoke to a teacher in June who was moving to a new school in September. She was already worrying about how it would go, whether she'd like it and if she had made a mistake by changing jobs. At that rate, she was not only going to ruin her summer but she'd be burned out before classes even started in the fall. I call such people "long-distance worriers." It's as if they want to get a head start so they can worry longer than everyone else. One of my patients called it "borrowing trouble from the future," a great phrase to describe this harmful habit.

Negative Filters: This describes a negative way of looking at things. It's like putting on tinted glasses so that everything looks darker and more ominous than it really is. If someone invites you to dinner and you look through your filter of suspicion, you question his motives and think: "I wonder what he wants." The filter of pessimism leads you to believe that things will work out badly. Defeatism causes you to assume you will fail at whatever project you undertake. When a friend invites you to play squash, you think to yourself: "What's the point? I'm just going to lose." Cynicism (or skepticism) generates doubt and overall negativity about things. These negative filters color what you see and experience, giving messages like "this won't work out" and "my success won't last." They undermine your mood and cause you to dismiss many of the good things and people in your life.

Comparisons: A mother gave up her occupation to stay home and raise her children. Years later, she and her husband went to a social function put on by his company. She spent the next week feeling depressed and demoralized. When I asked why, her explanation was a classic example of an undermining comparison. She met several career women at the party who impressed her with their intelligence and accomplishments. In fact, they so intimidated her with their poise and success that she felt worthless beside them. She began questioning her own life, her achievements and her abilities. The comparison made her feel bad about herself. She summed it up by saying: "I'm a wasted human being."

Undermining and self-defeating comparisons are a losing game. There will always be people out there for you to admire. But they don't have to become hammers with which you beat yourself over the head. Some folks refer to themselves as "the black sheep in the family" because they don't feel they measure up to their siblings. Others feel inept because they compare themselves with top-producing coworkers.

Comparisons are also made with movie stars and people in lifestyle ads. Have you ever gone to a movie starring Halle Berry or Brad Pitt? After the film you look in the mirror—and notice you don't look anything like Halle or Brad! It can be a real letdown. And the hunks and gorgeous women in lifestyle commercials (the ones playing beach volleyball and attending swell parties) can similarly undermine your self-concept. Comparisons with media images and TV characters can be a real trap. Imagine any doctor trying to live up to the image of *Marcus Welby M.D.*, a TV show from the 1970s (although physicians used to say *they* could be that good too—if they had to see only one patient a week!). Look at the lofty standards of fatherhood set by old classics such as *Father Knows Best* and *The Cosby Show*. Who could be so wise, patient, congenial, hard-working and decent as those two, week in and week out? Interestingly, there are far fewer idealized family figures on TV today. Maybe the viewers got tired of these paragons of virtue who made them feel so inadequate.

There's one irony to all this comparing: there are people right now who are not feeling good about themselves because *you're* the standard they're comparing themselves with and *they* don't measure up.

Another basis of comparison is the idealized standard many people set for themselves (their "ideal self"). These folks set up an image of appearance, behavior or performance that can't possibly be met. Then they dump on themselves for not measuring up. Sometimes they compare themselves with their own self at an earlier age when they were thinner, faster, stronger, more energetic, etc. A man lamented that he could no longer run as fast as he had ten years earlier. Even though he still enjoyed running, he let his slower pace gnaw at his feeling of satisfaction and pride.

Ruminating, Wallowing, Over-Analyzing and Second-Guessing: This tongue twister refers to people who think too much. Ruminating involves brooding, rehashing and stewing about things. It's like pushing the replay button on a tape recorder over and over again. These people don't let go of problems. A business executive was told he'd probably be transferred to another city. It wasn't definite and no specific time was set. He immediately got upset at the prospect of moving. The new town was small, isolated and cold. He dreaded the idea of living there. He became obsessed with this issue. It was on his mind all the time. It undermined his enjoyment of life for almost a year.

Wallowing involves immersing yourself in thoughts like "Poor me," "This is awful," "How could he do that to me?" It often leads to self-pity and self-absorption. One of my patients was jilted and deceived by a lover whom she couldn't get out of her mind, even months later. However, she was adding to her upset in a rather perverse way. She kept his picture in her wallet and looked at it longingly several times a day, tearfully dredging up the hurt all over again and indulging herself in misery.

Over-analyzing is a process of re-examining some issue repeatedly and from every conceivable angle, trying to discern some subtle meaning or significance. An insecure young man with too much time on his hands put his new relationship under a mental microscope. He dissected conversations to probe "What did she mean by that?" and examined the implications of how closely she sat to him in the movie theater. When I asked him if he was so intense about other things, he replied: "I analyze everything—unto *death*!" Over-analyzers also replay events and immerse themselves in the "If Onlys": "If only I had done this, if only I had said that," etc.

Another form of over-analyzing occurs in decision making. Some people weigh the possibilities back and forth in an endless internal debate. They sound like Tevye in *Fiddler on the Roof:* "On the one hand . . . but on the other hand . . ." This often leads to "Analysis Paralysis" where you analyze so much you end up taking no action at all. In 1989, I decided to buy a word processor; I was so overwhelmed by all the makes and models that I did nothing for months. Finally I was introduced to two experts by a mutual friend. We sat down on a Saturday morning and I said: "Enough of this dithering. Tell me what to buy and where to get it." They did and the computer was on my desk two weeks later. Left to my own devices, I'd still be pondering.

Second-guessing refers to re-examining some past decision or behavior and questioning whether it was good or bad. This internal conversation is usually loaded with "what if" and "if only" statements. "What if I had done such and such?" and "If only I had foreseen thus and so." As a brief exercise in learning from your mistake, second-guessing can be productive. But as an ongoing discussion, it's a waste of time. It's like the football coach who watches reruns of his team's championship loss all through the following winter. He learns nothing but suffers a lot.

In summary, *negative self-talk*, in all its varied disguises, is a losing game with great potential for misery and anguish. Worse yet, it's self-created. Techniques to neutralize these harmful messages are worth learning. Thought stopping, coping statements, diversion and affirmations are the skills to acquire. These will be discussed in Chapter 10. However, the first step in dealing with this inner voice is to become aware of it. Notice how it shows up for you. Write down some of the hurtful and harmful messages it conveys. Then realize it doesn't have to be that way.

CHAPTER SIX

Becoming Aware of Your Mind Traps

IND TRAPS ARE PATTERNS OF THINKING THAT create distortions or lead to problems and upset. These tendencies are often seen in sports. I used to be a mediocre golfer, but one day years ago I shot a terrific round. I couldn't wait to get out and play again. I felt I'd finally got the knack of the game. Was I ever wrong! My score was fifteen strokes higher, leaving me demoralized and disappointed. Then I realized why I felt such a letdown. I expected that, because I played very well one day, I could do the same again. But given my level of skill and experience, that expectation was unrealistic. The really good score was a fluke, not the forerunner of a trend. By setting my expectations so high, it was inevitable that I'd fall short.

Rigidity is another mind trap that shows up in sports. Some coaches play the percentages so faithfully that they often miss opportunities. The team that always punts on third down, the manager who always pinch hits a right-handed batter against a left-handed pitcher, the tennis player who always lobs against an opponent at the net: these rules make life predictable, but they show no imagination or flair, and since they fail to take many other important factors into account, they often backfire.

There are several mind traps that can cause problems in life as well as in sports. Perfectionism, over-identifying with roles, misinterpreting situations, taking things personally and all-or-nothing thinking are among the tendencies discussed in this chapter.

Unrealistic Expectations

Have you ever noticed that New Year's Eve is rarely as good as you'd hoped? You make all these elaborate plans, spend a bin full of money and come away feeling dissatisfied? What you expect is the celebration of a lifetime. When you get only a pleasant time it feels like a real downer. When your expectations are unrealistic, nothing can live up to them.

If you have a job without aggravation, you don't have a job.

MALCOLM FORBES

People with unrealistic expectations put themselves in a bind. Since what they expect is unrealistic, it almost certainly won't occur, and they will feel disappointed, upset, frustrated or even angry. Yet they often don't realize their expectations are unrealistic and that they are caught in a trap of their own making. The way out is to recognize that what they seek is highly unlikely and to modify their demands accordingly.

How do you know when your expectations are unrealistic? Sometimes only experience will tell you. But sometimes it is more obvious. For example, people who expect to be right all the time and never make mistakes are destined for trouble. Years ago I lamented to a colleague how upsetting it was to think I might make a serious mistake in my work even though I'm very careful. She said: "You've got it wrong. It's not that you *might* make mistakes, it's that you *will* make mistakes. If you think you can practice medicine for thirty years and never make a mistake, you're dreaming." How's that for a hard-hitting lesson in life? But it makes perfect sense.

Another unrealistic expectation is that everyone will like you—especially if you're nice to them. The fact is that *not* everyone will like you no matter what you do. A shy, single man I know has just started dating. But he's got a realistic outlook to counter his fear of rejection when he asks people out. He says: "You can't get a yes ten times out of ten; somebody's going to say no." Even in a landslide election many people vote for the other candidates. And no entertainer, no matter how popular, ever got a 100% endorsement from the public.

Some people think they can do it all. They get edgy if they fall behind. I subscribe to several magazines, but over the years I've accepted that I can't read all of them every week. I don't even try anymore. I asked a heart specialist how he dealt with the large and pressing demand for his services from family doctors. In the field of cardiology, where the stakes are high, there can be a lot of pressure on consultants to see "just one more patient." His answer was instructive: "First, I recognized that I couldn't do it all. Then, it was just a matter of deciding where to draw the line."

Unrealistic expectations are among the causes of burnout. When people set their goals too high (like a nurse setting out to relieve all suffering or a teacher expecting all his students to master algebra) the result is always less than anticipated. Most people accept the shortfall between their dreams and reality and modify their expectations accordingly. Those who simply strive harder and work longer hours fall into a cycle of effort and disappointment that leads to exhaustion and disillusionment.

People also have unrealistic expectations of others. When some folks marry, they do so expecting their mate to change certain characteristics or behavior. One woman knew her husband was shy and uncommunicative but expected him to change as he got more comfortable with her. When his behavior continued, she became angry and insisted he deal with his problem. Many parents expect their teenagers to have neat and tidy rooms. To measure the unreality of that expectation, just take a survey at your next social gathering and find out how widespread is the phenomenon of the teen's messy bedroom.

Realistic Versus Reasonable

Some expectations may be *reasonable* but still not *realistic*. If most teens have messy rooms, maybe that's the norm for these kids. It seems reasonable to expect them to clean up every so often, but that doesn't make it realistic. It's reasonable to expect motorists to thank you when you let them into traffic—but how many of them actually wave in appreciation? It's reasonable to expect that people I lend books to return them to me, but I've learned from bitter experience that such expectations are often not realistic. So just because an expectation makes sense to you (is "reasonable") doesn't mean it is likely to happen (is "realistic").

One of my patients used a coping statement to remind him when his expectations were reasonable but unrealistic. When someone let him down, he would say to himself, with a wistful smile, "Welcome to the real world."

Perfectionism

The most extreme form of unrealistic expectation is perfectionism. Very high expectations are often unrealistic but occasionally can be met. However, perfection is virtually impossible. One man told me: "I'm a perfectionist but I'm not perfect—and *that* drives me crazy."

Glenn Gould was a world-famous pianist, renowned as a concert and recording artist. At the height of his career he stopped giving live concerts. When asked why, he said that audiences and critics were expecting perfection, and anything less was unacceptable to them. Worse than that, he felt that patrons were listening carefully to see if they could detect a wrong note or flawed passage. The pressure of their impossible expectations drove one of the world's greats from the concert stage. It just wasn't worth it to him anymore.

The closest anyone ever comes to perfection is on a job application form.
UNKNOWN

Expecting perfection always results in disappointment. The reality that life delivers will always fall short (except for those few transcendent moments that are as brilliant as they are rare). So whenever you feel upset by a situation, ask yourself if your expectations are too high or unrealistic. If they are, modify them accordingly. This doesn't mean you should not do your best or strive for excellence. Just don't set yourself up by expecting too much.

This message is best summed up in a phrase I heard years ago: "When all else fails, lower your standards." A woman came to grips with this notion in her search for a spouse. "You won't find a mate who is perfect," she said. "You have to find someone whose faults and imperfections you can live with (and who can live with yours!)." A man came to terms with his perfectionism this way: "Making mistakes isn't all bad. It's just life."

Over-Identifying with Roles

Professional athletes lose a lot when they retire from sports. They leave behind the excitement, camaraderie, fame and money. But for many the biggest loss is their identity. They have thought of themselves as a baseball or tennis player for so long that it becomes their self-concept. When they become an ex-boxer, skier or whatever, they often don't have a new identity to step into.

I once heard a physician describe himself this way: "I'm a doctor first and everything else second." The "everything else" included his roles of husband, father, son, brother, neighbor, etc. A second-level executive in a company referred to himself more often as "a Level 2" than he did by his name. Then one day he told me he'd had lunch with "two Level 2s and a Level 4." He admitted: "I live my job. My job is my life."

These are examples of over-identifying with roles—usually a job or title or professional designation. "I am a nurse," "I am a teacher," "I am a lawyer" are phrases you hear every day and don't think twice about. But a lot of these people really *think* of themselves in those terms. It's as if they really *are* their job or title.

I sometimes tell my patients that I'm not a doctor. "I'm David Posen—and I *do* medicine." Medicine is my occupation, my vocation, my profession. It is what I *do*. But it is not who I *am*. If I switch jobs tomorrow and become a teacher or a carpenter, I will still be David Posen. When I play tennis or go to a movie or play with my kids I am not a doctor, I am simply David Posen. I keep my identity separate from the work I do.

Is this just a semantic distinction? No. The difference becomes important if I have a bad day at work (and we all have them). Maybe I've made a mistake or missed a diagnosis in my role of doctor. Those days are upsetting to me. I go home feeling disappointed or dispirited *as a physician*. But if my identity, my self-definition, my personhood were all tied up in my "doctorness," then I would go home feeling shattered and worthless *as a person*. I would feel devastated and unworthy as a person. That is about as awful a feeling as anyone can have. So to protect myself from such feelings of personal despair, to keep from being vulnerable to this kind of deep emotional assault, I separate my *self* from my role or work (which is only a *part* of my life). As my friend at Harvard, Dr. Matthew Budd, taught me years ago: Your job is what you *do*; it is not who you *are*.

There are other dangers from over-identifying with roles or jobs or titles. In recent years thousands of people have lost their jobs. Many of these individuals felt lost without their employment. It wasn't just that they had lost the structure or challenge in their lives. They had lost the sense of who they were. Their identity was tied to work, and now they felt like ships without anchors or rudders.

Tying your self-concept to work can also produce over-commitment to the job. Work consumes too much of your time and energy and leads to neglect of your family and personal life. This imbalance is dangerous because it leads to overload and burnout. Your work literally becomes your life. Then you invest yourself totally in that one activity to the exclusion of the other areas of your life.

Those who are most vulnerable to over-identifying with their work are people in the "helping professions" (doctors, nurses, therapists, social workers, teachers, clergy, lawyers, etc.) and business executives. The risk of burnout is highest in these groups.

Another problem arises when people see their value in monetary terms. Salaries, raises, bonuses and promotions take on symbolic importance in terms of self-image. A woman moved east from a high-paying job in Western Canada and she took a secretarial post at a much lower salary. "I hated myself for taking this job. I sold myself for bargain-basement prices," she lamented. "I want a new title. I've outgrown the 'secretary' label." She viewed her salary and her title as a measure of what she was worth as a person. I told her: "You are not your job—or your salary or your title." To which she replied: "Then I don't know who I *am*."

People can also over-identify with roles in their family. The roles of "wife" and "mother" can become emotionally complicated. Some women think of themselves as "Mrs. John Doe" or "Wife of . . ." (as Sondra Gotlieb, married to Canada's former U.S. ambassador, titled her book), and they lose their sense of themselves in the process. More than once I've seen a woman sign her name "Mrs. B. Jones" where the B. is her *husband's* initial. Thus, even when she signs her name, there is nothing of *her* in the signature. Then there is the label and identity of "mother" to reckon with. For some women (and men, for that matter) the highest level of self-actualization and fulfillment is to bear and raise children. When this leads to happiness and personal satisfaction, everyone wins. But if a parent loses themself in the role of "mother" or "father," it can lead to self-neglect, low self-esteem and a loss of identity. These parents consistently put their own needs after those of their children and get their self-definition through their kids.

The child-rearing years can be hard enough if approached in this way. But the real crisis comes when the children leave home. At that time many parents may feel that they lose their prime function and meaning in life, their identity as individuals. They need to be reminded that they have a substantial existence as people in their own right, not just as caregivers or relatives of others. To prevent this loss of identity, parents need to maintain their sense of themselves in addition to their roles as mother or father. Self-care, a social support system and enjoyable activities are all important ingredients of a balanced life, leading to a sense of *self* separate from roles within the family.

If it's dangerous to confuse your circumstances with your self, what are the antidotes to this tendency? One is to use short phrases ("coping statements") to keep things in perspective. Examples include: "I am not my job/title/label or salary," and "My job is what I do, not who I am." When things get pretty thick at work, it's helpful to remind yourself that "It's only a job." The idea is not to demean the job or your responsibilities, just to put work in context. View it as part of a full and balanced life, not as the overwhelming (or only) thing of importance. Another attitude I suggest is "healthy detachment." This means removing yourself emotionally from your job enough to protect you but not so much that you are ineffective. In medicine, nursing, social work, teaching and law I advocate "detached caring." This means caring enough for patients/students/clients to give empathy and concern but not so much that you lose your judgment or become devastated if anything happens to them.

Misleading Interpretations

In 1989 the Toronto Blue Jays acquired a new player named Mookie Wilson. Actually his name is William, but he is known strictly by his nickname. Something interesting happened the first time I saw him play. When Mookie came to the plate, the crowd started booing loudly. I was taken aback at this hostility from his home crowd. I was even more surprised to see people smiling as they booed. Most bewildering, however, was that Mookie was smiling too. Clearly there was more going on here than met the eye. When I listened more carefully, I realized that the sound filling the stadium was not "B-o-o-o-o-o" but rather "M-o-o-o-o-o-k-i-e." It sounded exactly like booing but it was really an affectionate cheer for a popular new player.

This misinterpretation demonstrates an important principle. As Dr. Albert Ellis explained in his model called Rational Emotive Therapy, emotions are rarely caused by actual events. The way you *interpret* events determines how you feel and react most of the time. When your interpretations are inaccurate, they can lead to problems and upsets. So misinterpretations are another kind of losing game—because things are often not what they seem.

A common situation illustrates this principle. Have you ever been speaking to someone and they start to yawn? How do you feel? Do you get a little uncomfortable or feel uneasy? You may even react more strongly and feel irritated or angry. But what's really happening? Is it the yawning that's upsetting you? No. The yawn is simply an event. If you get upset, it's because of the interpretation you've made of the yawn. You may feel the person is bored—or, even worse, that *you* are boring them. Or you may feel the person is not interested in you—or that you're not very important. It's not the *yawn* that's causing your upset; it's the *meaning* you've given to it. Now, what if your interpretation was that the person was tired because she didn't get enough sleep last night? Are you going to be upset? Probably not. Or maybe she just needs more oxygen. That's not going to offend you. Some people yawn when they're nervous—or when someone else yawns. When you give the event a different meaning, your emotional reaction changes accordingly.

I know a salesman who let an interpretation ruin his weekend. He received a call from one of his best customers on Friday morning. The caller asked to meet with him and his boss the following Monday morning. Not wanting to sound paranoid, the salesman didn't ask what it was about. He tried to sound casual and confident as he set up a time for the meeting. He then spent the whole weekend stewing about what the client wanted. His assessment was negative and he assumed he was in big trouble.

By Monday morning he was dreading the meeting. But when he arrived, a big surprise awaited him. The customer was so pleased with the company's product and service that he wanted to give them an unusually big order. The meeting was to find out if they could handle such a large shipment and to work out the details. The salesman left the meeting with a large commission and a wrap-around smile. But he had suffered needlessly for days. All from a faulty interpretation.

People interpret not only things that happen but things that *don't* happen. A couple hired a contractor to renovate their cottage. After giving a down-payment, they heard nothing from him for weeks and he never returned their phone calls. The husband was doing a slow burn! His assessments of the situation were: "He's unreliable; I'm being shafted; now that he's got my money he doesn't care," etc. The evening after I spoke to him, the workman called to say his son had been rushed to the hospital and was very sick. He said: "My mind has been totally preoccupied. I'm sorry."

Taking Things Personally

In baseball, it's not uncommon for a batter to be hit by a pitched ball. The hitter's reaction usually reflects his interpretation of the event. If he thinks it was an accident, he will accept the situation and trot on to first base. But if he thinks it was intentional, he will get angry and may even run out to attack the pitcher. He's most likely to get mad if he thinks the pitcher was trying to send him a *personal* message (as opposed to a general intimidation tactic). As with the interpretation of the yawning, though, this assessment is based on guesswork or mind-reading and can be quite inaccurate. Taking things personally is a common form of misinterpretation.

When you personalize other people's behavior, you set yourself up to be insulted or hurt. In most cases, people's actions are about *them*, not about *you*. Think about your own behavior. How many times have you been curt or impatient with someone who has done nothing to upset you? When you get short-tempered with your children, isn't it usually because of *your* mood rather than *their* behavior? You generate a lot of unnecessary distress when you take other people's moods personally.

It seems to be human nature to take things out on other people. When you get angry, you often lash out at someone other than the person with whom you are upset. A classic example is when my son (then age four) asked for a cookie near suppertime and I said no. He got angry, and his little brother, who happened by at that moment, got bopped just because he was small and handy. It's like the frustrated worker who comes home and kicks the dog.

One way you take things personally is by assuming that other people's behavior is aimed at you. What a lot of needless upset that creates. And, when you think about it, personalizing is rather self-centered. Presuming that events in the world revolve around you reflects a rather inflated view of your own importance. People are usually far too involved with themselves to be thinking about you. In a novel I read in high school one of the characters asks: "So tell me, what do you *really* think of me?" to which the other person replies, after a pause: "Well, to be honest with you, I *don't* think of you."

Some people personalize business decisions. It's one thing when you get a performance review that is unmistakably about you. But when corporate decisions are made (departments shuffled or closed, promotions given, jobs reassigned), many factors are involved and individual considerations are often the least of them. With mergers, downsizing, takeovers and the like, the bureaucracy may steamroller over people. Such events should be kept in perspective. Many baseball players are traded these days less because of their performance than to get rid of their huge salaries. Real estate clients may pull out of a deal because they have second thoughts, not because they want to shaft their agent. Patients change doctors or dentists for all kinds of reasons, many of which have nothing to do with the quality of care they received. Yet many professionals feel personally slighted by such occurrences.

How can you stop taking things personally? There are several things you can do. An obvious one is to check it out with others. If you feel slighted by a co-worker you've always gotten along with, have a chat with him. Tell him you've noticed a change in his attitude and ask if something is troubling him—about you or about anything else. Be supportive and concerned, not challenging or defensive. He will often assure you it has nothing to do with you. He may not even realize his behavior toward you had changed.

It also helps to notice how he behaves toward other people. One middle manager felt she was being undermined by her company president. The boss was countermanding her orders and undercutting her authority. Only when she observed the president's behavior with other managers did she realize it was a general pattern, not just aimed at her.

It's often illuminating to find out what's going on in the person's life that might account for their behavior. A college student was being picked on by a teacher and took it personally. When he looked into it, he discovered the teacher was a very unhappy person who had just split up with her spouse and had other personal problems.

Finally, there's one sticky fact to face about personalizing: some things *are* meant personally and some people really *don't* like you.

There's an expression: "Just because you're paranoid doesn't mean they *aren't* out to get you." So you have to acknowledge that sometimes your taking things personally is accurate, after all. And that can be hurtful. However, I'm convinced these occasions are in the minority. Realistic expectations tell you that *not* everyone will like you. You have to be philosophical and get on with your life in spite of it.

Who's Got the Problem?

A man was going to sell his house. A neighbor convinced him to rent it to her instead. He agreed. Then the neighbor told him she didn't like the wallpaper. The owner wanted to be accommodating, so he ripped out the wallpaper and started painting the walls himself. Alas, two cans of paint spilled, ruining the carpet, which then had to be replaced. After an exhausting and stress-filled weekend (and over $3,000 for broadloom and paint), the job was finished—whereupon the neighbor changed her mind and decided not to rent the house after all.

Lack of proper planning on your part does not constitute an emergency on my part.
UNKNOWN

When he told me this story (with a combination of drama and amusement), I asked him: "Who had the problem? Why did you make her not liking the wallpaper *your* problem? Even worse, while you were suffering unnecessarily, she wasn't suffering at all!"

Most victims of this type of scenario are Pleasers. Others are simply not assertive and allow themselves to be manipulated.

The "mind trap" is that the victims don't realize they're taking on someone else's problem. They take responsibility for something that is not (and *should* not be) theirs. And they're not aware of how they set themselves up. They just know they feel trapped and resentful. It may occur innocently. For example, an employee comes to you with a problem. You suggest a solution. He looks at you sheepishly.

"What's the matter?" you ask.

"I've never done that before," he replies; or "I don't know how to do that." Or maybe "I couldn't do that. Do you think you could speak to him?"

Before you know it you've said the fateful words: "All right, leave it with me. I'll take care of it" and you're stuck. The "helpless" employee has put you in the position of "Mommy" or "Daddy" and you've been lured into taking on their problem.

Every tax season accountants are inundated by pleading clients who, at the last minute, dump boxes of financial records on the desk, offer inane excuses about why they're late and expect their friendly accountant to bail them out one more time. No matter that these clients have been doing this for years. The accountant feels obliged to work into the night or weekend to accommodate the procrastinating customer. It's tough for those in a service profession to say no, but it's no fun being put upon by others either.

Another losing game is the trap of taking on other people's health problems. A mother anguished over her adult son who had asthma. Her son's destructive lifestyle (heavy smoking, careless use of medication, etc.) was triggering asthmatic attacks. The mother tried everything, from lecturing to nagging to pleading, but nothing worked. I finally asked her: "Who's got the problem?" She acknowledged it was her son's but felt she'd be pretty hard-hearted not to be worried. However, she was realizing there was only so much she could do. Beyond that she had to stop taking responsibility for the problem. Of course she would continue to be concerned. But for her own peace of mind she had to let her son make decisions and live his own life, as difficult as it might be to watch the result.

Another scenario could be called "The Dilemma of the Intermediary or Mutual Confidant." A woman told me about her mother and sister who were having an argument. Each felt she was right, and the two were barely on speaking terms. However, they were both calling my patient and telling her all the details of the argument, seeking her advice and support. The woman felt caught in the middle, confused, upset at both of them but empathic as well. She had allowed herself to take on both their problems simultaneously. I showed her that their fight was not her problem and that, if she found it stressful, she should tell them to stop involving her in their running feud. The real capper came at a family party some weeks later. The mother and sister kissed and laughed and behaved as if nothing had happened. The beleaguered woman could hardly believe her eyes. She was the only one still upset and she became furious with both of them.

Does this mean you should stop helping others or caring about their problems? Emphatically not. I'm not suggesting you look out for yourself alone and ignore the plight of others. You just need to be aware of when you're getting in deeper than you should. Sometimes the best help you can give people is *not* to help. Otherwise they don't learn to solve problems for themselves. The best indicator is how you're feeling. If you are comfortable getting involved and can keep your emotional distance, by all means help out. But if you're feeling distressed, manipulated or resentful, you'd do well to withdraw from further involvement.

What are the guidelines for dealing with problems that aren't yours? Detachment and disengagement are the keys. Tell yourself: "It's not my problem. It's not in my interest to get involved in this issue." And don't allow yourself to have a big emotional stake in things you can't control. Distance yourself if you realize you're getting drawn into a situation you can't resolve. Don't let others dump their work on you. It's one thing to help a motorist replace a flat tire; it's another for you to do all the work while he sits under the nearest tree, reading a book. Sometimes you have to be assertive or delegate appropriately. A business executive caught onto this enthusiastically and eliminated half the clutter on his desk within a week by reassigning all the tasks he'd taken on for other people. The phrase "Who's got the problem?" became the "open sesame" that allowed him to get control over his work life.

There is a corollary to the foregoing discussion: don't expect other people to solve *your* problems. Take again the teenager's messy room. Here, the parents are incensed by the chaos in their kid's room but the teen is either oblivious to the clutter or content with it. The dilemma centers around an interesting paradox: the parents want the child to solve *their* problem. On the surface the parents are saying: "We can't stand that mess in your room. Please clean it up." But underneath there is a different translation: "We have a problem with your room. And we want *you* to solve *our* problem by cleaning it up." Aside from the futility of this battle, the basic premise is flawed because people will usually not address issues that are not problems *to them.*

Rigidity

"I'm comfortable with things just as they are"; "That's the way we do things around here"; "I always do it this way." These are phrases from people who don't like change or trying new things. They're stuck to the status quo. Sometimes these folks are convinced their way is right. Other times they operate out of habit. And occasionally it's just old-fashioned stubbornness. One man supports his strong views with the motto: "I may be wrong but I am never in doubt!" The problem with this kind of thinking is that it limits options. The other dilemma is that real life situations don't conform to the rigid way these people think, leaving them at odds with their environment and fellow human beings. I once heard this problem called psychosclerosis—"hardening of the attitude."

I've been in a groove so long it's becoming a grave.
ANONYMOUS

One of my favorite stories is about a middle-aged lady who complained of exhaustion. Her life was overloaded with chores and she couldn't keep up. She felt totally out of control. In describing the mad rush of her morning routine, she said: "There are so many things I have to do before I leave for work."

"Like what?" I asked.

"Oh, like having breakfast and getting dressed and brushing my hair and teeth and making my bed . . ."

I interrupted to ask why she *had* to make her bed.

She looked surprised, as if this obvious concept was self-evident. "Well, uh, I've been making my bed all my life, I always make my bed, you *have* to make your bed."

I told her it wasn't imperative that she make her bed and then I made a suggestion: "Why don't you leave your bed unmade for the next two weeks and just see what happens?" She was speechless. But to her credit, this fifty-four-year-old woman, who'd made her bed every morning since age twelve, went along with my idea.

Two weeks later she returned beaming. She couldn't wait to report on her experiment. She hadn't made her bed for two weeks and nothing terrible had happened. In fact, it felt liberating. But the best part came next. "And do you know what else?" she asked, barely able to conceal her delight. "I stopped drying the dishes too! I just leave them in the rack to dry." And in that moment I knew this woman had freed herself from over forty years of rigidity in almost everything she had been doing. Once she realized she didn't have to make her bed, she could start to question other assumptions. This story is not about making beds or drying dishes. It is about *awareness* (of how she'd been restricting herself), about *choice*, and about *permission* to do things differently. Now if she's late or busy she knows she can leave the bed unmade and that's okay. Nothing *has* to be done *all* the time.

There's nothing wrong with being a creature of habit, per se. It depends on the circumstances. Some people are slow to replace old things but that doesn't have to present a problem. I still wear a pair of sandals purchased sixteen years ago. Even though they're almost worn through, they're comfortable and serve me well. My 1980 car ran extremely well for thirteen years and I was reluctant to give it up. The only one who had a problem was my dealer who wanted to sell me a new model. This is different from *rigidity* (or *inflexibility*), which reflects a reluctance to change. Rigidity becomes detrimental when it increases your workload, limits your ability to solve problems or react quickly to change, puts you at odds with the world or people around you or causes you distress.

The antidote to rigidity is flexibility. Keep an open mind. Go with the flow. Roll with the punches. Try new things, even if only for variety. Stay loose and light-footed so you can change direction quickly. Sometimes you will accidentally discover a better way of doing things. I always liked my tennis racket and thought the wide-bodied ones were some kind of cheating. Then I played with one just to see what it was like. Guess what I use now? Sometimes it's fun to drive a different route to work. Or interesting to change your office routine. If you're getting stale or into a rut, look for little things to do differently to spice things up. And especially if things aren't going well (in sports or in life), "Always change a losing game" is a motto worth remembering.

"All-or-Nothing" Thinking

Vince Lombardi, the legendary football coach of the Green Bay Packers, was fond of saying: "Winning isn't the most important thing—it's the *only* thing." There was no middle ground. Either you won or you lost.

There are several names for thinking in extremes. "Polarized" thinking, "black or white" thinking or "thinking in absolutes" are common descriptions of the tendency to see only the ends of a spectrum, while ignoring everything in between. The classic American symbol of this is the old Western movie. There were only good guys or bad guys and, just so you wouldn't miss the point, the good guys always wore white and the bad guys black. (There were a few exceptions like Hopalong Cassidy—but his *hair* was white.) The bad guys were venal, cruel, ruthless, uncouth, violent and evil liars; the good guys were upstanding, kind, patient, honest, decent, polite and good-looking. It made life simpler and the plot easier to follow.

Polarized thinking is a mind trap that creates problems in a number of ways. First, you overlook many options and possibilities if you see only the two extremes of an issue. Second, you become confused when things fall into the gray zone between your black and white reference points. Third, you get upset when things aren't just the way you want them (which happens a lot). Last, you push yourself to extremes if the only alternative to success is failure or disaster.

I asked a self-confessed Workaholic to cut down his work hours from sixty to fifty per week. He looked at me with disdain and replied: "Oh, so you want me to just goof off!" From his perspective, you either worked flat out or you were goofing off—there was no middle ground.

Many people who battle overweight think in extremes. One such woman was about to go on a "starvation diet" as the only alternative to her perceived "gross obesity." (She was about forty-five pounds over her desired weight. Still she considered herself "disgusting" and said she was "desperate.") Her all-or-nothing view of eating habits looked like this:

Starvation ◄————————————————————————► Gluttony

Together we discovered many stages along this spectrum. She realized it was not just a matter of one extreme or the other.

Starvation ◄——— Under-Eating ——— Sensible Eating ——— Over-Eating ——► Gluttony

A very cautious man spent his life "playing it safe" and avoided taking risks. He couldn't see anything between extreme caution and total irresponsibility. I asked him to define "irresponsibility" to which he replied: "Foolhardiness—like mountain-climbing without ropes." His spectrum looked like this:

Playing It Safe ◄————————————————————► Irresponsible Foolhardiness

There was nothing in between. After considering this, he realized there were many options between these two extremes:

Playing ◄──	Taking Small ──	Taking Cautious ──	Moderate ──►	Irresponsible
It Safe	Chances	Responsible Risks	Risk Taking	Foolhardiness

Most things in life are neither black nor white. As tempting as it is to think in simple terms, the good/bad, right/wrong, win/lose, success/failure, love/hate paradigms are too limiting and misleading to be the template for your thinking. You trap yourself needlessly when you think in terms of all or nothing.

In summary, mind traps are patterns of thinking that lead to problems and upset. They include unrealistic expectations, perfectionism, over-identifying with roles, misinterpreting events, taking things personally, taking on other people's problems, rigidity and all-or-nothing thinking. Identifying these patterns—and what they cost you—is the first step to dealing with them (*awareness*). The next step is to explore other, more constructive ways of thinking (*choice*). Be realistic; lower your expectations; separate your self from your roles in life (especially your job); question your interpretations and judgments—and check them out; detach yourself at times; be flexible; and learn to compromise and find the middle ground between extremes. All these mind traps reflect basic assumptions you've been making for years. The solution is to challenge and modify these suppositions. By doing so (*permission*) you will overcome the traps and change the losing game between your ears.

CHAPTER SEVEN

The Power of Beliefs

T HE QUOTES ON THIS PAGE FROM THE SPORTS WORLD HAVE crossed over into everyday usage because of their homespun charm and supposed wisdom. They have something else in common. The people who said them strongly believed them to be true—thus giving the ideas power.

Nice guys finish last.
LEO DUROCHER

We all have thousands of beliefs, most of which we never express in words. Some are important (like "you shouldn't cheat" and "you should treat others as you want to be treated") and many are trivial (such as "baseball should be played on grass" or "men shouldn't wear white socks with black shoes").

It ain't over till
it's over.
YOGI BERRA

One of the reasons beliefs are so powerful is that they are held to be true. There was quite a stir about clothes at the 1990 French Open tennis championships. Andre Agassi wanted to wear his colorful outfits, but tournament officials wanted him to dress more conservatively. Agassi even threatened to withdraw if he couldn't wear his usual apparel. Here were two opposing opinions, each held strongly by its proponent. One could paraphrase the beliefs as follows.

Agassi: tennis should be less purist and tradition-bound in its dress code.

Organizers: players should respect custom and wear white or something close to it.

There is no correct opinion here but each advocate believed his point of view was right, "the truth" so to speak.

Another reason for the power of beliefs is that they are usually held subconsciously; so you aren't even aware of them. This is demonstrated by the following story.

A man had an argument with his teenage son one morning because the boy was wearing the same clothes for the fifth day in a row. I asked the father why he was so upset.

"Because you should change your clothes every day," he replied.

"Who says so?" I asked.

He looked at me blankly at first, unsure whether to answer such a silly question. He was caught off guard because he'd never thought about this issue before. "Well, uh, my parents say so . . . I mean that's what they taught me . . . I mean *everybody* knows that!"

I said *I'd* never heard it, and anyway I didn't think it was true. He was shocked and seemed to back away, just in case *I* was wearing clothes that weren't fresh. I told him that, while his point of view sounded reasonable, I didn't think it was inherently *true*. It sounded more like an *opinion* to me. He struggled with that until I told him I'd lived in places where people couldn't change their clothes every day and nothing terrible ever happened to them. Slowly he admitted that maybe his assumption wasn't some cosmic truth after all. I suggested that his statement was really a belief (about how things *should* be) and that obviously his son had a different belief. This man was upset not because of what his son was wearing but because the boy was violating one of his beliefs about proper behavior. He had just discovered Belief #1 pertaining to this incident.

Then I asked: "What else bothered you about his attire?"

He replied with a question: "What will people say when they see him in those clothes?"

"What do you care?" I asked, a bit provocatively.

"Well, how my son dresses reflects on *me*." (Belief #2)

"Really?" I asked. "Do you think someone's going to walk up to him in the schoolyard and say: 'Hey, you were wearing those clothes yesterday! Who's your *father*?'? Anyway," I pointed out, "most of his schoolmates are probably doing the same thing, which means he's fitting in just fine."

He started to smile.

"What else upset you about this situation?" I inquired.

He replied: "I should be the boss in my house." (Belief #3)

"Oh really?" I said. "Wait till he's seventeen or eighteen and knows everything. That belief could be a dangerous assumption, especially if your son doesn't agree." I suggested that a more democratic approach would produce more domestic harmony than assertions of parental power.

He started to realize that the argument with his son (and his own upset) came from a series of beliefs he had about the way things should be. The problem arose when the son's behavior didn't conform to the father's belief system. It was notable that he had never articulated any of those thoughts until I started questioning him. He had held those beliefs for years without being *aware* of them. They were held implicitly, hidden from view. Because they were hidden, he was unaware of their impact and couldn't challenge them. That gave them greater power over him.

A third characteristic about belief systems is that they influence your thinking and behavior. If you believe that you cannot talk to a large group of people, you will avoid such situations or become extremely nervous when you're in that position. You're likely to stammer, forget words, mumble and so on. There is nothing inherently true in the statement "I can't talk to large crowds," but if you *believe* it, that alone will influence your performance. It's like the high jump, which is as much a psychological feat as a physical one. If you look at the bar and believe you can clear it, you'll usually make it over with ease. But if you think "no way can I jump that height," your feet will barely leave the ground and you'll hit the bar with your shoulder.

Beliefs also influence what you pay attention to and think about. Since you can't take in all the details of your environment, there is a subconscious selection process that determines what you notice and what you filter out. You often see what you want to see and suppress things that don't fit your assumptions.

Have you ever been really angry at some nasty person only to have the person do something nice? It ruins your mental picture, doesn't it? Here you've found someone you love to hate and they confuse you with behavior that's inconsistent with your view of them. You might rationalize their kind behavior ("It was probably an accident" or "Someone must have put them up to it"), but you might actually overlook it altogether. It just doesn't fit your belief system about them. Conversely, many parents are blind to their children's faults, the last to notice that they are bullying others or using drugs or stealing things. The parents have an idealized picture of the children and believe them to be wonderful—and then see only what is consistent with that belief. As objective as you want to be (or think you are), your beliefs shape your observations and thoughts more than you realize.

Your beliefs concern three domains:

1. **The nature of things and the world in general** ("Love conquers all," "You can't fight City Hall," "Money can't buy happiness," "Crime doesn't pay");

2. **Other people and how they should behave** ("Children should respect their elders," "Men shouldn't show emotion," "People should always be on time") and

3. **Yourself: what you can and cannot do and how you should behave and think** ("I can catch a football," "I can't do math," "I should visit my parents every Sunday," "I should give people the benefit of the doubt").

Origins of Beliefs

In previous chapters I recounted stories about belief systems: for example, Roger Bannister changing other runners' beliefs about how fast people can run and the woman who believed "You have to make your bed every day." Beliefs have a considerable influence over your life.

Many if not most of your beliefs are acquired early in life. As early as the cradle, infants learn that if they cry they will be fed, changed, cuddled, etc. (depending on how quickly they can "train" their caregivers!). They also learn that certain behavior will beget certain responses. For example, poking little sister will draw a rebuke, but hugging her will evoke approval. The learning experience of childhood leads to an entire belief system about how the world works, what you should and should not do, what you can and cannot do, what is rewarded and what draws punishment. Some of the messages from the past are stated explicitly ("You should wash your hands before meals" or "You should say please and thank you"). Others are implied or learned by observation, like "You sleep when it's dark out" or (during my own childhood) "Fathers go to jobs, mothers stay at home." No one ever said this; I just noticed that was how it was in our neighborhood and assumed that was the general pattern.

In working with patients and the losing games they play, I encourage them to discover their beliefs and where they came from. Some remember very specifically who taught them certain lessons, whereas others have no recollection. Phrases like "You must always be busy" and "Things have to be done 110%" come to light. A middle-aged woman with low self-esteem internalized these words from her father: "You're lazy. You can't do anything right. Everything you ever got you broke. You'll never amount to anything." Another woman, who has an abusive husband, accepts his behavior because she was taught that "a woman's lot is to grin and bear it, to suffer in silence and without complaint."

Lessons are often learned without being specifically taught. Children who are picked last for sports teams develop beliefs like "I'm not good enough" and "I'm a lousy athlete." Worse yet, that message often gets generalized into "I'm a lousy person" or "I'm a loser."

A Sampling of Beliefs

The range and variety of beliefs is fascinating. They cover every topic and human activity, from proper dress (men shouldn't wear summer sport jackets after Labor Day) to appropriate Christmas gifts. In the latter category, I heard about a woman whose live-in male partner gave her only a box of mixed nuts on their first Christmas together. She was mightily miffed, interpreting his gesture as uncaring, juvenile, cheap and insensitive. She had certain principles about gift giving and nowhere in her belief system did a box of nuts make it as a Christmas present from one's lover! This is one fascination about belief systems. You are generally unaware of your beliefs until you examine them. Then you realize you have a whole manual in your subconscious to cover every event and situation imaginable.

An intriguing belief I hear sometimes is: "Thinking good thoughts is tempting fate." People are often afraid to think about success because they might "jinx themselves" and thus bring about the opposite. Variations of this theme include "If things are going too well, something's going to get you" and "If you say you're feeling good, you'll pay for it down the road." Many people don't trust good times to last and believe that enjoying themselves too much is sure to bring retribution. One man put it this way: "Life is like a credit card—and eventually the bill comes in and you have to pay." Folks with this kind of belief system spend a lot of time looking over their shoulders instead of having fun.

Beliefs Based on Gender: There are endless assumptions about appropriate behavior based on gender—often called sex-role stereotypes. In an age of increasing awareness about sexism, these should be examined and most of them dismissed. Some are clichés, many are offensive and others are simply inaccurate. But many people (male and female) still hold these assertions to be "the truth."

Beliefs that "women shouldn't take jobs from men" and "women belong at home" are still held in many places. A woman in her late thirties told me: "The housework is *my* job and I have no *right* to ask for help." A working mother who wants to stay home with her children agrees with this notion but with a different slant: "Women shouldn't have to work and men should support them." A phrase I still hear from some females is "Women shouldn't enjoy sex." "Ladies don't chew gum" was an edict from the finishing schools of bygone days.

"Men shouldn't cry," "Men should be strong and stoical" and "Emotion is weakness" are among the beliefs that have been hamstringing males for generations. As a result of these assumptions, millions of men keep their feelings bottled up (at great cost to their physical and emotional health). Beliefs like "Men should be the breadwinners" and "Men should provide for their families" have been a yoke around the necks of males for decades, leading many to work two jobs to keep up.

Positive Beliefs: Your life is run by your belief systems. That isn't always a bad thing. Many beliefs are positive, helpful and supportive. "Hard work will always be rewarded" can be a constructive premise as long as it isn't taken to extremes. "People should honor their commitments" is a virtuous sentiment. One of the noblest beliefs I ever heard was my father's credo: "Just keep giving (to others) and the taking will look after itself," a code he lived by with wonderful results. And my mother-in-law had a philosophy that sustained her through many difficult times: "Everything happens for a reason— even if you don't know what the reason is."

Notice that none of these beliefs is "true" in any certain or measurable way. However, they are useful to those who believe them and live by their teaching.

Potentially Harmful Beliefs: On the other hand, many beliefs have a harmful impact. They represent a "losing game" that needs changing. It is useful to identify any detrimental assumptions that may be running your life and revise or discard them.

Negative beliefs include such sentiments as: "Sleep is a waste of time," "If people really knew me, they wouldn't like me," "I don't deserve to succeed," "I can't do anything right," "I'm scatter-brained," "The world is a fearful place," "It doesn't pay to be nice," "I'm not supposed to be really happy" and "I'm not the motherly type." These are all verbatim quotes from patients who were putting themselves down or seeing the world in negative terms, using statements they deeply believed to be true.

Limiting beliefs come in several forms, but the most common ones begin with "I can't." "I can't sing," "I can't remember people's names" and "I can't hit a golf ball out of the rough" are examples. These beliefs reduce the possibility of a positive outcome. They become self-fulfilling prophecies.

Years ago a good friend of mine told me to call him that evening at someone else's home. I said, "Okay, just a minute. Let me get a pencil to write down the phone number." This action was based on my unstated belief that "I can't remember phone numbers." He stopped me, saying: "You don't need to write it down. Just concentrate on the number and you'll remember it." He looked deeply into my eyes as he said this, making me an instant believer. I remembered that phone number for months. I even remembered the number long after I'd forgotten whose house it was!

Outdated beliefs reflect a world that used to be. A former school teacher of mine told me about how he met his wife. At the end of the Second World War, he was a 16-year-old lad who saw a young girl on the village green one Sunday afternoon. He took a real shine to her, but in those days a boy didn't just walk up to a girl and introduce himself or start chatting with her. The custom was that you had to have a formal introduction made by someone else. It took him months to arrange that meeting, his ardor and interest mounting all the time. Once they started "keeping company" (chaperoned, of course) and feelings grew between them, talk of marriage developed. But in those days men didn't get married until they were working and able to support a wife. So they put off marriage for years while he completed his education and got a well-paying job. I'm enough of a romantic to think those must have been wonderful times to live in (what with village greens, horse and buggy rides and all), but I can see the limitations and frustrations of some of those societal customs. These beliefs are now outmoded but not harmful.

Other outdated beliefs are more problematic. I've heard patients say: "Children have no rights," "Adults have rights, children have privileges (which can be taken away if they don't deserve them)" and, of course, the classic "Children should be seen and not heard." Women's role in relationships has also changed but many people's beliefs haven't kept pace. There was a time when women were legally viewed as "chattel" (property belonging to their husbands). Similarly, the husband was the "lord and master" of the household.

Individuals can hold outdated beliefs about *themselves.* Many who grew up with an older sibling still relate to that brother or sister in a subservient way, even though they are both mature, successful adults. A young man I know is a fine athlete, has a good build and is well coordinated. But he still thinks of himself as scrawny, awkward and weak because that's how he was until his mid teens.

Misleading beliefs often come from stereotypes. One woman was lamenting the "grubby appearance" of her teenage son. He had long hair and often didn't shave, and his clothes looked as if they'd been slept in. I asked her why his long hair bothered her and she replied: "Long hair leads to problem behavior." It just so happens her son's behavior had been irresponsible, but it wasn't the long hair that was doing it. I know some short-haired ne'er-do-wells and some terrific young people with hair down to their shoulders.

How often do you make assumptions about people based on their appearance? Women who wear sexy clothes may be labeled "loose," or men who wear ponytails are assumed to be drug users.

"Fat people are greedy and lack control" and "Bachelors over forty must be gay" are other misleading beliefs I've heard.

Inaccurate beliefs are the last group of harmful assumptions. These are the ones that are simply untrue. Of course, none of the beliefs I've been discussing are inherently "true" or "correct" (nor are they necessarily inaccurate or wrong). Their relative merits can be debated or discussed. But some beliefs are categorically false, even though there was a time when all were held to be "true." After all, everyone believed the world was flat until Columbus sailed off the edge in 1492 and came back to talk about it. Everyone "knew" that the sun revolved around the earth until 1543 when Copernicus said it was the other way around. It's helpful to remember such beliefs as touchstone examples that almost any premise you hold can be challenged and may some day be proven false. It is a good idea to maintain humility about your beliefs and remain flexible and open-minded when discussing such matters.

When I was in medical school, patients were kept in hospital for three weeks after a heart attack and not even allowed up from bed for the first week. By the time I had been in practice a few years, cardiac patients were routinely in a chair within a day of a coronary and out of hospital in ten days. Now it's not uncommon to be out in a week. These changes were not just because of new drugs and treatments. They were based on a fundamental shift in the beliefs doctors held about the damage sustained by heart attack victims, what was safe and what patients could tolerate.

This story of inaccurate beliefs had important consequences for a woman in her forties. She had been socially isolated through most of her life, avoiding gatherings because of her belief that she disliked being in groups. This was based on her discomfort in such situations. After pushing herself to socialize a couple of times, she started to look forward to these outings. "I feel more comfortable socially. I'm feeling more worthwhile. I feel I belong, that I deserve to be there. I now enjoy being in a group. I always thought I didn't enjoy that. I told myself I didn't." She was developing not just a comfort but an enthusiasm for an activity she previously believed she disliked. She went on: "What other things did I avoid because I told myself I didn't like them?" She cited speaking in front of others as another example. She used to shun such opportunities. Then she discovered she likes being the center of attention. She'd always believed the opposite about herself. She was pleased to find new activities that she had put off-limits. And she started to challenge other "truths" she held about herself. This woman's beliefs were not only inaccurate but limiting as well, stifling a gregarious nature she didn't realize she had.

In summary, beliefs are basic premises and assumptions that are held as objective "truths" and that guide our thinking, decisions and behavior. They include values, philosophies and ideas about the nature of things, other people and ourselves. Beliefs are held with certainty, viewed as facts or "the way it is." They influence what we notice, what we think and what we do. These assumptions are usually hidden or taken for granted, making them more powerful because they are less open to examination. Beliefs can lead to a losing game if they are limiting, inaccurate or held too rigidly, or if they conflict with the views and behavior of others. It is important to become aware of your beliefs, to notice what effect they have on you, and to challenge or even revise them when necessary. Changing beliefs will be discussed further in Chapter 10.

CHAPTER EIGHT

Looking at How You Behave

HOCKEY COACHES ARE AN INTERESTING BREED. They come in all shapes, sizes and temperaments. There are the brash and the reserved; the uncouth and the refined; the argumentative and the stoical. Some push their players hard, others are soft. Despite all the different styles, there are only two criteria by which coaches are measured: whether their teams play well and whether they win or lose. There's no right way to coach, but when one type of behavior doesn't work, the team usually finds someone else with a different approach.

People exhibit many different kinds of behavior, but like hockey coaches, some of their behavior patterns work better than others. The styles that don't fare well fall into two groups: those that are hard on the person and on others (Workaholics, Overachievers, Type As and Perfectionists) and those that allow the person to be pushed around by others (Pleasers, Caretakers and Victims). Some of these patterns may initially bring benefits, but eventually they either stop working or have more drawbacks than advantages.

Where do hockey coaches learn how to behave? Do they select a persona out of a catalogue? Is there a school where they pick up the knack of "kicking ass" or being charismatic? They probably evolve a style in one of three ways: they copy the behavior of someone they respect or who has been successful; or they try different approaches until they stumble on one that works; or they just do what comes naturally and see how far it takes them. Sometimes a way of behaving brings success for a while and the coach gets used to it. But as circumstances change, that style might not work anymore. What began as a winning game becomes a losing game. If the behavior becomes ingrained and the person doesn't change as events require, he will be left behind.

Most human behavior represents choices made early in life for one of three reasons:

1. You may have copied your parents or other important people in your life. I asked a woman who was both a Pleaser/Caretaker and a Type A/Perfectionist why she behaved that way. She said: "It was the way I was raised. My mom was like that. She deferred to my father and did everything for him. The hard-driving part comes from my dad. He's a perfectionist and always very time conscious."

2. You probably picked up some of the social conditioning to which all of us are subjected. In general terms, women were socialized to be Caretakers, Pleasers, givers and somewhat passive; males were conditioned to be strong, aggressive, work- and achievement-oriented. Even little children were treated differently according to their gender. These societal influences have been changing, but even subtle gender stereotyping can do much to shape your behavior.

3. You developed behavioral styles because they seemed appropriate to a particular situation. They either made you feel good about yourself or served some other specific purpose. There must have been a payoff once or you would not have bothered to repeat them. Then they became habits—familiar and comfortable ways of operating.

I know a middle-aged, successful businessman who is always in a hurry. He overloads his schedule, does everything fast and describes his life as "rushing, rushing, rushing." He's a classic Type-A individual. He also knows it's a losing game. His rushing creates *more* problems for him since he often has to redo things he did too fast and carelessly. He even plays golf quickly, whirling around the course as if someone were chasing him. When he allows himself to slow down, he takes five strokes off his score and enjoys the game more. When I asked when and why he began this race against time, he cast his eye back to age five. The Depression was on and he worked on the family farm. They all worked hard and fast because "the more we did, the more money we made." Later he worked as a delivery boy and again there was a monetary reward for working fast. He learned to do everything quickly because there was a payoff. Today he has lots of money. He doesn't have to hurry. But he does—and it's costing him.

Budd Schulberg wrote a book called *What Makes Sammy Run?*, exploring the frenetic behavior of one Sammy Glick from New York. Like Mordecai Richler's Duddy Kravitz, Sammy was a hustler, a man on the make. Although they are fictional characters, Sammy and Duddy resemble millions of real people who are Type As, Workaholics and Overachievers. I often ask these folks what makes *them* run. Here are some of their answers: "It makes me feel better about myself," "I feel productive, vital, important," "I feel my life has meaning because of my achievements," "I feel like I'm making an impact" or simply "I'm proving to my parents that I can be someone." It usually boils down to the issue of self-esteem—people trying to feel better about themselves. However, in most cases, it is either a futile quest or one that causes more problems than it solves.

Just as Type As often began their excessive striving as a quest for parental approval, Pleasers frequently began by also seeking favor. A young woman described how she tried to be Daddy's little girl. "I wasn't allowed to say no or show disagreement as a child. If I did, there would be an outburst of temper from my father. I'd be sent to my room or spanked. After a while, I would do anything to not raise his ire. I was afraid of him so I learned to be a Pleaser. I didn't know I had choices. Avoidance of his anger was my biggest motivator. But in addition I was never allowed to let my anger show." This is a classic example of childhood conditioning that produced behavior that served an important function at the time (escaping conflict and punishment) but does not serve this woman well in her adult life.

These behavior patterns constitute "losing games" because they don't work (self-defeating) and can even be costly (self-destructive). The self-driving activities (Type A, Workaholic, Perfectionist) lead to distress, overload and exhaustion. The self-neglecting styles (Pleaser, Caretaker, Victim) produce feelings of fatigue, resentment and helplessness. In other words, the payoff is relatively small in most cases and/or the cost is high. That makes these choices a poor trade-off and a self-punishing way to live. Let me explore each of these losing behaviors individually.

Workaholics

1. Do you work more than sixty hours a week?

2. Would you rather work than play or spend time with your family?

3. Do you feel edgy or like a fish out of water when you're away from work?

4. Do you often take work home or with you on holidays?

5. Is most of your reading work-related?

"Workaholic" means an addiction to work as a way of life. I apply the word to people whose lives are overwhelmingly dominated by work. They live to work, whereas most folks work in order to live. Work becomes the sole focus of their time, energy and thinking—to the exclusion of family, friends and self. Workaholism runs a spectrum, from mild to severe. Anyone who routinely works more than sixty hours a week starts to fit my definition of Workaholic.

Interestingly, many true Workaholics are happy with their lot. They toil long and hard not because they *have* to but because they *want* to. But there are many drawbacks. The most obvious is what happens to them when they are unable to get their work "fix." Illness, injury, loss of job and eventually retirement are four circumstances that can produce "withdrawal." Deprived of work, they feel empty. They also get restless and agitated when they're not on the job. Even short periods of withdrawal are stressful: a holiday or a long weekend feels like a punishment to be endured rather than a pleasure to be enjoyed.

For every happy and fulfilled Workaholic, I believe there are many more who aren't getting much joy out of their labor. A lot of people don't recognize themselves as Workaholics. I've identified several variations of this behavior. See if you recognize yourself among these categories.

The Eager Workaholic: This is the classic species described in Marilyn Machlowitz's book *Workaholics*. These people simply love to work. They thrive on it, they're excited by it, there's nothing they'd rather do. They enjoy the pressure, the stimulation, the challenge— and the power and prestige that often results. In addition, these folks are energized by work. They aren't drained and exhausted as most others are from long hours and high demands. The true Workaholics I know are vigorous, dynamic, charismatic people and seem to be getting a kick out of life. For them it works. And for this group, workaholism may not be a bad thing (although their families and friends, who rarely see them, might disagree).

The Reluctant Workaholic: These pluggers work long hours because they think they have to—for the money, to keep their job, in response to peer pressure or corporate culture, to satisfy demanding clients, etc. They work long hours but they don't like it. They're worn-down and dispirited but feel pushed by what they see as necessity. One such woman told me that in her field it was *impossible* to cut back or be unavailable when a client called. She worked seventy hours a week even though she would have preferred to work fifty.

The Pushover Workaholic: This person works long and hard to be well-liked, to please clients or customers and often because he can't say No. He's an easy mark if anyone wants to take advantage of him. I knew an accountant who would meet his clients anywhere, anytime, because he hated to decline a request. I urged him to regulate his hours. With a sheepish grin, he replied: "I can't. They won't like me if I do that."

The Temporary Workaholic: This is the person who burns the midnight oil for a limited time to achieve a specific goal. Getting started in business, bucking for promotion, making extra money to pay off the mortgage and trying to earn a raise are all legitimate reasons to work very hard *for a short period*. The overwork is simply a means to an end. A problem arises, though, when the temporary becomes permanent or the "reason" keeps changing in order to justify an ingrained Workaholic habit.

The Ambitious Workaholic: This individual is on the make and doesn't try to hide it. She is out for money, prestige, power—or all three—and simply sees overwork as the price of success. She wants to be where the action is, living in the fast lane and staying there.

The Robot Workaholic: These might have been temporary Workaholics who just fell into a rut and stayed there. They became Workaholics by default. To these folks, working long and hard is a habit, a way of life they've become used to. They've been doing it for so long, they don't even think about it anymore. They put one foot in front of the other and go on automatic pilot most of the time. It hardly occurs to them that it's a problem—or that there is an alternative.

The Turtle Workaholic: This person uses work as a way of hiding, pulling into his shell to avoid something he considers to be even worse. I worked in a hospital where one of the doctors stayed until eight or nine o'clock every night. I commented on this dedication to a colleague and received an amused reply: "Dedication? Hardly! He's got three kids and he doesn't go home at night until they're all in bed!" Avoiding home chores, child care, family obligations or other responsibilities is among the reasons these folks grind away at the job. Other "turtles" are avoiding intimacy or a relationship that has become stale or filled with tension.

The Inefficient Workaholic: This is the disorganized or slow worker who needs extra hours just to get the job done. The irony is that these unproductive people are caught on a treadmill going in circles: the overwork produces fatigue, which leads to inefficiency, which then requires more overwork to complete the task. They need sixty hours to do what should take only fifty. As one of these drones put it: "Workaholics aren't as productive as they think—but they are busy." Parkinson's Law states that "work expands so as to fill the time available for its completion." These people are living proof.

Most Workaholics I know are struggling and suffering. And as if their personal exhaustion and lack of pleasure aren't bad enough, there is also a huge price to be paid by *others* as a result of either neglect or abuse. Even happy Workaholics leave family and friends behind. They are home very little, leading children to think of them as visitors. The despair that mates feel can be heart-rending. Absence from major events and celebrations creates a lot of resentment. Some parents refer to themselves as "single parents," "work widows or widowers" or "house husbands" even though their mates still reside at home. And often even when Workaholics do come home, they are exhausted or preoccupied. They are there physically but are unavailable emotionally.

If the Workaholic is frustrated or short-tempered, the family often pays for all the flak that accumulated during the long work day. The resulting abuse can be verbal (insults and swearing), emotional (criticisms and put-downs) or even physical (pounding walls, throwing things or hitting people). The happy, fulfilled Workaholic isn't likely to be the culprit. But the reluctant, worn-down overworker might very well dump his emotional bucket at home, and then everybody loses.

Co-workers also suffer from the behavior of Workaholics. Verbal or emotional abuse can result if the overworker's fuse is short (administrative assistants could write volumes on this). Workaholics often expect others to work long hours too. The pressure can be direct (an order to work overtime) or indirect (giving someone a task late in the day or dropping not-so-subtle comments about "slackers" and "wimps" around the office). Workaholics can be absolute taskmasters or just daunting role models to keep up with. Either way, they can cause distress or burnout in colleagues who are not similarly inclined.

For most people, *workaholism* is a losing game. It leaves its followers socially isolated, underdeveloped in most other areas, and vulnerable if anything goes wrong in the work domain. Leisure, travel, entertainment and the company of others hold little appeal for them, leaving them bereft of life's variety and pleasures. They don't develop other interests or talents and become one-track individuals. Some of them even endanger their health by inviting more stress than they can handle. In Japan, the word *Karoshi* is commonly used. It means "death from overwork" and it is one price they paid for their phenomenal economic success in the latter third of the twentieth century.

There's a saying that might generate some sober thought for Workaholics: "No man ever said on his deathbed: 'I wish I had spent more time at the office.'"

Type-A Behavior

1. Do you feel you need to win at everything you do?

2. Do you enjoy—or need—to be the center of attention?

3. Do you drive yourself hard at work, at home and even at play?

4. Are you constantly struggling against time and often running behind schedule?

5. Do you get angry over little things, like small frustrations or when people let you down?

Two cardiologists from San Francisco, Drs. Meyer Friedman and Ray Rosenman, coined the term "Type-A behavior" in the 1970s to describe a constellation of traits common to their patients with coronary artery disease. The link between these Type-A characteristics and heart disease has been questioned by some in the scientific community. But one thing is certain: whether it predisposes to heart attacks or not, it is a very stressful way to live and causes numerous other problems. It is a losing game I can attest to from firsthand experience. I can also vouch for the benefits that come with modifying such behavior.

The trouble with life in the fast lane is that you get to the other end in an awful hurry.

JOHN JENSEN

There are three main components of Type-A behavior. These people are hard-driving, hyper-aggressive and excessively competitive; they have a strong sense of time urgency or what Friedman and Rosenman call "Hurry Sickness"; and they are quick to anger, a trait called "free-floating hostility." The authors estimate that 75% of the adult American population show Type-A tendencies, although the severity ranges from mild to extreme. You don't have to have *all* the characteristics to be considered Type A. It used to be much more common in males but is now appearing increasingly among women, especially those in the paid work force.

Hyper-Aggressiveness: Type-A individuals are hard on themselves and others. They drive themselves without mercy and do the same to their employees and co-workers, and even to their families. These people are out to win. They turn everything into a contest. A friendly game of tennis becomes a tournament, a casual game of gin rummy feels like high-stakes poker and even a game like Monopoly takes on cosmic proportions. Intense Type As need to win even when they're playing with their kids. You can see them get sullen if their five-year-old beats them at Snakes and Ladders. They'll even call foot-faults on their eight-year-old in a game of horseshoes at the cottage.

Another manifestation is their need to be the center of attention. They'll monopolize conversations without even realizing it. It's especially interesting when two Type As get together, each wanting the spotlight. I heard this definition of a conversation between two Type-A people: a competitive exercise in which the first person to draw a breath is declared the listener!

Hurry Sickness: Type-A people are always trying to do more things in less time. They walk, talk and eat fast. They hurry the speech of others, show impatience with slow talkers and even finish sentences for people. A classic place where their behavior shows up is in driving. Type As are always found in the passing lane on highways, driving over the speed limit and honking at any car that slows them down. They're great lane-hoppers if they think it will shave a few seconds off the trip.

Type As are notorious for squeezing as much as possible into any time frame. Their schedule isn't full until it's crammed. One of my patients showed up twenty-five minutes late for his appointment. His explanation was typical. He had a little extra time ("a window of opportunity") before our meeting so he ran an errand in the other end of town. Of course he got held up at the store and arrived at my office late—and breathless. He knew it would be a pretty tight fit, but Type As are famous for that kind of shoehorn routine.

Another characteristic is what Friedman and Rosenman call "polyphasic activity"—doing more than one thing at a time. It's now become a high art—known as "multi-tasking." Type As shave while showering, read while eating, dictate while driving, that sort of thing. Reading while watching TV seems to be a popular habit. One woman, not satisfied with that, *knits* while reading while watching TV. A man told me he watches five TV programs at once. I envisioned five different television sets like those in an appliance store, all tuned to different channels. But, no, he does it with a remote control and switches channels so often that he can track a sitcom, a documentary, one or two sports events and the news almost simultaneously. Is this impressive?

Impatience is another Type-A hallmark. Standing in line at a theater or waiting for a restaurant seat is very stressful. They fidget, pace or editorialize about how slow the service is. Faced with a long lineup, they're more likely to walk away and go hungry than slowly work themselves through the queue.

Type As also leave things to the last minute. They time everything tightly. It reminds me of when I was a kid waking up in the morning. School started at nine and I knew exactly how long my morning routine took (including breakfast, toilet, hair and teeth brushing, bed making, walking to school, etc.). Some winter mornings I'd lie there figuring out how to stay in bed a little longer (six extra minutes if I skip breakfast, another ninety seconds if I don't make my bed . . .), deciding which activities I could eliminate or abbreviate to buy me a few more precious moments under the warm covers. Type As program their whole lives like that.

Friedman and Rosenman call another Type-A trait "the quest for numbers." Type As enjoy acquiring things, from objects (like art or books) to money to achievements and accolades. They are less interested in quality than quantity and can usually tell you how many of something they have. After my 1965 summer in Europe a friend asked me, "How many countries did you bag?" He didn't ask if I had a good summer, what I enjoyed most or even which countries I visited—only how many. He knew who he was talking to though. I proudly answered "eleven," not telling him I spent less than a day each in Monaco, San Marino, and Liechtenstein. If I were to return to Europe today, I'd be content to visit one or two countries, but back then I was into volume. Type As can boast about the twelve pieces of art in their home but rarely look at them. They might accumulate 200 music CDs but listen to very few. Acquiring, owning, possessing—these are the things that Type As strive for. But using, appreciating and enjoying what they have—these are foreign to the Type-A person.

Free-Floating Hostility: One Type-A woman told me: "I used to live life in the emphatic tense." She was intense about everything—even trivial things. She was easily irritated, easily frustrated and quick to anger when mistakes were made (even by herself). Type As get impatient, snap at people and explode with very little provocation. These displays of anger often surprise or offend others, especially if they take the outbursts personally. Bystanders should understand that this anger is rarely because of *them*. It is a function of the Type-A personality and probably emanates from the hyper-aggressiveness. It is as if the anger is very close to the surface, breaking through easily and often.

Type As get angry not only at themselves and others but at inanimate objects as well. A phone that doesn't work is likely to be slammed down. A screwdriver might be thrown if it doesn't work. Coin-vending machines that malfunction are great triggers—

especially if they don't return the coins. It's as if these people are anger itself, just looking for a place to happen. Curiously the anger doesn't last long. But the next outburst may not be far behind. It's not a fun way to live.

Overachievers

1. Are you usually working on some project, like home renovations or taking night courses?

2. Do you feel you have to list your activities when someone asks "How've you been?"

3. Do you feel lazy or unsatisfied if you're not doing something to better yourself?

4. Do you look for praise when you accomplish something?

5. Does the satisfaction from your success fade quickly after it's over?

Overachievers are strivers. They are not people who just set goals and then work to achieve them (I call these folks "achievers"). Overachievers drive themselves to excel, to be the best and to accomplish more and more. And they are not satisfied for very long with their successes. Never content to rest on their laurels (or to rest at all, for that matter), they keep looking for new fields to conquer. When they were in school, the Overachievers sought As. When they reached that, they strove for A-pluses. Once they achieved that level, they aimed to be tops in the class and so on. As adults, they climb the executive ladder, lingering at each rung only long enough to set their sights on the next level. They take night courses and do community activities, accumulating credits and kudos as they get more involved. They never reach a point where they can comfortably say, "This is enough."

I often ask Overachievers what drives them. They usually had a parent whom they could never please or whom they *thought* they could never satisfy—the mother who asked "What happened to the other 5%?" when the child came home with a 95 in math, or the father who showed disappointment when his son didn't make the baseball team. One man told me: "I wasn't a big kid—and my father wanted a home-run hitter." Many children grew up feeling they didn't measure up—to an older brother, a favored cousin or their parents' expectations of them. Sometimes they weren't noticed except when they excelled at something. Now as adults they still strive to get the praise and recognition that was never forthcoming in their youth. Sadly, it is often withheld even in adulthood, so their struggle becomes a fruitless, losing game no matter how well they succeed in objective terms.

One problem with overachieving is that it's often futile. It doesn't impress the people it's aimed at, and it doesn't satisfy the striver either. The other problem is that it gobbles up huge amounts of time and energy, leading to exhaustion—physical and spiritual.

Perfectionists

Here's a little test to see whether you are a Perfectionist.

1. Do you always fold pieces of paper so the corners meet exactly? And if someone hands you a piece of paper folded asymmetrically, do you open it and then refold it "neatly"?

2. Do you make your bed with hospital corners? Are the sheets centered exactly on the mattress? Do the pillows sit precisely in place?

3. Are you intolerant of mistakes—yours and other peoples'?

4. Do pictures that are slightly crooked bother you until you straighten them? Do you pick pieces of lint off other people's clothes? Are all the items on your coffee table arranged to sit symmetrically?

5. Do you reread personal letters or emails you've written, correcting all errors of grammar and punctuation? If the letter isn't perfect, do you rewrite it carefully (like an essay in high school)?

If you do some or all of the things noted above, are you having fun? Do you drive people crazy with your exactness? Do you drive yourself crazy? Do you find it hard to sit and relax with so much imperfection around you? Have you noticed you spend a lot of your time attending to details and tidying up? Do you want to keep living like this?

The problem (and curse) of perfectionism is that it's unattainable and time-wasting and diverts your attention from important things. It is also a form of all-or-nothing thinking that is rigid and leads to distress and unhappiness.

A business executive told me: "If I don't give 110%, I feel like I'm cheating somebody." He added: "When I do something, I like to do it right." However, he was so demanding of himself that he soon got hopelessly bogged down in his new job. He finally realized what his perfectionism was costing him: "I can't get through my 'In Basket' because I'm a perfectionist." That's when he stopped writing every little office memo as if it were going to be framed in a museum and started to get on with his work. Perfectionists waste inordinate amounts of time, don't prioritize well, exhaust themselves with needless overwork and cause themselves endless delays and frustrations. A man told me he spends so much time each weekend washing his car and his wife's that he never has time for himself. I asked why he washed his cars so often. "I hate driving a dirty car," he said. But he didn't just wash off the dirt. He cleaned scrupulously, polished immaculately—and then searched for smudge marks he'd overlooked.

Pleasers

1. Do you put yourself out for others and feel you get little back in return?

2. Do you feel people take advantage of you or take you for granted?

3. Is getting the approval of others a high priority for you?

4. Do you appease others, being careful not to show your anger at them?

5. Do you avoid conflict at all costs—even when you know you're right?

Hang around your local tennis club and you'll likely hear the telltale cries of the Pleaser: "Sorry," "I'm sorry" and "Excuse me." They apologize for balls hit out of bounds, balls hit onto the next court and shots they hit too hard or too soft. Not all players are like this, of course. For many, especially in the heat of a game, anything goes. But like birds chirping in the morning, the "sorry" cry of the pleaser is common on community courts.

Pleasers are people who want to get along with others—to avoid conflict and/or to be well liked. In order to achieve these goals, they often do things

I don't know the key to success, but the key to failure is trying to please everybody.

BILL COSBY

they don't want to do, say yes when they want to say no and don't ob-ject when things displease them. I heard this definition recently: being a Pleaser is when your gut says "No" and your mouth says "I'd be happy to." They are also called appeasers, peace-makers and givers—and push-overs, doormats and milquetoasts. They don't stand up for themselves and they get pushed around, but they put up with it because they have a high need for approval. Pleasers don't want to make waves or cause a scene. The result is that they often please everyone but themselves.

The reason that being a Pleaser is a losing game was summed up by one of my patients: "Pleasing is a technique to get something, stay safe, avoid anxiety—but it usually generates resentment and hostility because it's not genuine." When Pleasers let people walk all over them or agree to do something they dislike, several negative things happen. First, they become vulnerable to others. They can be taken advantage of, manip-ulated, exploited and taken for granted. Second, they feel resentful of the other person and angry at themselves—yet they can't let on because then maybe the person won't like them. Third, they don't feel in con-trol of their own lives. They don't get what they want, and they put their own needs behind those of others (or deny them entirely). Last, they don't feel good about themselves. This is not the stuff from which healthy self-esteem is built.

Ironically, the people you please also pay a price: they receive the underlying (and often poorly concealed) resentment you feel toward them (even as you're doing favors for them). This story illustrates the point. A hard-working man toiled at his job six days a week. He longed to play golf but felt he should spend Sunday with his wife and children. Those Sundays got to be pretty long for all of them. He was restless and preoccupied. His family found him remote, edgy and unhappy. I sug-gested he take four hours off to play golf and spend the rest of the day at home. He seized the idea (and the permission I gave him). It was a toss-up as to who was happier, him or his family. Of course he was thrilled to be out on the links again. But they were equally delighted when he returned home relaxed and happy—and much easier to be with. In de-nying his own needs to please his family, he had actually done them a disservice because of the cranky mood he was in at home.

Interestingly, being a Pleaser *seems* easier and more expedient than speaking up and perhaps risking confrontation. But in most cases it simply trades one problem for another. It results in frustration and resentment and also sends the wrong signal to the person presuming on your time and goodwill. A woman told me she puts up with a friend who keeps her waiting and then talks incessantly, behavior she finds offensive. But nothing ever changes because she never speaks up. She told me: "It's easier not to say anything—you don't get into any hassles." However, she began to see that it was costing her in other ways. Their visits were stressful and unenjoyable. Her mood shifted between anger and boredom, and she felt she was wasting her time.

Pleasers often live their lives governed by *someone else's priorities*. They do what other people want them to, what they *think* others want, or what they think they *should* do rather than what they *want* to do. The question to ask is: according to whose agenda do you want to live your life? Taken to an extreme, some people even choose their line of work to please others—especially their parents. I know several people who reluctantly entered law or medicine or went into the family business in order to follow their parents' footsteps or to meet their wishes. I also know some who had the courage to defy parental pressure and drop out of courses or fields they realized were wrong for them. They recognized they were in a losing game and decided to change it.

Caretakers

1. Do you feel responsible for other people (relatives, neighbors, friends)?

2. Do you like it when people say they can't get along without you?

3. Do you take over jobs (e.g., ironing, carpentry, problem solving or chores at work) that others should be learning how to do?

4. Do you feel a need to be needed by others?

5. Do you resent people depending on you—but do nothing to change it?

There is an expression that the shoemaker's children often go barefoot. Another is that doctors take good care of their patients but not of themselves. I encounter people who are so busy looking out for others that they don't get around to taking care of themselves. It's not a good way to live. Think of the last snowstorm. Did you go out and shovel your front walk and driveway? Did it occur to you to shovel your neighbor's walk and driveway? If so, you're a very nice and thoughtful person. But what would you say about someone who does his neighbor's shoveling *before* he does his own? And makes a habit of it? And then finds himself too tired or with no time to shovel his own property? Wouldn't you consider that a strange order of priorities?

Caretakers think nothing of putting themselves out for others. I'm not referring to individuals who are just kind and generous with their time and energy. I'm talking about those who make it a way of life and who neglect themselves in the process. This self-sacrifice is wonderful for a while but as a permanent behavior it leads to fatigue, resentment and even self-pity. I knew a woman who on three separate occasions gave several hundreds of dollars (which she could ill afford) to people she felt sorry for. As a result she had to scramble for rent and food money for months afterward. And in all three cases, the recipients showed very little gratitude. Hers is an extreme case but it only makes the point more clearly: if you give away too much of yourself, you don't leave enough to take care of your own needs.

There's an old story about the boy scout helping an elderly lady cross the street. She then turns and hits him with her purse. The reason, of course, is that she didn't want to cross the street in the first place. That's another scenario Caretakers can get into. They "help" people who don't want their help. A mother kept "mothering" her adult son after he left home. She wore herself out doing his laundry and making meals for him, even though he neither asked nor encouraged her to do so. Then she lamented how unappreciative he was for all she was doing for him.

Some Caretakers need to be needed. Others just want to feel useful. Many are drawn to the "helping professions" like social work, nursing, teaching, medicine and law. Phrases like "I've lost myself in caring for others" indicate when the line has been crossed from simple kindness to caretaking. Helping your child with her firstborn is a wonderful pleasure. But running yourself ragged to relieve your child of her burden is excessive. It can also generate guilt or anger in the recipient.

Last winter we received a birdfeeder as a gift. We set it up in the backyard and enjoyed watching the different species of winged visitors. We also felt noble in helping birds find food during a cold and snowy winter. When spring came, a friend taught us a valuable lesson about both birds and people. She told us to take down our birdfeeder until the next winter. Her explanation was that if we left it up we'd make it too easy for birds to feed at our trough, and they would lose the ability to find food on their own ("in the wild" so to speak). Before long, the birds would lose their instinct to forage for food and would become dependent on us. We did them no favors by creating that dependency. It disempowered them.

Not long after, a beleaguered woman told me she had no time for herself in the evening because she had to help her teenage daughter with her homework. Actually it was worse than that. She had to stay up past her own bedtime because her child wanted to watch TV first. So they rarely got started before 10:00. (The Pleaser in her accepted this arrangement.) I asked why she was so involved in this homework. She informed me that she'd been doing it for so many years her daughter was now unable to do it alone. Her helping had produced a dependency that was costly to both of them: it diminished the teenager's competence and inconvenienced the mother. All because her tendency to caretaking had gone too far. This kind of behavior is also a form of enabling. Your actions, costly to you, promote a form of behavior that is not in the other person's best interest either. So both people lose. A game with no winners is certainly a game to give up.

Victims

1.   Do you feel that other people and outside forces run your life?

2.   Do you just accept it or react passively when things don't work out as you'd like? Do you feel powerless to do anything about it?

3.   Are you often struck by the fact that bad luck seems to follow you?

4.   Do you often blame others for the way you feel (angry, guilty, frustrated)?

5.   Are you attracted to strong personalities? Do you let other people take over your life?

Al Capp created the comic strip "L'il Abner" in which he had a character named Joe Btfsplk. Wherever this man went there was a raincloud over his head. The weather five feet away was sunny and bright, but Joe lived in a perpetual gloom that *seemed* to be external. Many people live like this, convinced there are forces beyond their control that are shaping their lives. This is not to suggest people aren't victimized at times—by tragedy, illness, exploiters, etc. I am referring, however, to the many people whose victimization is more apparent than real or who are, in fact, victimizing themselves.

A woman was telling me about all the pressures on her from other people: demands from her family, from community organizations she served and from friends. She felt obliged to call her mother every day, chauffeur her children around, run errands, attend meetings and spend weekends at a cottage that her husband enjoyed but which she resented. When I questioned her, she told me she had no choice in these matters. The conversation went like this:

"It sounds to me as though you feel trapped. It's as if someone else is running your life."

"Someone else *is* running my life."

"Who?"

"All the people who *touch* my life."

"Do you see yourself as an agent of choice or not?"

"Not!"

"But *you* have to give them *permission* to run your life, don't you?"

"Somewhere along the line I abdicated responsibility for my life and I haven't done anything about it—except to complain."

Unlike the Pleaser who decides to say yes, and to avoid conflict, Victims don't even see that they have a choice. It feels as if everything is happening to them and they're powerless to stop it. Other words to describe this feeling include helpless, vulnerable, weak and stuck. It's a very unpleasant way to live.

There is a passive quality to the way Victims think that is reflected in their language. Here are some examples. "We can't seem to find babysitters"; "How come all these troubled people gather around *me*?"; "I never speak to my friends. Nobody seems to call anymore"; "I'd like to play tennis more often—if someone would force me into it. If left to my own devices, I'd never get around to it."

A common but subtle form of Victim thinking is contained in these phrases: "He makes me so angry," "She always makes me feel guilty," "He makes me feel stupid" and "She really intimidates me." The fact is that people don't *make* you feel anything. They simply behave and interact. Whatever feelings you have in response are generated by *you*. As Eleanor Roosevelt put it: "Nobody can make you feel inferior without your consent."

Other telltale phrases of Victim thinking include: "I can't do anything about it," "It's not my fault" (for some people it's *never* their fault), "I have no choice" and "I have no say in things." Granted there are times when all these phrases may be true—but not nearly as often as you think. Take, for example, a situation where you walk into a crowded movie theater and the only empty seats are singles. So you and your companion split up to watch the film. On one hand, you could say you had no choice but to sit separately. On the other hand, what's to stop you from looking for a row with two vacant single seats and asking the people between the chairs to move down one place each to create two adjacent empty seats? I've done this many times and people are always accommodating. This is a case of taking initiative to change a situation (in a way that's acceptable to all involved) rather than feeling powerless to influence circumstances that, on the surface, appear to be unchangeable.

Here is a useful concept to identify the forces running your life. *Locus* is a Latin word meaning "place." The phrase "locus of control" refers to the place where the control in your life resides. If you are in control of your own life, you would say you have an *internal* locus of control—the control rests within you. Similar concepts include being responsible for yourself, independent, autonomous, taking initiative, being proactive and empowered. If you operate as a Victim, you have an *external* locus of control, where you feel forces act on you from outside yourself. Other words to convey this include helpless, dependent, contingent, being a follower, being reactive and disempowered.

Combinations of Losing Games

There is a lot of overlap between the various games described here. As a result, many people display characteristics of several of these traits. For example, many Type As are also Overachievers and/or Workaholics. Caretakers are often Pleasers, and both groups have their share of Victims. Sometimes, the combination of behaviors presents internal conflicts. For example, a Type-A person who is also a Pleaser can find herself in an interesting dilemma. On the one hand, she's highly competitive and likes to win in everything she does. On the other hand, she doesn't like to offend or antagonize people. So what does she do when she's winning a tennis game but sees that her opponent is getting upset or even resentful? Does she ease off and give him a few points? Does she subconsciously throw the game so she won't feel guilty? Does she say: "That's his problem and I'm going to whomp him"? Or does she leave the court saying, "I think I hear my mother calling me"?

Here is a man who combines several of these losing patterns. He is a Type A/Workaholic/Overachiever/Pleaser who realizes his behavior is not benefiting him. He's a middle manager running a small department in a large company. The Type-A part of him is always in a hurry and he gets very impatient if things move slowly. His workaholism is reflected in his very long hours at work and having "no time for myself." His Overachiever said, "I have to do things that *other people* see and comment on—and that *I* can see results of." The Pleaser in him said: "Criticism can destroy me." And underlying all this came an expression of poor self-esteem (which is the impetus for his push to succeed): "I never felt I was good enough—but I always *wanted* to be first." To others he appeared to be highly successful. However, despite all his hard-driving efforts, his self-esteem was not improving. In addition, his behavior created a number of problems: fatigue, frustration, distress, feeling under pressure and always being in a hurry. He was on a treadmill of his own making and finally recognized the futility and the cost of it all.

In summary, many behavior patterns turn out to be losing games because they don't produce the desired results—or even if they do, there are many negative trade-offs. *Workaholics*, *Type As* and *Overachievers* often get a lot done, are admired by others and may become successful and rich. But they are very hard on themselves. The cost to them is fatigue, stress, anxiety and frequently alienating others. *Perfectionists* do splendid work—but a lot less (and with more hassle) than if they were less demanding. *Pleasers* may be well liked and avoid conflict, but they give power to other people, exhaust themselves, feel resentful and not in control of their lives and are frequently taken for granted. *Caretakers* get a lot of satisfaction and praise, but they neglect themselves and run the risk of exhaustion or even burnout. *Victims* avoid responsibility and may be taken care of by others, but they are just as likely to be abused and exploited. In addition, their feeling of powerlessness leads to a lot of uncertainty and anxiety.

All of these losing games can be changed. The first step in the process is to be aware of when you're playing them.

CHOICE

CHAPTER NINE

Making Choices

ICTURE THIS: YOU'RE LOSING IN A FRIENDLY game of tennis. Nothing is at stake except your pride and desire to win. But as you get farther behind, you start to get upset. Feelings of frustration emerge, you get down on yourself and start into your negative self-talk routine. You become dispirited and discouraged. The game isn't fun anymore. You're now playing two losing games: the one on the scoreboard and the one in your head. The result is emotional (feeling tense and annoyed) and physical (you play even worse, leading to more upset). What a cycle to get into!

You step off the court for a pep talk and some friendly advice to yourself. You note that you're playing poorly, your thinking is negative and you're allowing the score to sabotage your enjoyment. It's time to change your losing game.

There are three ways you can turn things around. First, change your strategy. Do things differently: mix up your shots, move the ball around, settle down to basic strokes—nothing fancy. Second, change your thinking. View the game as an opportunity to practice your skills, make the quality of your shots more important than winning the points, appreciate the exercise and don't worry about the score, enjoy the fresh air and concentrate on having fun. By changing your attitude about the game, you decrease the pressure you've created when winning becomes your primary goal. The third thing you can do is to get your mind off the game occasionally. Look around while you're switching sides, say hello to other people, stop to towel off or have a drink. Such diversions act like "time-outs" and calm you down when you're taking things too seriously.

From Sports to the Game of Life

Whenever you're aware that your game isn't working, the next step is to explore the choices available to you. As noted in the previous scenario, there are three main options: do something to change the situation, change the way you think about the situation, or get away from the situation (temporarily). Let's see how this applies in real life.

An executive assistant is at work late on a Friday afternoon. In an hour she'll be off for the weekend. The weather's great and she's got friends coming over for a barbecue. She's tidying up some loose ends when her boss comes in and tells her he needs some work done before she leaves. It will take about two hours. He's imposed on her at the last minute like this many times before. It's all she can do to conceal her anger. She forces a smile to hide her rage, sits down to the work and feels her neck muscles tighten and her stomach knot up. She feels trapped, powerless and ready to throw her keyboard through the window!

This woman is now involved in a losing game, albeit not entirely of her own making. She has learned to monitor the signals of a losing game so she is aware of what is happening. She notices the telltale muscle tension, palpitations, flushing and abdominal tightness. Mentally, her mind races and she loses her focus. Emotionally, anger and frustration are the dominant symptoms. In terms of behavior, she starts drumming her fingers and bouncing her right knee. These are all signals she's learned to notice. They help her detect the losing game within minutes. She's also aware of what the game is. The situation is not just the request from her boss. It includes her reaction to the work he's asked her to do. It is her self-talk and her interpretation of his action that is really fueling her upset.

The stage is now set for her to explore her *choices* for changing this losing game. She has many options. She could stay and do the work requested. But she could also change the situation. Her options include saying no, taking the assignment home, coming in on Saturday morning, delegating it to someone else, talking her boss out of it (showing him why it can wait till Monday), negotiating time off next week as a trade-off for staying late, chastising him for being so disorganized and taking her for granted, quitting her job on the spot, and so on. These are all alternatives to doing what she's been asked. Of course, some of these options have unpleasant consequences that she has to consider. But the important point is that, even though the situation seems to be one in which she is powerless, she has many choices. The issue of choice is one I will refer to again and again. The message to remember is this: you always have a choice even if you don't exercise that choice.

Even if she chooses to go along with her boss's request, she can reduce her distress by changing her attitude toward the situation. By *thinking* differently about it, she can decrease her upset or even create a winning game out of a losing one. She can view this moment as an opportunity to score points with her boss, or see it as part of the job in which everyone's expected to pitch in from time to time for the common good. If her boss is thoughtful and generous in other ways, she may see it as a reasonable trade-off for favors she's received previously. Perhaps he has personal problems she knows about that explain his behavior and with which she can sympathize. Maybe staying late will allow her to miss the Friday-afternoon rush hour and still arrive home close to her usual time. By changing the way she thinks about the situation, she can minimize its stressful impact.

The third way of dealing with this upsetting event is to get away from the situation. This involves either physically removing herself or at least getting her mind off the situation and onto something else. Taking a short break can do wonders at such a moment. A quick walk before she sits down to work, a trip to the snack bar or washroom, a brief chat with a co-worker, a phone call or some other activity will allow her to get her attention off the immediate state of affairs and let her anger cool down. Relaxation techniques can be helpful at times like these: a few deep breaths or shoulder rolls can restore her feeling of balance and calm.

One thing is certain: any of these three ways of dealing with a stressful situation is preferable to suffering, seething or self-pitying. Actually, the best approach is to use elements of all three. This game plan (which is diagrammed on the flow chart on the next page) is constructive and offers lots of choice. It provides an organized approach and confers a feeling of control. It directs your thinking at a time when you most need to avoid flying off the handle.

STRESS MASTERY FLOW CHART

What's Changeable and What's Not

This is how the game plan is used. When you recognize the signs of a losing game, the first question to ask is: "Is this situation changeable or not?" The answer isn't always obvious. For example, a situation may *appear* unchangeable until you think about it. A rule of thumb is that any situation created *by* people is usually changeable, because *people* are changeable. Decisions can be reversed, plans changed and laws altered. Don't assume things are carved in stone when they're not. On the other hand, things that happen *to* people are usually not changeable and have to be dealt with differently. Heart attacks, birth defects, injuries, deaths of relatives or friends, house fires and failed businesses are among the unchangeable circumstances that you have to cope with and learn to accept.

If a situation is changeable, the next question to ask is: "Can *I* change it?" For example, your child may be on drugs or your partner abuses alcohol. That's changeable, but you aren't the one who can change it—your child or partner is the only one who can do that. This doesn't mean that you can't influence the situation, but the ultimate control is not in your hands. Another way of asking this question is: "Is this something over which *I* have *control?*" Many circumstances are changeable *but not by you,* and you have to know when and where to draw that line. You should also ask yourself: "How upset do I want to get over things I can't control?" It's better to save your energy for things you can do something about. Things that are changeable—but not by you—mostly involve other people's behavior and certain business or government decisions.

If your company is taken over and your job is eliminated, technically something can be done to change that—but it's not within your power or control.

A third question to consider is this: "Even if I *can* change the situation, is it worth the effort or cost or the likely consequences of doing so?" For example, you may have been treated unfairly at work. You could challenge your employers through your union (if you belong to one), through your lawyer or by your own efforts but it may be more aggravation than it's worth in time, money and energy. You have to decide for yourself. But whether you choose to pursue something or not, it's helpful to recognize that you have a choice.

There are two main ways to change a situation: one is within the situation, the other is by leaving the situation. (Leaving in this sense means permanently leaving, as distinguished from diversion and distraction, which are temporary. A short walk, a movie or a holiday are diversions; you then return to the situation, but you're fresher because you've had a break.) If you don't like your job there are many ways to change things *within* the situation: change your hours, alter your job description, delegate more, manage your time better, etc. Leaving the situation would be quitting the job altogether. If your marriage isn't working out, you can discuss your problems, spend more time together, read books about relationships, be more cooperative, seek counseling, etc. Or you can leave the situation by getting a separation or divorce. If you dislike your house, you can renovate, redecorate, landscape, etc.—or you can leave by selling the house and moving to another dwelling.

I generally advise people to try to change a situation from within before deciding to leave, but this is an individual choice and there's no hard-and-fast rule. In a job or relationship, it makes sense to see if the situation is salvageable before moving on. Leaving can sometimes look like the easiest option, but you burn your bridges that way. Also, even if your attempt to overcome the problem is unsuccessful, at least you will know you did your best and you won't have to wonder later on if you did the right thing by leaving.

A Personal Example

Let me demonstrate how this game plan looks in action. The first example is my own experience as a family physician, a job I found increasingly stressful near the end of my seventeen-year career. I was aware of this by noting the physical signs (primarily fatigue and low back pain), the mental signals (trouble concentrating and being less decisive at times), the emotional tip-offs (feeling irritable and impatient) and the behavioral clues (like knee-jiggling and restlessness).

Since the situation was changeable, I had three broad choices. I changed the situation in a number of ways. I gave up obstetrics and emergency-room shifts, which I found particularly stressful, and did more stress and lifestyle counseling, which I enjoyed. I started my office hours earlier and booked physicals in the morning when I was fresh. I delegated more responsibility to my nurse, who was only too happy to have the extra challenge. I altered my method for keeping patient records and adopted a new bookkeeping system.

In addition, I changed my attitude toward my work. I focused on the positives: the pleasure I got from my patients, the variety of problems I got to see, the comradeship with doctors and nurses at our community hospital, being my own boss and the sense that my job was meaningful. I also modified my expectations and stopped trying to be all things to all people all the time. Another extremely important attitude shift was to remind myself that I wasn't trapped—that I could do something else if I wanted, that the door to choice was always open.

There were also many diversions and distractions to get my mind off work. I played several sports, tooted my trombone in the local orchestra, went to movies and plays, socialized a lot, read constantly and took frequent holidays.

The result of utilizing this three-pronged approach was to reduce my stress to a comfortable level, which allowed me to practice medicine for several more years. Eventually I exercised the other "change the situation" option by leaving general practice and taking up a new career in counseling and teaching.

What to Do in Case of Fire

Now let's look at a situation that was *not* changeable: a fire that gutted the house of a woman I knew. Fortunately no one was home, so there were no injuries, and the house was not badly damaged structurally. She was understandably upset for a few days, but something interesting happened when she re-entered the house on the third day. Since she expected everything to be destroyed or damaged beyond repair, she was thrilled to find some things were salvageable. She made a game of seeing how much she could recover and viewed every item that was intact or restorable as a bonus. Thus she completely reversed her perspective, focusing not on what was lost but on what she could find.

She changed her attitude in another significant way. She saw the insurance money as a chance to improve the house. Instead of seeing the fire as a disaster, she started to view it as a golden opportunity: "Now I'll decorate the house the way I wanted it in the first place but could never afford!" In thinking differently about the fire, she found a way of winning something in an otherwise losing situation.

A Father's Frustration

Now let me cite a situation that was changeable but later became unchangeable. It involved a bright and capable teenager who was nevertheless failing in school. The story was related to me by his father, a well-educated professional man who was extremely upset by his son's poor performance. The boy had been an excellent student and his parents had high hopes for him. Now that he was failing, his father was frustrated, angry and worried.

Realizing this was a changeable situation, the father employed a variety of different strategies, none of which succeeded. He talked to his son and his teachers. He learned that the young man wasn't studying or doing his assignments. So he organized a meeting with the boy, his teachers and the school principal. Nothing changed. He bribed and rewarded him. He threatened and punished him. All to no avail. He had done everything he could think of to change the situation and had run out of options.

At this point, the father realized that, although this was a changeable situation, it was not changeable *by him*. It was a matter beyond his control. Thus it had become, de facto, an *unchangeable* situation from his point of view. His choices were therefore limited to changing his attitude toward the situation or not thinking about it at all (diversion and distraction).

He began thinking differently about the matter. "Maybe it's not so terrible that he's failing after all. In fact, perhaps the *best* thing would be for him to miss his year. That would probably smarten him up pretty quickly." He even started to think it wouldn't be the end of the world if his son didn't go to college—an unthinkable idea only months earlier. Maybe if the boy worked for a year or two, he'd get his priorities straight and clamor to go to university. He also wondered: "Why am I more upset about this than my son is?" In addition he said: "One of my roles as a parent is to teach my children responsibility. Sometimes I can do that verbally. But other times I have to stand back and let him make mistakes and learn from the consequences. This appears to be such a time." Finally, he put his son's school grades in a larger context: his overall development. He acknowledged his boy's many other attributes and was pleased with the way he was turning out. The young man was respectful and cooperative at home, had good values and nice friends, was not abusing drugs or alcohol, played sports, etc.

The other thing this man did was to stop dwelling on his son's academic performance as if it were the central issue in his *own* life. He refocused on his work, his wife and other children, his hobbies and his friends. Gradually he spent less and less time stewing over the topic that had seemed so crucial a short time before. He had moved from the losing game of worry and anger and trying to control his son's behavior. In its place he created a new and comfortable game of "live and let live," involving a different perspective and some optimism that things would eventually work themselves out.

In summary, there are many ways to change a losing game. However, they fall into three main categories: changing the situation, changing your attitude toward the situation and getting away from the situation. Often the best approach is to use elements of all three. Changing the situation can be achieved *within* the situation (by changing the objective circumstances or by changing your own behavior) or by permanently *leaving* the situation. Now it's time to look at each of these areas of change in more detail. Because I believe changing the way you think is the most important and powerful kind of change, I will begin by revisiting "the game between your ears."

CHAPTER TEN

Change Your Thinking

PORTS PSYCHOLOGISTS HAVE BECOME A PART of athletics. They show players how to enhance their natural physical skills by using their minds as an ally instead of an obstacle. Teaching athletes to relax, stay focused, have a positive attitude, overcome fear and doubt, be upbeat and encouraging—this is the psychologist's role. But can you really change the way you think? Is it possible to alter your beliefs and attitudes and how you look at things?

Many people view thoughts as being beyond their control, involuntary impulses that just pop into their heads. It's quite a radical notion that you can shape and choose your thoughts, deciding what you will think about and for how long and in what way. However, it is possible and everyone has the ability to do it.

My patients have demonstrated this ability to *choose* how and what they think. One business executive had been in conflict with his boss for years. He started feeling better when he voluntarily changed his attitude. He announced to me: "I've decided not to let him get to me anymore." A young woman had been hassled by her ex-husband and began laughing while telling me about it. When I asked what was so funny, she replied: "I'm laughing because it doesn't do me any good to be pissed off."

On a personal level, I've learned to do this too. If a problem comes up at work that I can't deal with at the time, I make an appointment with myself to think about it during my lunchtime run. I put the subject on hold until I have time to mull it over at my convenience. Such is our ability to program and channel our thinking.

Some of the worst games you can play are in your head. And of these, negative self-talk is about the most punishing of all. As noted in Chapter 5, the little voice in your head talks to you in a variety of harmful ways. However, you don't have to just sit back and listen. There are alternatives to this hurtful activity.

Antidotes to Negative Self-Talk

Occasional negative self-talk is natural and inevitable, but for many people, it's a way of life. The question is: what can be done about it? How can the voice be silenced, dimmed or neutralized? Here are some suggestions.

The first step is to acknowledge the presence of your negative voice. Awareness is the initial stage in taking control of your life. Just noticing your inner voice and monitoring its messages is very instructive. You may be surprised at the frequency and nastiness of the statements. Many people find it helpful to write down these thoughts for a few days to appreciate the range and hurtfulness of them. Once you're tuned in to this damaging communication, the next stage of eradication is *choice*.

Your internal voice is like a recorded message that keeps playing. You cannot turn off the voice entirely but you can alter the negative content and replace it with something positive. This is the element of *choice*. You can choose to stop the harmful message and to reprogram the voice to say things you want to hear. You don't have to be a victim of your thoughts. Give yourself *permission* to employ some of the following techniques as an alternative to negative self-talk.

Thought Stopping

The first technique is called thought stopping, a form of behavior modification introduced in 1928. It is elegant in its simplicity and does exactly what it says: it stops unwanted thoughts. Picture yourself walking down the street with a friend who keeps putting himself down. You listen to this guy dumping on himself for a few blocks. Finally, when you've heard enough, you turn and tell him to knock it off. He might be surprised at your reaction. If you yell at him, he may even be shocked. And the more jolted he is, the more likely he is to stop saying those destructive things about himself.

Thought stopping is exactly like this scenario except you are both the negative talker and the irritated listener. As soon as you notice the harmful voice in your head, you yell something sharp and loud and jarring to stop yourself. "Stop it," "Cut it out," "Enough" and "Cool it" are examples of crisp and snappy messages that cannot help but grab your attention. At first, I suggest that people actually shout these remarks to get the full force of this technique. (Of course it would be prudent to do this at times when you are alone—like driving in your car or being at home by yourself.) Once you've caught onto the idea and shocked yourself a few times, you can yell a little more quietly, until you are just saying the words. Then you can progress to whispering and eventually to just saying the words silently in your head. The objective of this technique is to disrupt the negative statements.

I first learned about thought stopping from Dr. Eva Feindler, a psychologist from New York. Since then I have picked up two variations of this technique from other colleagues. A physician friend of mine teaches his patients to hold their left arm out in front of them with their hand cocked up so that the palm is facing them. Then they project the unwanted thought onto their palm. Finally they take their right hand and loudly clap it against the outstretched hand while yelling the words "Stop it!" In this way they literally squash the thought they have projected onto their hand. This technique uses three senses at once (visual, auditory and kinesthetic), producing more impact.

Another approach is to put an elastic band loosely around your wrist. Then, whenever an unwanted thought enters your head, you snap the elastic band and silently say "Stop it." Although these techniques sound unsophisticated, they absolutely work. Practice for several days and you'll quickly master them. An excellent description of this skill appears in *The Relaxation and Stress Reduction Workbook* by Martha Davis, PhD.; Elizabeth Robbins Eshelman, MSW; and Matthew McKay, PhD.

Thought stopping is like switching TV channels or turning the set off when something unpleasant comes on the screen. You wouldn't think of watching something terribly upsetting just because it happened to be on. You have the freedom to interrupt the program at any moment. Thoughts in your head have no more hold on you than unwanted TV images.

However, thought stopping alone is not enough. If you interrupt negative thoughts but don't replace them with something else, the thoughts are likely to reappear. So you need to divert your thoughts to other things. Thought substitution and diversion are the two ways of keeping unwanted messages from returning after you've jolted them out of your thought stream.

Positive self-statements are a great antidote after you've used thought stopping to interrupt the negative messages. A woman who kept dumping on herself about her weight found some very positive features to admire. Her substitute thoughts included phrases like: "I have a warm smile" and "Everyone tells me how beautiful my eyes are." These were the self-compliments she chose to focus on and feel good about.

Diversion is the other way of keeping unwanted ideas from returning after you use thought stopping. It's like saying "Let's change the subject" and proposing a new topic of conversation. Years ago my wife and I were in Florida on holiday. There was a hostage drama going on in the Middle East that was protracted and grisly, and we'd watched some of it on CNN. One day, we were on our way to play golf and I began thinking about what it would be like to be on that plane. Within minutes I'd gotten myself very upset with negative images and thoughts. Finally recognizing what I was doing, I said to myself (silently): "All right, David, that's enough. You're just upsetting yourself." Then I did three things to divert my attention away from the hijacking. I opened my window, turned on the radio and started chatting with my wife. I'd had the disturbing thoughts, employed thought stopping and used diversion, all within a minute, and none of it was telegraphed to my spouse sitting inches away. This is how quiet yet effective the process of thought control can be.

There are many forms of diversion and distraction. You can pick up the phone, grab a magazine, start a conversation, go to the fridge, take a walk, read your mail, visit the bathroom, turn on the TV, take a few deep breaths, etc. Or you can just focus your attention on something else. Looking out the window, daydreaming or planning your weekend are all ways of shifting to a different and pleasant channel and keeping the harmful messages from re-entering your mind.

Coping Statements

Coping statements are another way to neutralize negative self-talk. These are little phrases you say to yourself that contain advice, wisdom and encouragement. They are like slogans or mottos; little catchphrases to calm you down, lift your spirits and change your perspective. They can be used alone or as a follow-up to thought stopping. Examples include: "It's not worth it," "Life's too short," "This too shall pass," "I did my best," "It'll all come out in the wash," "Lighten up," "Who needs the hassle?," and "It's okay to have an off-day." Coping statements are a combination of down-home wisdom, basic philosophy and common sense. Some coping statements become famous. Doris Day made a lot of money in 1956 with a song called "Que Sera Sera—Whatever Will Be Will Be." Paul McCarney's was "Let It Be."

Sometimes coping statements are like a pep talk. Instead of worrying endlessly about a job interview, a woman used phrases such as "I'm sure I'm as good as the other candidates," "I'm as prepared as I can be" and "They'd be crazy not to hire me." She also kept feeding herself helpful advice: "Just stay calm and relaxed," "Take your time" and "Smile and keep it friendly." These statements filled her mind and left no room for the undermining thoughts that had plagued her.

Affirmations

In 1923, a Frenchman named Émile Coué introduced his philosophy of auto-suggestion with this phrase: "Every day, in every way, I'm getting better and better." This well-known positive self-statement is a classic example of an affirmation. Coué repeated this to himself many times a day until it became the truth for him. Because of the way he stated it and the frequency of his repetitions, his mind accepted it as being true. Thus he established a new "reality" for himself simply because he wanted to believe it.

The power of affirmations has been known for a long time. Books like Norman Vincent Peale's *The Power of Positive Thinking* and Napoleon Hill's *Think and Grow Rich* are based on this premise. Dr. John Lilly said: "In the realm of the mind, what you believe to be true is true."

Your thoughts have incredible power over you. Negative thoughts become reality. Even the destructive, insulting judgments you make about yourself become "the truth" for you. But as damaging as these negative thoughts are, they are not a permanent part of you. They were learned and therefore they can be unlearned.

Affirmations are positive, constructive, validating assertions that you make about yourself. You can literally reprogram your internal voice to produce positive messages as a replacement for the harmful voice of the past. You simply decide to talk to yourself in the affirmative rather than the negative. And you can do this by choice, voluntarily and consistently.

You have far more control over your thoughts than you realize, and you can learn the skills to put that control to good use. Negative self-talk is one of the greatest destroyers of human potential, but methods exist for overcoming it. You're not stuck with what your internal voice says, no matter how long or persistently it's been polluting your thoughts.

Refuting the "Shoulds"

The bossy side of your internal voice can also be countered with the use of thought stopping. You can talk back to the voice as you might to a bossy person. Assert yourself, resist the message. When your self-talk is badgering you and telling you what you *should* do, tell it what you want to do instead.

Which Tense Do You Live In?

Of all the self-destructive emotions articulated by your internal voice, worry, regret, remorse and resentment have something in common: they are all related to either the past or the future, not the present. As such they are a waste of energy. Thought stopping, coping statements and diversion help to get rid of these unwanted thoughts. But learning to live in the present is of great benefit as well.

Have you ever watched a tennis player get so upset about a bad shot that he loses the next point as well? What marks a top athlete is the ability to concentrate on each moment as it comes, totally focused on what is happening *right now* and oblivious to everything that preceded it. The best competitors have learned to "live in the moment" as if it were frozen in time. One of my patients put it this way: "It's like a fastball coming at you. You swing and hit it or miss it and then it's over. It's too late to re-swing. And dwelling on it after the fact just interferes with your ability to hit the *next* one."

The same principle applies to life. You can't focus on the here and now if your mind is regretting something from the past or worrying about things in the future. Many people tell me they live so much in the past or the future that they don't live in the present at all. This is regrettable but changeable. Learning to live each moment, one at a time, is an excellent way to shut off the destructive thoughts relating to past and future. It will enhance the quality of your life immeasurably.

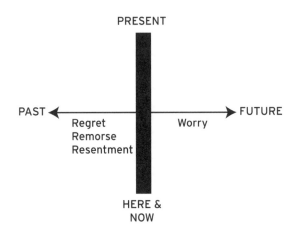

Worry about the unknown has an implied "what if?" attached to it. And the images you conjure up in your mind are usually worse than what eventually happens. I used to get called to our emergency department to see acutely ill patients. The nurses would describe someone gasping for breath or going gray, and I would roar off to see them with my thoughts full of impending disaster. The stress I put myself through bordered on cruelty. When I arrived, palpitating and anxious, I'd often find a patient looking rather well compared with the expectation I'd created in my mind. This happened often enough that I decided to take a new approach to these calls. I chose not to worry until I got there. I reminded myself about all the "false alarms" of the past when things worked out fine. This approach kept my thoughts (and emotions) in check.

One of my favorite quotes is from the French philosopher Montaigne: "My life has been a series of catastrophes—most of which never happened!" Worrying before the fact is a wasteful activity. It reminds me of the joke about a guy who receives the following telegram: "Start worrying—details to follow." My philosophy is this: "Don't worry until you know you have something to worry about. If there's nothing wrong, you'll save yourself a lot of grief. And if there *is* something wrong, you'll have all the time in the world to worry about it *then*."

Let me return to the school teacher in Chapter 5 who was worrying in June about her new job at a different school come September. She was just starting her summer vacation and already fretting about the fall. I told her it was appropriate to have some concern about a new job, but I felt she was starting rather early. I asked her how many days of worry she thought this job change warranted. She laughed, then she winked and said, "Three." We jokingly agreed that she would put the worrying off until the last day of August. She could start stewing then—if she still wanted to. I hinted that she could even mark her calendar to *remind* her to worry—in case she totally forgot! She recognized three things from this: that worry was unnecessary and wasteful (*awareness*); that she had a *choice* about whether she'd worry and for how long; and that she could give herself *permission* to put the worry out of her mind for as long as she wanted and to bring it back only when she wanted—if at all.

This story brings out another point. I make a distinction between worry and concern. To me, concern is appropriate and constructive; it implies interest in and caring about a person or thing. It is in proportion to the issue being considered, not excessive, and it leads to productive action like making plans or solving problems. On the other hand, worry is excessive, unfocused and unhelpful. It can range from being fretful all the way to catastrophic thinking. Worry is often so pervasive that it immobilizes people instead of leading them to take helpful measures. I think of concern as an intellectual, positive exercise. By contrast, worry is an emotional and negative pursuit.

Worry can intrude even when you don't want it to. There are many ways of dealing with it, including thought stopping, coping statements and diversion. Here are three other approaches. One is to talk to someone about it. Share your fears. Vent your feelings of anxiety or dread. Expressing your feelings helps to reduce them. It also allows people to assist you by offering useful suggestions, giving emotional support, encouraging you or even helping you laugh about the situation. One of the biggest losing games you can play is to suffer alone and in silence, bottling up your emotions and keeping your feelings inside you. People who suffer alone suffer a lot. Let people you trust (family, friends, colleagues or therapists) help you through difficult times.

The second approach is to write about what worries you. Ask yourself "what's the worst thing that can happen?" and think about how you would handle it. Sometimes confronting the worst-case scenario puts things in perspective. When you do this on paper, it's sometimes called "creative or constructive worrying."

Third, set aside time for worrying so it doesn't consume your thinking. Make an appointment with yourself and defer all your fretting until that time. Then brood all you want and get it over with all at once.

As for regret, remorse and resentment, these three poisonous emotions can be relieved by letting go of the past. Resentment is animosity toward someone else. One man had been angry with his sister for years about some money she owed him. They had had no contact and he felt upset whenever he thought about her. As we talked about it, he said: "Maybe I need to let go of the bad feelings I have toward my sister. Part of me is still bloody mad and would like that money back. Most of me would like to just let it go. I think it's making-up time." He reached that conclusion by working through his feelings but also by realizing how much damage the resentment was causing him. He had an *awareness* of his anger and what it was costing him. He recognized that he had *choices* that included calling his sister and making up. So he gave himself *permission* to take action. He went to visit her and, despite his apprehension, he was able to bury the hatchet once and for all.

Remorse and regret involve upset or disappointment in yourself. I saw a man who had been beating up on himself for his entire adult life. One day I asked him what terrible shame he was hiding, and he confessed to me that he had committed a crime as a teenager. It was a robbery in which no one was hurt. He was caught and served a prison sentence. He had paid his debt to society but was still punishing himself. I asked what it would take for him to forgive himself. He said he'd always wanted to repay his victim but had no idea where he was. The compromise we devised was that he would donate a similar amount of money to charity as a symbolic act. He was finally able to discharge the remorse he had carried for so long.

I was once contemplating a big decision in my life and debating whether to take the plunge into a new venture. In discussing it with an uncle, he said something I never forgot: "The only things in life I regret are the things I *didn't* do." He went on to say that we all make mistakes. It's a part of life and of growth. Accepting that fact helps to put events into perspective. You can't rewrite history. Somehow you have to make peace with your past. Self-forgiveness and letting go of regret are parts of that process. Looking back and suffering is neither wise nor healthy. Don't look back—except to celebrate the past or to learn from it.

Beliefs

In Chapter 7, I discussed belief systems and how the beliefs you hold shape the way you think, act and feel. The first step in dealing with beliefs is to become aware of them. Although you hold most of your beliefs subconsciously, bringing them to conscious awareness is not too difficult. The next step is to evaluate their impact on you. If it's negative or limiting, you should challenge those assumptions and even revise them. You can choose other beliefs that serve you better—and the benefits of so doing are considerable.

Whether you believe you can do a thing or believe you can't, you are right.
HENRY FORD

Changing harmful beliefs can be a liberating experience. It's like taking off a thick coat on a hot day, or setting down a heavy load you've been carrying unnecessarily. And the consequences are not just psychological but behavioral as well. Here are a few success stories to illustrate the point.

A patient I was seeing had used sleeping pills for over two years and felt he couldn't sleep without them. He even declared: "I need the Serax to fall asleep," and he was quite certain about this. I encouraged him to go off medication, and we developed a seven-point plan for his evening routine. I also urged him to challenge his belief about the need for medication. He discontinued his Serax over a weekend, during which the certainty that he needed pills began to recede. After two weeks off medication he reported sleeping "remarkably well," which surprised him. He then stated (with real conviction): "I'm in charge of this. I can go to sleep. I was hooked on this drug. I don't need it now!" By arbitrarily changing his behavior, he not only altered his night-time pill-taking routine, he proved to himself that his belief had been untrue. The result was a new, positive and totally opposite belief to replace the old one. And the belief change supported the behavioral change.

New beliefs can lead to the blossoming of an inhibited individual. A woman in her thirties who could never please her father grew up with low self-esteem and a notable lack of confidence. She was filled with beliefs that began with "I can't." Then she developed health problems and her doctor insisted she quit smoking. Despite her misgivings, she succeeded. This led to a new belief. She announced: "There's nothing on earth I can't do," after which she went out and got her driver's license. Next she took an assertiveness training course and became more outspoken and self-determining. She was on a roll and feeling like a world-beater. With every success, her conviction that "there's nothing I can't do" was strengthened.

Changing beliefs can make a crucial difference in business. A salesman came to see me about work stress. He found calling on customers very difficult, becoming apprehensive and sweaty and often coming away without an order. When I asked him what was going through his mind before he stepped into his prospects' offices, he recounted a litany of negative self-talk messages based on the assumption that he would fail. It was a pep talk that would get any football coach fired on the spot. Why was he programming himself so negatively? He was an engaging chap who believed in his product, and I saw no reason why he couldn't convince people to buy from him. I suggested a new routine with his customers. He began arriving for each appointment a little early and sat in the waiting room, telling himself he could make this sale and pumping up his confidence. He quickly started getting results. He began making sales when he started believing he would, and he set up a positive self-fulfilling prophecy.

"The Pygmalion effect" is a phrase referring to the power of beliefs to produce a desired outcome. In George Bernard Shaw's play *Pygmalion* (later made into *My Fair Lady*), Eliza Doolittle was turned from a guttersnipe into a sophisticated lady by the tutoring of Professor Henry Higgins. But first he had to believe such a transformation was possible. Furthermore, he had to get Eliza to believe it too. Becoming what you believe you can be is the fabric of every success story. Wilma Rudolph was a remarkable athlete who overcame childhood polio to become an Olympic gold-medal sprinter. She had great dreams, determination and discipline. But she also had to believe she could succeed.

In summary, when negative self-talk plagues your brain circuits, you are not stuck with these undermining messages. Thought stopping, coping statements, affirmations, thinking in the present and creative worrying are constructive alternatives. Choosing from among these positive options will lead you away from the harm of your internal chatter.

As for belief systems, the first step in dealing with their power is to bring them to awareness. Ask yourself: "How do you feel employers should treat their workers?" or "What do you think about athletes using steroids?" or "What's your picture of an ideal family?" and you will uncover your beliefs about these things. You will likely discover views you didn't know you had. When something upsets you, ask yourself what's bothering you and why. If you're having difficulty overcoming a harmful behavior (like overloading your schedule), question yourself about why you're stuck. The answers will often reveal hidden assumptions and unconscious beliefs that are limiting you.

The second step is to recognize that these beliefs are *not* inherently true. They are merely opinions, your thoughts about how things are or should be. It is more accurate to say "I think" or "my opinion is" rather than "I know" or "the truth is."

Third, evaluate whether your beliefs are harmful to you, holding you back or misleading you. Challenge them and see which ones should be modified, revised or discarded altogether.

Last, replace your harmful assumptions with positive and constructive beliefs that support and empower you. In short, identify your losing game and replace it with a winning one.

CHAPTER ELEVEN

Reframing—Choosing the Way You Look At Things

HOW CAN A COACH KEEP HIS PLAYERS FROM being dispirited when the star of the team is injured? This is the challenge that faced Tom Webster of the Los Angeles Kings when Wayne Gretzky missed the first two games of the 1990 play-offs against the Calgary Flames. He obviously succeeded in motivating his players because L.A. won both those games. My guess is that Webster appealed to their pride by asking them: "Are you going to let people think you're nothing without Gretzky? Are you going to let them say this is a one-man team?" This is a classic example of reframing, turning adversity to advantage by changing the way the players looked at the situation. They didn't just win in spite of their star's not playing. I suspect they won because the Great One was out of the lineup and because their coach knew how to use that as a motivator instead of a setback. You often hear phrases like "A blessing in disguise" or "every cloud has a silver lining."

The greatest weapon against stress is our ability to choose one thought over another.
WILLIAM JAMES

Reframing is a skill that allows you to see things differently and can be used to solve problems, relieve upsets and turn losing games into winning ones.

Let me borrow a wonderful word game from Dr. Joel Goodman, well-known writer and lecturer on humor, to illustrate the concept of reframing. Look at the following and state out loud what appears to you:

```
OPPORTUNITY
ISNOWHERE
```

More on this in a moment.

Of the many ways in which you can change the way you think, none is as creative or powerful as the art of reframing. This is a technique for choosing the way you look at things, for choosing your attitude and perspective. We all do this naturally on occasion. Sometimes a different interpretation occurs spontaneously and makes us feel better about a situation. For example, a teenage patient of mine came down with infectious mononucleosis. His mother was upset by the news, but he seemed rather pleased with the diagnosis. I asked him why he was smiling. "I have two tests next week. Now I won't have to write them." It turns out he wasn't prepared for either subject. His illness took him off the hook. Instinctive or accidental reinterpretations like this are unpredictable and irregular. However, reframing is a skill that can be learned and practiced so that reinterpretations occur predictably, by intention and design.

Getting back to the word game. You may have seen "Opportunity is now here." Or you might have read "Opportunity is nowhere." Maybe you saw both. You may have thought "Opportunity I snow here." but ruled it out because it didn't "make sense." If you're really creative you might have read it in a circle: "Opportunity erehwonsi." Since the first two interpretations seem most plausible, let's deal with those. The big question now is: which of these two is the right answer? That is, of the two possible interpretations, which one is correct?

In my seminars there's often a split on this question as people debate which one they agree with. Some say "Opportunity *is* here" as if this is some universal truth. Others say it "is nowhere" with equal certainty. However, based on the way the letters are presented, there is no right or wrong answer. Each is equally correct and valid, taken on its own terms.

A similar example is illustrated on the next page. Is the glass half empty or half full? Again, either or both answers are correct, depending on your point of view or frame of reference. This is the key to reframing: there is no single right answer in the way we interpret things. However, if your interpretations are that "Opportunity is now here" and "the glass is half full," your life will be different (and better) than if you see "Opportunity is nowhere" and "the glass is half empty." So, given that there is no *correct* answer, you might as well pick the interpretation you like and that serves you best. As Joel Goodman notes: There is more than one meaning to the same "reality."

Is the Glass
Half Empty
or
Half Full?

There are many ways of seeing and interpreting events in life. If you can appreciate that one point of view is no more correct than another, then you can start picking the ones you like and that make you feel better. The quality of your life will be influenced by the kinds of interpretations you choose to make. Here are some examples of this profound and useful concept.

Going to Expo in Style

My older sister broke her leg while skiing on March 5, 1967. The date is important because that was just before Expo 67 opened in Montreal, and she and her husband had "passports" to attend in July. She was put in a long-leg cast (hip to toe) for three months. But on June 5, X-rays showed the fractures hadn't mended and she was told the cast would have to stay on for another three months.

Aside from the obvious letdown and the prospect of dragging the cast around through a hot summer, she was particularly upset to have to miss Expo. Someone asked why she couldn't go to the World Fair. "With a cast and crutches?" she replied. To which this person came up with a perfect "reframe": "You think you can't go to Expo because you're in a long-leg cast? Not only *can* you go in a long-leg cast but the *best* way to go is in a long-leg cast! They'll put you in a wheelchair, take you to the front of every line and treat you like a VIP." Which is exactly what happened. While millions of visitors (myself included) stood for hours in long lines under the hot summer sun, my sister was escorted around like royalty and saw the whole fair in two days. Her friend had taken an apparently negative situation and reinterpreted it in a positive light. This is reframing.

"I Never Thought of it That Way"

Here is a story about reframing other people's behavior. Planning a wedding can be an exciting, joyful experience. Which is why a couple I know were so upset when their daughter and intended son-in-law announced their engagement. By the time they told her parents the news, they had already made all the wedding plans and her family had no input whatever, nor any of the shared excitement of the preparation process. To make matters worse, the groom's parents were involved from the outset, making their exclusion even more hurtful.

I asked them who paid for the wedding. The young couple financed most of it, and *his* parents paid for the rest. My suspicion confirmed, I reframed the situation this way: "I think the kids were out to save you from upset, not to hurt you. They knew you couldn't afford to throw a wedding [the bride's parents had serious financial problems] and didn't want to put you in an uncomfortable position. If they had come to you at the beginning, you would have been faced with two unpleasant options: to pay for a wedding you couldn't afford or to feel guilty because you couldn't pay for it. But by waiting until all the plans were made to share the good news with you, they spared you that dilemma. I think what they did was considerate and kind, even though it looked insulting and hurtful." The woman thought for a moment and then said: "I never thought of it that way." When something has been reframed in a believable and useful way, people often respond with that phrase (and their eyes light up at the same time). It's like a moment of discovery.

The key to these examples is that the reinterpretations were entirely plausible and didn't contradict any of the known facts. Reframing is not a gimmick or a word game or a self-deception. It is a way of reinterpreting situations in genuine ways that still fit the facts. If the reframe isn't completely logical and credible, it will have no power and therefore no benefit.

Here are some questions to ask yourself that will help you to reframe stressful situations:

1. How else can I look at this situation?

2. Why don't I think of it this way?

3. Is there another point of view I can take?

4. Are there any positives or benefits or opportunities to notice?

5. What can this teach me?

6. What would I tell a friend in a similar situation?

There are many different ways of reframing. Here are several categories with examples of each.

Choosing a Positive Interpretation of an Ambiguous Situation

Opportunity isnowhere and a glass half full or half empty are examples of situations that are ambiguous. They are neutral and can be interpreted in more than one way.

Yawning can be taken many ways. The person may be bored, tired, nervous, needing oxygen or even reacting to the power of suggestion when someone else yawns. When I was speaking in public, I used to find people yawning a little off-putting until I realized I had a choice of how to take their behavior. Now I just assume it's their problem and is unrelated to me. I'm sure I'm wrong at times, but it feels a lot better *for me* to view it that way. (Mind you, if I'm addressing an audience and they all start yawning, I'll have to rethink my reframe!) A really positive interpretation would be that people feel so comfortable with me that they can yawn whenever they feel like it.

Silence between two people can be very uncomfortable for some folks. But it's totally subjective and can be taken in many different ways. It can mean respect or reverence, it can reflect intimidation or anger, it might mean shyness and so on. Silence can also be a measure of the comfort between two people. They don't *need* to talk all the time. So if silence in social situations bothers you, pick a less upsetting way to view it.

Changing jobs is a neutral event that can be taken many ways. Some people see it negatively, as an act of failure, surrender or irresponsibility. Alternatively it can reflect courage and flexibility. One man sees it as an adventure. Another has an interesting belief. He equates changing jobs to career success: "If I'm changing jobs every two to three years, it's a sign to everyone that I'm successful."

Weather is one of those things that are usually neither good nor bad. It all depends on your point of view. My twin sister is one of those Pollyanna types who can look out on a sunny day and say: "Oh great, we'll go bicycling and have a picnic," but if it's raining, she'll exclaim:

"Oh great, we'll build a fire and curl up with our books." You can never throw her a curve.

Choosing a Positive Interpretation of a Negative Situation

There are great benefits to seeing opportunity and possibility instead of problems and adversity. The key here is that you are not changing the situation itself but simply changing the way you look at it.

Several of my patients have requested urgent appointments with me when they lost their jobs. In two cases they were taken aback when I smiled and said: "Great, now you can get on with your life." They thought I was callous and cruel until I explained my reaction. Both these people had been telling me for months how much they hated their jobs. They had recounted upsetting incidents at work in vivid detail. Yet when I suggested they seek other employment, they wouldn't hear of such a drastic solution.

I told them their bosses had done them a favor by firing them. They had made the decision these patients were reluctant to make on their own. I reframed the firings as a liberation—they were no longer trapped in lousy jobs and now had the freedom to pursue more satisfying work. I predicted they'd soon be happier and better off than they could have imagined. In both cases, people who had walked into my office feeling like their world had collapsed walked out feeling optimistic. And both soon landed good jobs.

In a related incident, a woman was passed over for a promotion. She greeted the news philosophically and I commented on how well she had reacted. She said: "I look at it this way. If I had gotten the promotion, it would have meant longer hours and working harder. By not getting the promotion, I was able to have my workload and hours cut back." She had set this up as a win/win situation. She had instinctively reframed the situation so that losing the promotion had a positive aspect to it.

Looking for Benefits When They Aren't Obvious To You

Let's take an example of reframing a situation involving change. In professional sports, being traded from one team to another is a common occurrence. With little or no warning, whether he likes it or not, the player finds himself in a new town with new teammates and coaches.

Suddenly there is a change in job, city, housing – and a loss of friends, familiar surroundings and support system.

How do professional athletes deal with this? Their most important tool is their attitude, the way they choose to think about what happened. I did a seminar with the staff of a sporting-goods company, and I asked them to put themselves in the shoes of the departing player and reframe the situation: *come up with positive ways to look at being traded.* Here's the list of positive angles that the group came up with:

• The other team wanted me.

• It's a new challenge.

• Maybe it'll be a better fit for my skills.

• Maybe I'll get more playing time.

• It's a chance to start over, a fresh start.

• I'll meet new friends and teammates (or possibly reunite with former teammates).

• It's a chance to progress, to move ahead in a new organization.

• There will be an opportunity to negotiate a new contract.

• I'll finally get to wear sweater number 7.

• The climate is warmer.

• It's a chance to play on a winning team.

• It's a nice city to live in.

• Look who they gave up to get me!

• It's a chance to play with Joey Votto or LeBron James!

• Maybe I can really help this team, be a leader.

The Chinese word for "crisis" is written with two characters. One of the characters stands for "danger"; the other represents "opportunity." Thus a Chinese person sees two possibilities in the word *crisis*. In English, crisis has a distinctly negative connotation. In the realm of reframing, the Chinese interpretation is very instructive because it invites you to find a positive meaning. So whenever you deal with a crisis, focus on the opportunity concept (positive) instead of the danger idea (negative). More about this on pages 162–63.

A common form of reframing is to choose to view something that didn't work out as a learning experience rather than a mistake. Sometimes I'll use a joke in my lectures that doesn't go over well. I used to feel uncomfortable being the only one in the room smiling. Now if a joke bombs, I simply tell myself not to trot that one out again and keep right on rolling. You can learn as much from things that don't go well as from those that do. By seeing everything for its learning potential, mistakes become far less upsetting. As a friend of mine said, after a project we'd put together fizzled: "We're not smarting—we're *smarter.*"

This story came to me from Dr. Robert Shaw, a Berkeley psychiatrist. Apparently Thomas Edison was working on the incandescent lightbulb in his lab at Menlo Park. Someone asked him how things were going and he replied: "Great!"

The guy said: "Really? Have you got a prototype for your patent?"

"No," replied Edison.

"So what do you mean it's going great?"

"Well," said the great inventor, "I've now discovered twenty-two ways not to build a lightbulb!" What he realized, of course, was that he could view every unsuccessful experiment as a failure *or* as a learning experience in the inevitable trial-and-error process called research. Every idea that didn't work out brought him that much closer to the one that would eventually succeed.

Choosing a Neutral Interpretation of a Negative Situation

Years ago I saw a young man with stress symptoms. He listed five problems causing his distress. As we discussed the various issues, he started to think differently about them. Then one day he announced that he had reviewed his troubles and decided that two of them were "problems" and the other three were just "situations." I was impressed that he could redefine his dilemmas—and, by doing so, lessen their stressful impact. One of these upsets had to do with an old friend who owed him money. He said: "Either he'll pay me or he won't. My life won't change much either way. It's not a big issue anymore." He chose to see this as a situation ("the way it is") rather than a problem that had to be solved. He taught me a valuable lesson.

When my second son was born, my first son was twenty-seven months old. He was pleased to have a little brother, was very gentle and affectionate with him and showed no visible signs of resentment. However, about a month later he began biting his fingernails, which he'd never done before. My wife and I were concerned about this behavior and wondered how we should deal with it. I sounded out a few of my colleagues who worked with kids and got some excellent advice from a child psychologist friend of mine. He said: "I'm not sure how I'd deal with it but I can tell you that if you make it a problem, it will *become* a problem." I immediately grasped that the issue was not the nail-biting but our *attitude* toward it. If we chose to see it as a problem, we would be upset. And we would likely hover over him or urge him to stop (which would raise his anxiety level and probably lead to more nail-biting). By deciding it was merely a "situation" we relaxed, ignored it most of the time and occasionally kidded him about it. He stopped biting his nails about six weeks later—and never started again.

Reinterpreting the Motives or Intent Behind People's Behavior

I got an urgent call one Monday morning from a man in great distress. He was mad as hell at his teenage son for throwing a party on Saturday night while he and his wife were out of town. This young boy had invited a couple of friends over, but many other teenagers showed up and more arrived later. There was no booze or drug use and no damage to the house, but the police were called by a neighbor at 3:00 a.m. because of the noise. That ended the party, and the youthful crowd departed.

The father was furious because he had warned his son not to throw any parties while they were away. In exploring his anger, it was clear that he took his child's behavior as defiance. He felt his trust had been betrayed and his authority flouted. I asked his wife what she thought of these goings-on. After all, it was her son and house too and she didn't seem particularly upset. Her response turned out to be a perfect reframing for her husband. She said: "Look, he's young and naive and not very assertive. He's insecure and wants to be well liked. I think the word got around that some kids were over at our place and everyone decided there was a party going on. Things got out of hand and he wasn't able to stand up to them. I don't think he planned this or had any devious intentions. I think he just got swept up in the events and didn't know how to stop them." Given this boy's age and other things I'd heard about him, I thought her assessment was probably accurate. It was certainly as credible as her husband's interpretation. Slowly the father agreed he may have misjudged the situation and jumped to conclusions too quickly. With that new perspective, his anger and stress rapidly diminished. He felt much better by reframing the reasons for his son's behavior.

A sociologist friend of mine made a statement that has stayed with me for the past forty years. We were talking about someone whose behavior was very offensive, and I was making him out to be a repugnant and despicable individual. My friend was more charitable. He looked at the man's background, which had been one of neglect and abuse. He recognized that he was an isolated and lonely person who was unhappy with himself and his life. He summed it up by saying: "I think he's really a *sad* man, not a *bad* man." I immediately saw his point and my anger gave way to compassion. I have used this reframe dozens of times over the years to remind myself that most obnoxious people are more sad than bad. They don't walk around in foul humor, mad at the world, out of conscious intent. They are victims of their own behavior as much as (or more than) the bystanders whom they happen to affect.

Putting Events into a Different Perspective or Wider "Context"

Umpire Ron Luciano quotes baseball pitcher Mike Marshall in his book *Remembrance of Swings Past*. The star reliever said: "Let's keep it in perspective. These are baseball games. It's not someone in my family having major surgery. It's nothing that's going to permanently affect my future life." Many people ask themselves: "Is this going to matter in six months (or days)?" If the answer is no, they don't bother getting upset.

Being able to see the bigger picture and view things in perspective changes your outlook considerably. Every major-league baseball team has a few players who pull the team down. It's easy to dump on these guys. But there is another way of looking at them. Consider that only 3% of all professional players actually make it to the Big Leagues. So any major-leaguer is already among the elite in the sport. Even the worst of them are better than the 97% of pros who never make it to the "Bigs." You have to decide with whom to compare a player: the best of the 3% or the 97% who never get out of the minors. Your judgment of any player depends on the basis of your comparison, your frame of reference. It's all in how you choose to look at it.

So it is with many situations in your life. Say you invested $10,000 in the stock market in 1999. Imagine that, by cleverness and luck, your portfolio was worth $100,000 by 2007. You would have been very pleased. Then came the global recession in 2008, and your stocks lost half their value. Suddenly they were worth only $50,000. The question is: did you lose $50,000 (your paper loss) or did you make $40,000 (based on your initial investment)? The answer depends on which time frame you use as a reference. If you compare with 1999, you won. If you think of 2007, you lost. Both frames of reference are valid, just as the glass half full is also half empty. But one will make you feel good (quintupling your money in nine years isn't too shabby) whereas the other (losing half your money in one year) may make you want to drink hemlock. Take your pick.

In diagram form, it looks like this:

Frame One

But by enlarging the frame, it looks this way:

Frame Two

The way you choose to look at this will not change the facts of your portfolio, but it will change the way you feel about your financial situation.

A common way of using the expanded frame is illustrated by the Chinese proverb "I felt sorry for myself because I had no shoes until I met a man who had no feet." People often put things in perspective by comparing their situations with those worse than their own. By doing this, their problems don't look so big after all. I knew someone whose comparison was with himself. He survived a cancer scare. He had a tumor picked up at a very early stage. After successful surgery, he was pronounced cured. But the experience put a lot of things in perspective for him. Events that had previously been a big deal to him now seemed rather insignificant. His tumor became a touchstone and he began asking: "Compared with my tumor, how important is this situation?"

A quote from writer Richard Bach beautifully summarizes this concept of changing the frame of reference: "What the caterpillar calls the end of the world, the Master calls the butterfly."

Humor Based on Reframing

Suddenly changing the frame of reference is the basis of a lot of humor. When you tell a joke, you establish a certain premise. Then, at the last second, you change the context, which is what creates the punchline. A classic example is the story of the drunk who decided to go ice fishing. He walked out on the ice with his saw and fishing pole and picked a spot to make his fishing hole. He was just about to saw through the ice when he heard a loud voice from above: "There're no fish there." He thought that was strange but simply shrugged his shoulders and walked to another spot on the ice. As he was about to start sawing, he heard the voice again: "There're no fish there." Now he was starting to feel spooked. He walked over to yet another place to make his hole when again he heard this disembodied voice from above: "There're no fish there." Thoroughly rattled, he looked up and asked: "Are you God?" The answer came back immediately: "No, I'm the arena manager!"

Here is another example of how changing the frame of reference changes the way you look at things—and brings a laugh at the same time. An Israeli kibbutznik was visiting a Texas rancher. Most kibbutzim in Israel are relatively small by Texas ranch standards, and this Texan was trying to impress his visitor with the vastness of his land holdings. In his most elaborate Southern drawl he bragged: "I'll tell you how big my land is. I can get in my car at dawn and start driving across my ranch. And by nightfall I would not have reached the far side of my property." "Yes," said the Israeli mildly, "I also had a car like that once." Seeing humor in upsetting situations is a wonderful way to reduce stress. It's a form of reframing that releases tension through laughter and is a great skill to develop.

Seeing What's There Instead of What's Missing

When Babe Ruth hit sixty home runs in one season, he also led the league in strikeouts. Not too many people were focusing on his strikeouts. Reggie Jackson was another home-run hitter who struck out a lot. Many weekend athletes get mightily upset at their bad shots and the mistakes they make during a game. They'd enjoy themselves a lot more by appreciating the good shots and not dwelling on the errors. Even lousy golfers get off a few good smacks in a round. Savoring those moments is what makes the game pleasurable for them. (Goodness knows *their* scores are not a source of great joy!)

Some people worry more about what's missing than what's there. It's like throwing a party for twenty people, of whom eighteen attend. Some folks would spend half the night upset about the two who didn't show up instead of enjoying the company of the eighteen who did.

When people are ill or injured, they often focus on all the things they can no longer do. I urge them instead to notice all the activities they can do, including things like reading and listening to music that they may not have made time for previously.

Regaining Control in Situations Where You Feel Not in Control

Another time that changing the way you think can be very helpful is when you feel powerless or not in control. This often occurs when someone is bullying or abusing you. The culprit can be a stranger but is usually a boss, partner or parent. In explaining this form of reframing, it may appear that I am advocating that people put up with abusive behavior from others. Nothing could be farther from the truth. I strongly urge patients to redefine or leave such relationships, be they in the work, family or social domain. However, reframing can play two useful roles. The first is to reduce the stress of situations that people choose not to leave (or cannot do so quickly). The second is to help them become empowered, to gain the strength and confidence to stand up to bullies and to eventually leave if the behavior doesn't change. In a sense, the reframing is an interim measure and part of preparing for a more definitive resolution of the problem.

This kind of reframing reminds me of an incident from my high school days. One of my best friends was being reprimanded in class. In fact he was being thoroughly excoriated. The teacher's face was flushed, his neck veins were bulging and he was literally bellowing. My friend stood placidly at the back of the room with a look on his face that was somewhere between bored and bemused. I was stunned by his composure. He had tuned the teacher out completely. After class, I asked him how he stayed so calm during this attack. He smiled and said: "The problem with you, Pose, is that you take those things too seriously. He was just blowing off steam as far as I was concerned. You take it too personally."

People who can detach themselves emotionally in the face of abusive behavior from others save themselves a lot of stress. This kind of self-protection involves a form of reframing. Instead of seeing yourself in the picture (as participant or victim), you place yourself outside the frame and take the position of observer. That way, whatever is going on doesn't affect you directly. You still see and hear everything, but it's as if you're standing behind an invisible shield or wearing an asbestos suit to protect you from the heat.

A woman described to me a scene in which she was being yelled at by her boss. Her vivid description of him pacing back and forth, shouting and spouting off was followed by the statement: "I mean, he was really losing it." I asked how she was feeling at the time. "At first I was very upset and intimidated. But the longer he went on, the less seriously I took him. I mean he was irrational. He was like a caricature of some dictator and after a while it was almost funny." She had reframed his behavior from being menacing to being something between comical and pathetic. And the more she was able to distance herself emotionally from the force of his words, the less effect he had on her.

You can use this approach to deal with people who throw tirades. Whether it's a customer or client, a relative or boss, if you can keep your distance you can keep your cool. I suggest you actually take one discreet step backward—to detach yourself physically and to pull back emotionally. Then observe the abuser as if you're looking through a one-way mirror or protective glass window. Keep reminding yourself that this person's behavior is more a reflection of them than of anything you may have done to provoke them. Look at them in the same detached way you would watch a two-year-old having a temper tantrum. Say things to yourself to remind you that you are outside the frame, like "If only he could see himself" or "Look how flushed she's getting" or "I wonder if this is going to be released on the Internet."

In abusive relationships between couples, it's a lot harder to remain dispassionate and detached, especially because partners usually know each other's frailties and can pick exactly which buttons to push to get a maximum response. Nonetheless, emotional detachment can be achieved. In most of these cases the perpetrator is feeling insecure or highly stressed. Reminding yourself of that is a good way to start. Recognize that the person who looks so strong and fearsome is, in fact, lacking in self-esteem and/or feeling not in control at the very moment they are yelling at you. Realize that chronically abusive people are almost always trying to make themselves feel good by making you feel bad; they're trying to win by making you lose. Once you see through their outburst, it's easier to keep from being taken in by it.

Another form of reframing to gain control is to remind yourself you always have a choice. I worked for a year in the Canadian Arctic. I was on an open-ended contract, which meant I could leave whenever I chose. Most government employees worked on a two-year contract, which obliged them to stay for twenty-four months (except for vacations). Some of these people felt trapped by that arrangement. When it gets cold and dark above the Arctic Circle, people can get depressed or develop "cabin fever" from being indoors so much.

One day I was counseling a woman who was feeling desperate to go south. I urged her to see she had a choice, that she wasn't really stuck there. She thought I misunderstood her government agreement. I told her I was aware of her contractual obligations but that she was still free to leave any time she wanted. The only cost to her would be the price of her transportation (otherwise paid for by the government), the probable loss of a reference letter and the self-knowledge that she had breached her contract. I said, "I'm not advising you to leave. I just want you to know that, if it comes to a crunch, you *can* leave. You're not a prisoner here." That awareness shed new light on her position. She stopped feeling trapped and gradually came to grips with the situation. My reframing didn't make the weather warmer or the darkness lighter. It just made her feel more in control of her circumstances by reminding her that she had a choice, even if she didn't choose to act upon it.

When you change the way you look at things, the things you look at change.
ALBERT EINSTEIN

In summary, you can choose how you think about things, and by doing so, you can change a lot of seemingly losing games into winning ones. Reframing is a technique to change your perspective about situations in a way that makes you feel good. But it's not a gimmick or a word game. It is a valid, credible way of viewing things based on the premise that there are many plausible interpretations of most events. However, negative thoughts will *drain* you (and so will negative people), whereas positive thoughts will *energize* you. And you have a *choice*. So look for the upsides and benefits as much as you can.

This skill can be learned and used purposefully and consistently. My wife will often ask: "How can we reframe this?" when we're faced with an upset or disappointment. This is the spirit with which reframing can be used.

I want to end this chapter with one of my favorite examples of reframing, which is also a wonderful philosophy of life. This sentiment comes from the book *Shoeless Joe* by W.P. Kinsella (from which the movie *Field of Dreams* was made):

Success is *getting what you want.*

Happiness is *wanting what you get.*

CHAPTER TWELVE

Attention and Focus— Choosing *Which* Things You Look At

I T'S FUNNY HOW LITTLE THINGS can catch our attention. I was eating breakfast one dark winter morning at 7:00 A.M. Munching on my toast and reading the paper, my eye was suddenly drawn to something small on the floor just at the edge of my peripheral vision. It was a pint-sized centipede that had just moved. It grabbed my attention no less than a rat or a mouse would have done. What was that all about?

The science around attention and focus is quite fascinating. In her outstanding book *RAPT: Attention and the Focused Life*, author Winifred Gallagher explores this subject and explains concepts that relate to some of the losing games we play, particularly our tendency to dwell on negative thoughts and upsetting situations.

Our stress not only results from the *way* we think about things, but also reflects the amount of *time and attention* we give to things. It relates to what we notice, what we focus on. Take, for example, five people walking along the same block on Fifth Avenue at the same time and in the same direction. One is looking at store windows as he/she strolls by. Another is looking down at the paving stones of the sidewalk. A third is looking at the sky, the soft clouds and the sunshine. A fourth is people-watching, observing each pedestrian that walks by. The fifth is taking in the whole streetscape—the buildings, the street, the cars and the crowds. Here are five people in the same place at the same time, but they're all having a totally different experience based not on their surroundings, but on what they're choosing to look at. Our observations, perceptions and reactions are all affected by what we give our attention to.

Your quality of life depends on what you choose to pay attention to.
WINIFRED GALLAGHER

Two Kinds of Attention

This raises a question: how much of what we notice is voluntary and how much is not? Winifred Gallagher describes two kinds of attention. She calls them "bottom-up" and "top-down." *Bottom-up* attention is hard-wired into our brain stem and is there for self-protection and survival. Any change in our environment—any movement, sound, touch or smell that could signal danger—is immediately and automatically sensed. It "grabs" our attention. Bottom-up attention is automatic, involuntary and stimulus-driven. It serves us well unless and until there's too much of it, which can lead to constant distraction and sensory overload in our complex and dynamic world.

Top-down attention is different. It comes from our higher levels of brain function located in the cerebral cortex. It relates to what we choose to focus or concentrate on, whether it's the book we're reading, the report we're writing, the mountain stream we're watching, the music we're listening to, etc. After a visit with friends, my wife might say, "Did you notice the curtains in the living room?" or "Did you see that beautiful painting in the front hall?" My answer is usually no. I was looking through the window at the back yard and scanning the books on the shelf in the den. Top-down attention is deliberate, voluntary and goal-oriented. It relates to what interests us and what we choose to pay attention to.

How Attention Affects Feelings

Ms. Gallagher talks about two other aspects of attention and focus: their effect on, and relationship to, mood. She calls them "outside in" and "inside out."

Outside in relates to the emotional impact things have on us based on what we're *noticing* or looking at. Gray skies can drag you down while bright sunshine can cheer you up. My wife and I walk on the ravine trails in our neighborhood. We pass rabbits, chipmunks and cute dogs along the way and we smile. Large, fierce-looking dogs make us feel a little wary and unlikely to reach out and pet them. Once we encountered a coyote and walked a very wide—and cautiously brisk—path around it.

Not only do external stimuli affect our mood, but we can intentionally *change* our mood by deciding to focus on other things. If a graphic

TV crime drama upsets us, we flick the channel to a sit-com. If heavy rock on the radio is jarring we can switch to soft, soothing classical music. We can alter our experience and emotions by deciding where to direct our attention.

Inside out speaks to the research showing that how we *feel* will influence what we *notice*. For example, she cites "eye-tracking experiments" where subjects are directed to look at the central object in a visual display. If they are then asked to think of something pleasant—thus evoking a positive emotion—"they take in significant peripheral material, despite the earlier instruction. In contrast, subjects who remain in a neutral or negative state continue to focus on the display's central element and tune out the surrounding stimuli." One implication of this is that if you're feeling depressed, your field of focus becomes constricted and you tend to dwell more on the upsetting aspects of your situation rather than seeing the bigger picture or context.

Focus On What's There

Gallagher's book about where we put our attention relates to the aspect of reframing that I call "Focus on what's there, not on what's missing." One of my metaphors is the United Way campaign in Toronto in the mid-1990's, during the height of a very serious recession. The goal, as I recall, was set at $52 million. The campaign raised $50 million. A lot of people were talking about the two million dollar shortfall, the resulting need to reduce funding for certain agencies and the fact that the goal—which was arbitrary to begin with—was not met. But I was thinking, "There's a big recession going on. People are hurting badly and feeling scared about their uncertain financial future. But in spite of that, they donated *50 million dollars* to the United Way. Instead of focusing on the shortage, can we not celebrate the fact that 50 million dollars was raised in a very difficult economy?" I looked at that campaign as a huge success, given the circumstances. Others viewed it as a failure because the full amount wasn't raised.

How often do we do this in our everyday lives? For example, when people are overloaded at work (and who isn't these days?), there's a tendency to go home at the end of the day feeling dispirited and discouraged about the things that didn't get done. Some folks even berate or beat up on themselves about the stuff they never finished, or the unanswered phone calls and emails. Wouldn't it be kinder, more constructive—and just as accurate—to think back at all the things they *did* get done and acknowledge themselves for that? To say, "That was a really productive day. I worked hard, stayed on task and accomplished a lot." How often do we focus on someone's faults and give little notice to their positive attributes? It all depends on which side of the ledger you choose to look at.

What Does Change Mean To You?

In 1995 I gave my first presentation on how individuals can manage and cope with change. It was a time of great upheaval, largely a result of downsizing at work, a wave of new technology and the economic recession. People were really struggling with the speed and extent of the changes going on. Since then I've given dozens of seminars on what I've come to call "Change Mastery."

I often start by asking people "What does *change* mean to *you*? Either specific changes or change in general? What words come to your mind?" I then gather the group's input and write the words on a flipchart, dividing them into two lists. Here's a sample of what they often look like.

Anxiety	Growth
Distraction	Exciting
Fear	Opportunity
Loss	Progress
Frustration	Learning
Stress	Challenge
Hassle	Improvement
Confusion	Adventure
Unknown	Novelty
Uncertainty	Hopefulness
Chaos	Stimulating

My main message is that change means different things to different people. Some see it in negative terms while others—especially those who welcome and embrace change—view it in positive ways.

But there's another message here. If change is going to happen, whether we like it or not, the way *we experience* the change will be strongly influenced by the way we look at it. I ask my audiences whether the second list (the positive words) is just as valid as the first list in terms of looking at change in general. They all agree that it is. Then I ask which list will help them to accept and adjust to the change and to handle it better. They all agree that it's the second list. And, as the principle about reframing teaches us, we have a *choice* in how we look at things. In terms of resilience and adaptability, attitude is hugely important. In fact, one could say that **attitude is everything**.

From Reframing to Refocusing

So I think there's another helpful step beyond *reframing* a situation: it's choosing to *focus* on the interpretations that best support you and lower your level of stress and discomfort. For example, in the face of change, which of the two lists do you want to pay attention to? This is a conscious choice you get to make, as opposed to the automatic, subconscious choices we all make so often.

Please note that I'm not suggesting we ignore or negate or deny the negative impacts or feelings. In fact, it's important to *acknowledge* these. But it's not helpful to *dwell* on them for too long. At some point we can make a conscious decision to focus on the positives, the benefits, the upsides as a way of coping and dealing with the situation.

There's an allegory from Native American Aboriginal lore that goes something like this. A man is telling his friend about the fierce debates that go on in his mind between opposing points of view about different issues. Some of the thoughts are negative while others are positive. He tries to decide on these matters but, in the process, he often experiences a tremendous amount of conflict. He says the battles are very stressful. He concludes by saying, "It's like two dogs fighting inside my head." His friend asks him, "Which dog usually wins?" His answer: "The one I *feed* the most." In other words, the one I focus on, the one I give most 'air time' to. Your attitude and mood are very often the result of what you choose to pay attention to.

Pay attention to what you pay attention to.

UNKNOWN

Different Meanings to the Word "Crisis"

The word *crisis* doesn't usually evoke happy thoughts. If someone tells you they're having a crisis, you don't say, "Oh that's great! Can I come over? I'll bring deli and beer. We can have a crisis together." You're more likely to wish them well and ask them to call you back when things settle down. In English, the word has a negative tone, even a stressful one. But in Chinese the word crisis is written with two characters and pronounced "way gee." The ideogram looks like this:

Each character stands for a different concept: one for *danger*, the other for *opportunity*. In essence, the Chinese writing invites you to re-frame the situation. It sees both sides of the issue. Very importantly, it acknowledges the downside, the upsetting or stressful aspect of it. It doesn't try to whitewash or deny the negative side. When patients come to see me having encountered setbacks or bad news in their lives, I am always respectful in letting them talk about what's happened and giving them time to express and experience their emotions. It might be an illness or death in the family, the loss of a job or the end of a relationship. It's important to recognize and respect what has happened and the feelings that have resulted.

But then, gently—and it may be one or two visits later – I will often ask if there has been anything positive that's come out of the experience. An illness in the family might have brought them closer to that person or given them the opportunity to be helpful. The loss of a job might actually bring a sense of relief in some ways (e.g. the end of their long daily commutes or work that wasn't very fulfilling) or a chance to step back and reflect on a possible career change.

Once people can see both sides of an issue, the next choice is which of those factors they want to focus on. Do they want to keep lamenting the (very real and legitimate) negatives and losses, or do they want to give more attention to the positives, real and potential?

Too often at work and in life we focus on the "danger" part of situations and fail to acknowledge the "opportunity" side. Dan Sullivan runs a very successful training program for entrepreneurs and professionals called The Strategic Coach. He says, "Some of our best opportunities in life come to us cleverly disguised as problems." Learning to solve problems leads to progress and growth. The problems become a stimulus for us to be creative and to make breakthroughs and discover abilities in ourselves we would otherwise never uncover.

The Attitude of Gratitude

Another aspect of where we choose to put our attention relates to stepping back and looking at our lives as a whole. When patients go through difficult times, and especially if I find they're feeling sorry for themselves, I ask them to do a gratitude list. I ask them to think of all the things in their lives for which they are thankful—and I encourage them to make it a long list! Big things and little things; major things and mundane things. This accomplishes two purposes. One is to show them all of the many blessings they have been overlooking or taking for granted. The other is to encourage them to start noticing on an ongoing basis, all the wonderful things in their lives that they hadn't been acknowledging or paying attention to.

Here's a sample of my own gratitude list to illustrate the range of things I'm referring to and the fine detail that you can get into when you look closely:

- My good health (I count my blessings on this one every day)

- My family, nuclear and extended, to whom I'm very close

- Our lovely home

- My close friends

- Our great neighbors

- Living in Canada

- Warm sunshine on spring and summer days

- Good movies

- Good music (everything from Mozart and Gershwin to Louis Armstrong and Willie Nelson)

- Rockport shoes (this one always gets a laugh but they did wonders to relieve my back stiffness when I was on my feet all day)

- Interlochen (I spent five amazing summers at the National Music Camp) in Michigan

- Weekend crossword puzzles in the *Toronto Star*

- Malcolm Gladwell, one of my favorite writers

- Playing tennis and golf

- Playing my trombone in the Oakville Wind Orchestra

- The taste of orange juice first thing in the morning

- Taking a hot shower

- My favorite foods, including onion soup, barbecued steak and asparagus

This is how specific you can get. But then you can keep noticing *other* things that give you pleasure or for which you feel grateful. If you start to put these things on a list and pay attention to them, it will change your attitude about your life. It will also put some of the negative things that happen into different perspective and a larger context.

I will leave the last word to Winifred Gallagher from her "eye-opening" book, *RAPT:*

> *"Deciding what to pay attention to … is a peculiarly human predicament, and your quality of life largely depends on how you handle it."*

CHAPTER THIRTEEN

Keeping and Using Your Sense of Humor

 VERYTHING IN LIFE IS EASIER if you can laugh about it. With all the layoffs and downsizing in recent years, the air around most workplaces has been thick with tension for a long time. A similar scenario played out in the mid-1990s. But someone at the Hospital for Sick Children in Toronto decided to blow some humor through the fog of worry by putting up the following sign in the outpatient department in 1996:

Life is too serious to be taken seriously.

OSCAR WILDE

DUE TO CUTBACKS, THE LIGHT AT THE END OF THE TUNNEL WILL BE TURNED OFF UNTIL FURTHER NOTICE.

Did this affect the rate of restructuring? No. Did it create any new jobs? Hardly. Did it lighten the mood and lessen the stress even a little? You bet. Humor isn't about changing what happens. It's about changing our reaction to what happens. And those who use humor as a coping strategy are generally more resilient and adaptable when faced with change or difficult situations.

Humor Reduces Stress

Laughter relieves tension. You cannot laugh and feel tense at the same time. Physiologically it's not possible. Because the minute you laugh you relieve the tension. I watched this happen one day in my office. A woman was telling me about her experience the night before when she tried on her bathing suit. It was April and they were preparing for a Caribbean cruise. She'd gained some weight over the winter and her suit didn't fit. This brought up a lot of weight issues for her and triggered some painful memories and emotions. I was just listening as she talked about those feelings when suddenly she stopped. Her face changed, she smiled and then said, "You know what? I've just solved my problem. This year I'm going to swim in the dark!" With that we both burst out laughing and the tension disappeared. It was as if she'd decided in that moment to stop feeling sad and frustrated and down on herself. Seeing the funny side of her situation enabled her to pull herself together and raise herself up, to find the words and wit to break the mood. Was this woman a standup comic or humor writer? No. She was simply a person who was willing to be playful and, like millions of others, had the ability to find amusement in everyday situations. We can all tap into our sense of humor, and benefit from it.

Humor doesn't have to produce a thigh-slapping joke to be helpful. Think of a meeting you were at where things were getting pretty tense. Then perhaps someone said something funny and everybody laughed. That night you told the story to a friend, but the joke fell flat. You finally said, "Well, I guess you had to be there." That's probably true. Because if you weren't there to feel the tension, you couldn't experience the relief of the remark that broke it. In the right circumstances it doesn't take much to generate a laugh. And the humor is a gift to everyone in the room, because they all benefit from the laughter.

Laughter in the Workplace

Nowhere is humor more needed these days than at the office. When times are tough, people tend to get serious and intense, and one of the first casualties of this somber mood is laughter. Yet humor can be the perfect antidote to those uptight feelings. Dr. Joel Goodman, a humor advocate and academic from New York, uses the phrase "From grim and bear it to grin and share it." Create a playful, fun environment in your office and people will beat a path to your door to work with you.

> *Question:* Is the glass half-empty or half-full?
> *Answer:* The reengineering department says
> that there's just too much glass!

I was doing a seminar for a company that had downsized, resulting in everyone being asked to do more than they had before. We were talking about reframing, and one of the participants said he worked at a counter in which he not only served the onsite customers but those who phoned in. Then he was given the added responsibility of being the trouble-shooter for staff problems. There were times when he was besieged from all sides and felt overwhelmed. "At times like that," he said, "I reframe the situation in a way that really helps. I say to myself, 'I love it when they fight over me!'"

What's Funny about Change?

Workplaces have seen huge amounts of change in the past 20 years. Now, there's nothing inherently funny about change. But if you look, you can find or create a wealth of humor in change situations—or any other situation, for that matter.

For example, there's the old line to use when you're snowed under by the sheer volume of work to be done: "I feel like a mosquito at a nudist colony. I know what I'm supposed to do. I just don't know where to start."

When I interned in Edmonton, we earned the princely sum of $4,300 for the year. For this we worked an average of 80–100 hours a week (including on-call coverage every other night and every other weekend). Sometimes we grumbled about being "paid slaves," and one of us said, "Do you realize we're earning less than a dollar an hour?" to which someone else replied, "You're wrong. We're earning about $50 an hour—but they're *paying* us less than a buck an hour!" But the best line of the year came from a surgical resident (he didn't make much more than we did): "I am wealthy, not in the magnitude of my possessions but in the modesty of my requirements!" Given that we had barely enough time to sleep, much less enjoy leisure pursuits, there really wasn't much opportunity to spend our meager salary anyway.

Merger mania has been part of the business landscape for many years and will likely continue. Sometimes the possible names for merged entities are very funny. For example, if El Al airlines of Israel decided to merge with Alitalia, the Italian national carrier, they could call the new company "Val, I'll *Tal* Ya." And here's one that was passed to me after a seminar I did on humor in the workplace: "Did you hear about the merger between Xerox and Wurlitzer? They wanted to manufacture a reproductive organ!"

Stretch your humor muscles by thinking up your own merger scenarios and create funny names for them. For example, if Chock Full o' Nuts joined with Beef Jerky they could form a company called "Chock Full o' Jerks."

Good-news, bad-news jokes are a great way of injecting a bit of humor into tense situations. Again they don't have to be hysterically funny to be welcome. For example: "The good news is that we're finally going to have some free time around here. The bad news is we just lost our major client." Or: "The good news is that with this cell phone my staff can reach me anywhere. The bad news is that with this cell phone my staff can reach me anywhere!"

We're often faced with difficult decisions at work where none of the options is appealing. Woody Allen had a line about the no win dilemma: "More than any time in history, mankind faces a crossroad. One path leads to despair and utter hopelessness, the other to total extinction. Let us pray that we have the wisdom to choose correctly."

You might have a no-win situation at work, such as when you feel you can't please your boss or you can't do anything right. It reminds me of the man whose aunt comes to visit and brings him two neckties as a gift. This guy doesn't even wear ties, but to please his aunt he puts one of them on for dinner that night. He's waiting for her to notice and be pleased with his gesture. After a few minutes she looks up from her soup and says, "So what's the matter? You didn't like the other tie?"

Humor about Health

Illness creates unwelcome and often painful changes in our lives. Humor can at least give us a welcome respite. When my father was very ill, he was hospitalized several times. It's ironic that, despite our upset and worry on those occasions, there were also moments for laughter. My dad never lost his warm sense of humor, even in his final few days, and we rarely passed up an opportunity to kibbitz with him or find something funny about what was going on. The lightness and laughter were blessings to all of us.

One of my patients developed breast cancer and was devastated with fear. Before her surgery she met the surgeon in his office and he explained what he intended to do. He'd remove the lump and as little other breast tissue as possible (called a "lumpectomy"). If there was evidence of spread to the lymph nodes, he'd have to do a mastectomy. In summing up, he said, "You'll either have a small dimple in your breast — or you'll look like me!" She loved the joke, and she appreciated his trying to help ease her tension. This surgeon, by the way, was a skilled, kind and empathetic man whom his patients adored. His remark was made in the context of a caring, concerned consultation. It was neither flip nor disrespectful. He knew this patient, understood how she herself used humor and took his lead from her.

Unfortunately she did require a mastectomy. On her first visit back to see me, she related, with a hearty laugh, what her best friend said when she first saw her after the operation: "So which side did they do?" Again the context was important. This was a loving friend who shared her dry sense of humor. The comment was therefore welcome and appreciated.

Norman Cousins wrote a landmark book called *The Anatomy of an Illness* in which he related the benefits of laughter for him when he was battling a painful, degenerative disease called anky losing spondylitis. He decided that conventional medicine was not offering him sufficient improvement. So he prescribed laugh therapy for himself. He asked people to bring him old Marx Brothers movies, which generated real belly laughs for him. Deep laughter actually stirs up the body in a positive way—humor specialists call this an "internal massage." It improves the circulation, increases oxygen intake and stimulates the release of endorphins, the feel good brain hormone.

Humor can also be useful in dealing with illness of close relatives. Multiple Sclerosis is a difficult and disabling disease, often affecting relatively young people. When I was in training, I cared for a man who developed MS and was confined to a wheel chair. Not long after, research on a promising treatment was reported in the popular press. Early tests on monkeys showed hopeful signs. The next day his wife came in with the newspaper and jokingly said, "I'm going to start him on a diet of bananas. After all, if it works for monkeys ..."

When I heard that comment, I knew this couple were mobilizing one of the best coping mechanisms—humor—and to me it was a sign that they were dealing constructively with his pain.

Humor to Ward Off Fear

One of our greatest weapons against fear is humor. We make jokes about things we're most afraid of, like death. Again, Woody Allen: "I don't believe in a life after death, but I'm taking a change of underwear anyway." And this line was attributed to Harry Truman: "It reminds me of the man who woke up to find himself lying in a coffin. He said, 'If I'm not dead, what am I doing here? And if I am dead, how come I have to go to the bathroom?'"

Fear of Alzheimer's disease has led to a multitude of jokes. Humor is one of the few weapons we have as yet against this unfortunate condition. Here's an example: "Two good things about Alzheimer's — you keep meeting new people and you can hide your own Easter eggs."

We also tell jokes about areas in which we feel uncomfortable or insecure. That's why there are so many gags about sex. For example: Two sophisticated eight-year-olds are talking. One says, "Hey, I found a condom on the veranda last night." The other asks, "What's a veranda?" (You didn't really expect me to tell a racy story here, did you?)

A line I heard from a guy on his fiftieth birthday went like this: "I'm not as good as I once was. But I'm as good *once* as I *ever* was!"

Humor about Transitions

One change we all experience is the passage through different stages of life, from infancy and childhood to adolescence, to young adulthood and on through middle age to retirement and old age. Some of these transitions are difficult, even painful. The loss of faculties as we age is of particular concern to seniors, and a lot of people fear the fading of eyesight, hearing, memory and sex drive. This creates very fertile ground for humor. Laughter is one of the best weapons we have to deal with situations over which we have no control.

An elderly but avid golfer had to stop playing because his vision was deteriorating and he could no longer follow the flight of the ball. His friend said to him, "That's no problem. My eyes are fine. I'll come along and watch the ball for you." The golfer was grateful and delighted. They set out to play. On the first tee, the golfer took his drive and got away a very nice shot. His friend did as he promised and kept his eye on the ball's flight. He said, "I see it. I see it." As they strolled off the tee toward the ball, the golfer asked, "Which way did it go?" His buddy replied, "I forget!"

At a recent class reunion one of our classmates gave a presentation on "Memory and the Aging Brain." It spawned two memorable lines.

One guy quipped, "The older we get, the clearer our memory becomes for things that never happened." To which someone retorted, "Yeah, the older you get, the better it *was.*"

When my uncle was eighty-two and slowing down physically, he lost none of his great sense of humor. We were talking to him about plans to do something next year and he said, "I don't know. We'll see. These days I don't plan that far ahead. I don't even buy green bananas anymore."

Retirement holds great appeal for some people, while others view it with trepidation. Wives are notorious for fearing the time when their husbands will be home all day, every day. This gives rise to lines like "I vowed to take him for better or worse—but not for lunch," and "Since he retired I have twice as much husband and half as much money."

Couples growing old together provide fodder for stories like this one. A couple in their eighties are sitting in the living room when the husband decides to go to the store. He asks his wife if she wants anything and she says some ice cream would be nice.

"What flavor?" he asks. "Vanilla?"

"OK."

"Why don't you write it down so you don't forget?"

"I won't forget. Do you want any sauce on it?"

"Sure. Chocolate. But why don't you write it down?"

"Vanilla ice cream, chocolate sauce. I'll remember. Do you want nuts on top?"

"Yes, thank you. Walnuts. I wish you'd write all this down."

"I'll be fine. See you in an hour."

One hour later he returns. He shuffles across the living room to where his wife is sitting and hands her a brown bag. She opens it and takes out a bagel with lox. She looks at him with an expression of frustration and exasperation. "You forgot the cream cheese!"

How Do I Look?

Another area of transition we all go through has to do with physical appearance. As we age our bodies change shape, wrinkles develop and hair turns gray or drops out. As a follicly-challenged individual, I've noticed a lot of jokes about baldness over the years. I liked the T-shirt that said, "All males have a certain amount of testosterone. If some men want to waste theirs growing hair, that's up to them!"

Or how about: "Men who go bald from the front are thinkers. Men who go bald from the back are sexy. And men who go bald from the front *and* the back just *think* they're sexy!"

Sometimes friends can use humor to help us adjust to new stages. Timing, kindness and sensitivity are paramount. Here's a sample from my twenty second birthday. I was already starting to lose my hair and was feeling a bit touchy about the subject. It was the end of my third summer on staff at the National Music Camp in Michigan. A surprise party was thrown in my honor at which the following song was sung (to the tune of "On Top of Old Smoky"):

> *On top of Old Posen*
> *All covered with hair,*
> *That is until lately*
> *Now the* hair *isn't* there.

It went on for several verses. I didn't know how to react; I laughed and felt like hiding at the same time. One of my pals put it in context for me: "This room is filled with your best friends. We know you're sensitive about your hair and we thought it was time you lightened up about it. In this whole room you're the only one who notices or cares. The rest of us love you just the way you are."

Their use of humor was one of the watershed moments in my eventual acceptance of an inherited family trait.

It's OK to Be Playful—at Any Age

Humor is more than jokes and laughter. It's also about playfulness. As we get older we often lose our youthful exuberance and willingness to goof around. What a shame! The word silly is usually a putdown word, as in "Stop being so silly. Act your age." But actually it's a wonderful word that comes from the Middle English word selig, which means "prosperous, happy, healthy and blessed."

Playfulness is as much an attitude as it is an activity. It's about seeing things in a light and offbeat way. Being playful is like looking through a fun filter, viewing the world through a light-giving lens. (My son is wonderful at this. When he was three, he fell through a slightly ajar front door and tumbled onto the floor. Within two seconds he said, "Look who just dropped in!" When he was 10 we went horseback-riding, and while the horses were being saddled, he walked up to one of them and said, "Hi, Molly. Why the long face?" Humor and play are an innate part of who he is but for others it's a skill that can be acquired through practice.) Playfulness is about being joyful and free and clowning around. It's about taking yourself less seriously and giving yourself permission to have fun. Playfulness can include loud ties, funny T shirts or funky hats. When safe sex became a societal concern, a friend of ours showed up at a party wearing a pair of very colorful earrings fashioned from small condoms. Talk about a conversation piece!

When I opened my practice in stress management counseling, I received several coffee mugs with funny sayings on them. One was a Garfield cartoon with this line: "You are entitled to my opinion." A friend gave me a small pillow embroidered with: "My Decision Is Final. The Answer Is Maybe." Years ago, I learned how to juggle. I keep three small colored beanbags on my desk at work and every so often I take a short juggling break. It gets me out of my chair, gives me a short exercise break and reminds me to stay loose and playful. It's hard to take yourself seriously while you're juggling beanbags. As someone said, "Having fun is more important than being funny."

Humor and Creativity: the Perfect Match

In dealing with certain situations, humor isn't helpful only as a stress reliever. Its other benefits include waking up our bodies (laughter is a great energizer), bringing people together (for team building and group cooperation) and enhancing creativity. This latter function reflects the fact that the part of the brain (located on the right side) that controls humor also controls creativity. It relates to our ability to think conceptually, in ideas and pictures rather than words and logic. You *get* a joke, you don't *understand* it. If someone has to explain it to you (which you process in your analytical left brain), it's not funny anymore.

The more people learn to see humor in situations, the more they develop the ability to see things in different ways, which is the essence of creativity. When I was in high school, the clock had stopped in the room where we studied French. A student put a sign up beside the clock that read, "This clock doesn't work. Why should I?" Everyone thought that was terribly clever. But our French teacher went one better. He put up a sign next to the first sign that read, "Time passes. Will you?"

Problem-solving and being innovative are ways of stretching your "creativity muscles." Creativity is one of the elements of resilience—and resilience is a key survival skill in our rapidly changing world. So laugh, stay loose and think laterally!

Most things in life are not funny in themselves and the humor comes from how we choose to *look* at those things.

Jerry Seinfeld and Woody Allen make a healthy living finding humor in everyday situations. Most of us will never be that funny, but we can have fun trying. And remember, he who laughs—lasts!

CHAPTER FOURTEEN

Getting into Shape—
Choosing Your Lifestyle

MAGINE YOUR FAVORITE BASKETBALL PLAYER showing up for a play-off game. Picture him feeling tired, hungry, cranky and stiff. Also a little light-headed from the two beers he just drank and a bit shaky from the coffee he had to perk him up. He does not inspire much confidence from you nor fear from the other team. He is not a very formidable foe. In fact, he looks like a washout!

It's unthinkable that someone would show up for a competitive sports event feeling so wasted and unprepared. And yet a surprisingly large number of people report for work every day in this kind of condition. They arrive to the challenges of their job feeling out of shape and out of sorts. Small wonder they perform below their capabilities and suffer a lot of stress in the bargain.

If I had eight hours to chop down a tree, I'd spend six sharpening my ax.

ABRAHAM LINCOLN

If you're looking for a classic example of a losing game, poor lifestyle habits are hard to beat. I have patients who eat one meal a day, usually a pig-out at supper. They go to bed too late so they wake up tired; then they sleepwalk through their day, barely able to function. They smoke a pack a day, leaving them breathless on stairs and coughing a lot. Their alcohol intake is three or four drinks a day, taking the edge off their reflexes (mental and physical). With up to five or ten coffees a day, their nerves jangle and their hands shake. Exercise consists of walking from house to car; leisure is a word they never use and no longer understand, and it's been years since they've had a holiday. Boy, are these people having fun!

And yet talking to them about lifestyle change and good health habits is often difficult. Many react indifferently or even negatively when they hear about a healthy way of life. Some get defensive ("Here comes the lecture my mother used to give me") or their eyes glaze over, anticipating the "good health message." Others just find the idea corny and dull.

The fact is that good health habits aren't very exotic or exciting. Let's face it, there are more thrilling things in life than going for a walk or eating broccoli. As Johnny Carson put it: "I know a man who gave up smoking, drinking, sex and rich food. He was healthy right up to the time he killed himself." A heavy drinker and smoker told me that "living on exercise and fresh air is not very romantic or adventurous" (as if his dissipated lifestyle was either of those things!). And then there's the issue of effort. Good lifestyle habits seem like such a hassle to some people. An out-of-shape businessman told me: "I don't know if I can *handle* being healthy—it's a lot of responsibility." Taken all together, these objections make lifestyle change a hard sell.

Despite all the resistance, however, even my most reluctant patients grudgingly admit they would feel better if they ate well, got adequate sleep, exercised regularly, stopped smoking, drank less alcohol and caffeine and had more leisure time. My aim in counseling my patients is to tap into this latent awareness. I use a piece of logic that applies both to sports and to daily living. If people are rested, well-fed, fit and in a good frame of mind, they are more resilient and adaptable when it comes to dealing with the events of everyday life. They perform better. They're more resistant to stress and handle it with greater ease. And they have an increased sense of well-being. Some of the most mundane changes in daily habits yield benefits far greater than expected. The changes may seem too simple to be so important. But don't overlook their power. You'll be delighted with the results. One patient, who became a real convert, told me with some surprise: "Lifestyle change is such a simple but profound solution."

Lifestyle as Metaphor

There is another reason I encourage lifestyle changes. Choosing to make a change has symbolic benefits as well. Lifestyle habits are often a metaphor for the way people function in other aspects of their lives. Making changes in the lifestyle sphere has a spillover effect into other areas.

The first symbolic benefit relates to taking control of your life. For example, if you give up smoking, you stop the habit of putting dried tobacco leaves in your mouth, setting them on fire and inhaling the smoke (which sounds pretty perverse when you think about it!). Giving up cigarettes is what you do in the realm of everyday reality. But on a *symbolic* level, you are taking control of a part of your life that you had not controlled before.

Here's a story that illustrates how the symbolic benefit of lifestyle change can spread to other areas. One of my patients was drinking six to eight cups of coffee a day. I explained the stimulant effect of caffeine and asked her to give up her coffee for three weeks. I suggested she wean herself off over seven to ten days to avoid withdrawal headaches. Five weeks later she was still drinking four or five coffees a day. Her explanation was: "I want to change very gradually. I feel overwhelmed by rapid change." I explained that this exercise was not just about caffeine. It was about taking control of her life. That sparked her interest and her resolve. Nine days later she was off caffeine, eating better and walking almost daily. She was feeling good, was sleeping better, had lost a few pounds and had no more of "the terrible feeling I get from coffee" (dizziness and nausea). She was very pleased.

One week later she quit her job. This seemed rather abrupt (especially since she hadn't found another job yet), so I asked what precipitated such a major decision. She said, "Once I realized I was dragging my heels on the caffeine, I recognized I was doing the same thing with my job. I've wanted to quit for a year but kept procrastinating and rationalizing why I shouldn't."

If you want to take control of your life, lifestyle habits are a great place to start. For one thing, *you* are the only one who controls them. Who else decides whether you eat breakfast or drink coffee? Furthermore, your daily living habits are among the few things in life that you *can* fully control. With relationships, your job and other people's behavior, partial control is about all you can achieve. But when it comes to your lifestyle choices, you are the boss.

A second symbolic benefit of lifestyle improvement is that it's an excellent place to practice change. Some of the changes advocated in this book are difficult to make, taking time and determination. By comparison, most lifestyle changes are relatively simple. It's not that complicated to go to bed earlier, take a walk or drink fruit juice. Lifestyle alterations are tangible and specific, are generally easy to make and confer almost immediate benefits. Most people notice results within days or weeks. Also, these changes give them a feeling of momentum and confidence to take on other, more difficult challenges.

Confronting lifestyle change has another benefit: it reveals your inclination to make excuses. People's tendency to dodge responsibility usually comes out in lifestyle discussions. Excuses they wouldn't accept from their own children gush forth when suggestions are made about good eating habits or lightening up on the liquor. A pleasant lady told me she doesn't like walking because "I had to walk hills as a girl" and, if that wasn't good enough, "I don't like walking alone." "I don't like listening to music because my brother used to play music too loud." She refuted everything I suggested. This woman had a problem for every solution. As I gently reflected her conversation back to her, she saw how often she limited herself by making excuses. Take note if *you* allow alibis to block you from worthwhile things in life.

Lifestyle change is also a good place to become a problem solver. I know business people and professionals who are valued for their creativity at work but seem unable to transfer that ability to their own lives. One highly paid executive was a crackerjack at solving corporate dilemmas—but couldn't figure out how to get juice at the office "because all they serve is coffee, tea and pop." I know a conference leader who can schedule a seminar beautifully—but couldn't find time for his own evening bike ride. In confronting their lifestyle difficulties, people improve their ability to solve problems.

Where Do You Stand?

When I see new patients, I ask them a number of lifestyle questions. This inventory is summarized in the questionnaire on the next page. I invite you to take a few minutes to fill it out. It will help focus your attention in the following discussion.

There are many factors that influence your lifestyle choices, most of which you may be unaware of. Take any aspect of your lifestyle (nutrition, exercise, leisure, alcohol, etc.) and ask yourself when you started doing it and why. Messages from the past (from parents, teachers, etc.) may be one reason. Or you might have been copying the example of someone else. A child psychiatrist told me that 90% of children's behavior results from modeling behavior of others, not from what they were told.

Social pressure could have started you on some path. (Did you start smoking to be one of the gang, or begin drinking to fit in?) Whether

---

PERSONAL LIFESTYLE INVENTORY PART I (WHERE ARE YOU NOW?)

NUTRITION
How many times per week do you eat
Breakfast? ___ Lunch? ___ Supper? ___

DAIRY: How many times per week do you have
Milk? ___ Cheese? ___ Eggs? ___ Yogurt? ___

PROTEIN: How many times per week do you eat
Chicken? ___ Fish? ___ Meat? ___

VEGETABLE: How many times per week do you eat
Cooked Vegetables? ___ Salads? ___

FRUIT: How much fruit do you eat per day? ___
How much juice per day? ___

GRAINS: How many times per week do you eat
Cereal? ___ Whole Wheat Bread? ___ Bran Muffins? ___

FLUIDS: How many glasses of water do you drink per day? ___

Do you eat "JUNK FOOD" (cookies, candies, donuts, cake, ice cream, pop, potato chips, etc.)?

❑ Never ❑ Rarely (less than once per week)
❑ Occasionally (once per week) ❑ Often

Do you eat FRIED FOODS (french fries, deep fried chicken or fish or veggies)?
❑ Never ❑ Rarely ❑ Occasionally ❑ Often

Do you eat FAST ("on the run," "on the fly")?
❑ Never ❑ Rarely ❑ Often

SLEEP
Generally speaking, do you sleep
❑ Well? ❑ Fair-Good? ❑ Poorly?

What time do you generally
Go to bed? _____ Turn lights off? _____ Get up? _____

How many of those hours do you think you're actually asleep? _____
Do you awaken feeling Rested/Refreshed? or Tired?

Do you sleep longer on the weekends? _____ If so, how many extra hours? _____

Do you take naps? _____ How often? _____ For how long? _____

EXERCISE: How often? _____ For how long? _____
What type? _____

SMOKING: Cigarettes? ___ Cigars? ___ Pipe? ___ per day

ALCOHOL: Beer? ___ Wine? ___ Liquor? ___ per day or week

CAFFEINE: Coffee? ___ Tea? ___ Cola? ___ Chocolate? ___ per day direct or subtle, these pressures to conform can be very strong. Your self-esteem can also influence your choices. If you don't feel good about yourself, you might do things to please or impress others—or give in easily to peer pressure.

Aside from these factors, you may have drifted into unhealthy lifestyle choices by inattention or default. It's as if these things evolved while you weren't looking. Whatever your habits may be, just remember you chose them at some point and for some reason. It's helpful to assess which of your choices are beneficial and which are not. It isn't a matter of right or wrong, good or bad, moral or immoral. It's a question of whether your lifestyle choices support your sense of well-being or undermine it. In considering those that aren't serving you well, ask yourself whether you still feel the need for these activities or if you're ready to give them up.

Healthstyles: Ingredients of a Healthy Lifestyle

The following list is a set of positive guidelines for daily living. Compare these suggestions with the personal inventory you filled out and see what kind of shape your lifestyle is in. If you're playing some losing games, the following discussion might help you make better choices.

Where to Start

Even motivated people wonder where to begin in revising their lifestyle habits. Do they quit smoking right off the bat or ease into it? Do they make several changes at once or one at a time? I have found an approach that works well with my patients. It starts with things that are easiest to do and that yield the biggest payoff. Each step makes people feel more in control of their lives, thus making the next steps that much easier.

Give Up Caffeine

In terms of immediate payoff, I know of no single lifestyle change to rival the benefits of giving up caffeine. Testimonials from patients often include phrases like "I can't believe how much better I feel," "It's fantastic," "I'm amazed at the difference" and "It's unbelievable." Caffeine is found in coffee, tea, cola drinks (like Coke and Pepsi), chocolate and energy drinks. Because it is a stimulant, caffeine produces a response in the body similar to a stress reaction. In addition, a large amount of sugar often accompanies caffeine. Since refined sugar also has an energizing and stimulant effect, adding it to caffeine is like a double whammy.

HEALTHSTYLES: LIFESTYLE KEYS TO HEALTH AND SUCCESS

1. Eliminate caffeine (coffee, tea, cola and chocolate and energy drinks).
2. Regular meals, balanced diet, minimal junk and fried foods, eat slowly.
3. Good fluid intake (six to eight glasses of water or other liquids per day).
4. Alcohol in moderation (one or two drinks per day maximum).
5. Don't smoke. Don't use recreational drugs.
6. Adequate sleep (based on your requirements).
7. Regular exercise (at least thirty minutes, three times per week; aerobic; fun; do a warm-up).
8. Balance between work and leisure. Make time for family and for self.
9. Time-outs regularly and as required.
10. Regular holidays (take them before you need them).
11. Establish and nurture relationships. Develop a support system.
12. Learn to relax—including relaxation skills.
13. Manage your time. Don't overload your schedule.
14. Manage your money. Don't get over-extended.
15. Do something for yourself every day.

The best way to know what caffeine is doing to you is to get it out of your system for a while. I urge all my patients to give it up totally for three weeks and observe the effects. I present it as an experiment: "Try it for three weeks and see what happens. If you don't notice a difference, you'll go back to it and nothing will be lost. But if you feel better without it, you will learn a lesson to benefit you for the rest of your life." Very few people resist, and virtually all find it easy to do because caffeine is not strongly addicting. In fact, I haven't met a patient in twenty-five years who couldn't give up caffeine within a week or two. Some miss the routine or the taste, but no one has trouble giving up caffeine itself. I guesstimate that about 80% of my patients feel better without it, and many of them feel dramatically better. They report improved sleep, increased energy, feeling more calm and relaxed and being less irritable. There is also great improvement in things like heartburn and aching muscles. Of the remaining 20% who report no difference, a significant number notice the stimulant effect when they go *back* to caffeine. They feel "jolted, buzzed, hyper, a rush," things they hadn't noticed before. Most patients stay off caffeine or consume much less after this experiment.

People can generally tolerate one or two caffeine drinks a day, but some find even one too much. No matter what your intake is, you should taper off gradually (decrease by one a day, down to zero) because stopping abruptly often leads to bad "withdrawal" headaches. For the duration of the experiment, don't even drink decaffeinated coffee because it still has a small amount of caffeine. Be aware that some drugs (especially pain killers) have caffeine in them. The accompanying chart shows the caffeine content of common dietary sources.

Food	Serving Size	Caffeine (mg)
Coffee, brewed	250 mL (1 cup)	80-179
Cappuccino or Latte	250 mL (1 cup)	45-148
Coffee, instant	250 mL (1 cup)	81-106
Espresso, brewed	30 mL (1 oz)	64-90
Coffee, decaffeinated	250 mL (1 cup)	3-15
Coffee liqueur	45 mL (1 ½ oz)	4-14
Coffee, instant, decaffeinated	250 mL (1 cup)	3-5
Decaffeinated espresso	30 mL (1 oz)	0
Iced Tea, sweetened	355 mL (1 can)	22-64
Tea, leaf or bag (black)	250 mL (1 cup)	43-50
Tea (green, oolong, white)	250 mL (1 cup)	25-45
Tea, decaffeinated	250 mL (1 cup)	0-5
Herbal teas	250 mL (1 cup)	0
Energy drink, various	250 mL (1 cup)	80-97
Diet cola	355 mL (1 can)	25-50
Cola	355 mL (1 can)	37-38
Dr. Pepper (regular, diet)	355 mL (1 can)	41
Chocolate, dark	1 bar (40 g)	27
Hot chocolate	125 mL (½ cup)	5-12
Milk chocolate bar	1 bar (40 g)	7-10
Chocolate milk	250 mL (1 cup)	5
Milkshake, chocolate	125 mL (½ cup)	2
Ice cream, chocolate	125 mL (½ cup)	2

Source: "Canadian Nutrient File 2007b" http://www.hc-sc.gc.ca/fn-an/nutrition/fiche-nutri-data/index-eng.php, 2010.

I suggest you taper off the evening and afternoon caffeine first because the drinks closest to bedtime interfere with sleep. This is true whether you think you're sleeping well or not. Some people can take caffeine late in the day and still fall asleep easily and stay asleep until morning. They assume the caffeine is not interfering with their sleep. However, many of these people admit to waking up tired in the morning. The reason is instructive. The value of sleep is based not just on how much you get (quantity) but also on how well you sleep (quality). Caffeine disrupts the sleep cycle even in people who think they're sleeping well. It keeps you from reaching the deepest levels of sleep (Levels 3 and 4). It is this deep sleep that rejuvenates you physically (as contrasted with the dream or REM sleep, that is thought to produce mental and psychological benefit). The following diagram from Jon Shearer, a sleep expert in Ottawa, shows a normal sleep pattern (each cycle takes about ninety minutes) and what happens as a result of caffeine. Notice that the first two cycles of the night are the ones in which you reach Level 3 and 4 sleep; subsequent cycles reach only Level 2.

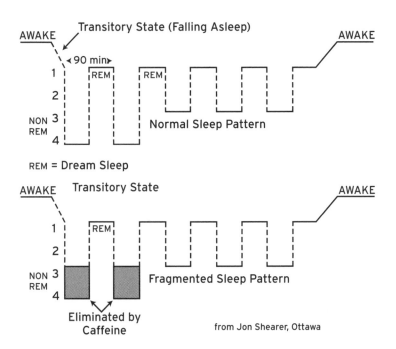

Get More Sleep

The next issue I look at is sleep. The surest way to start your day feeling off balance is to wake up tired. You feel as if you have one foot in a hole all day. It happens to everyone on occasion, but it's perverse to make it a routine. Whenever someone tells me they're tired, my first question is "How much sleep are you getting at night?" I often hear answers like: "Oh, about six, six and a half hours." To which I ask: "How much sleep do you think you need to function at your best?" The reply is often immediate: "Eight!" My next inquiry is: "Then why aren't you getting more sleep?" This leads to all kinds of interesting reasons, stories and excuses. But for most people the solution to the fatigue problem is simply to get more sleep.

This is such an obvious piece of advice that many people overlook it, possibly because they can't believe it's that simple. But it makes two important points: (1) Sometimes the remedy is obvious and easy to apply. (2) If you know what the problem is, fix it. Some people have gotten so used to fatigue they've become resigned to it. They accept lethargy as a natural condition to be endured. That's what I call a losing game.

Good "sleep hygiene" is a combination of common sense, discipline and a willingness to make some trade-offs. The payoffs are enormous. Here is a list of basic tips regarding sleep (Nature's best restorative):

1. Determine how much sleep you need to function well. Then get it.

2. Go to bed and wake up at the same time each day.

3. Develop a bedtime routine to wind down (bath, reading, soft music, etc.).

4. Clear your mind of problems and worries. Think calm and pleasant thoughts.

5. Don't watch TV in your bedroom, and especially not at bedtime.

6. Avoid caffeine within eight to ten hours of bedtime.

7. Avoid exertion and overeating in the mid-to-late evening.

8. Avoid sleeping pills.

9. Avoid alcohol as a bedtime sedative—it leads to early-morning wakening.

10. Don't nap in the evening. When you wake, you'll be infuriatingly awake.

"Power Naps" or *"Cat Naps."* There's one kind of nap that is helpful for daytime fatigue. It consists of a short sleep (between five and twenty minutes) that has a rejuvenating effect. If you sleep longer than twenty (and especially thirty) minutes, you risk waking up groggy and sluggish. But the short nap is remarkably refreshing. Not everyone can fall asleep at will in the middle of the day, but if you have this ability, the power nap may be a real boon. If you can't actually fall asleep, some form of relaxation exercise (muscle relaxation, meditation, imaging, etc.) will be equally beneficial. I advise people to sleep in a sitting or partial reclining position so you'll waken more easily. If you get too comfortable, an hour can slip by and you feel listless from oversleeping.

Improve Your Nutrition

As nutritional expert Adelle Davis said, "You are what you eat." It amazes me how many people don't follow the simple, common-sense rules for healthy eating. I hear stories of individuals skipping meals, grabbing food on the run or even standing up to eat. They belong to the "Eat It and Beat It" school of nutrition. Some folks almost inhale their food, as if they don't realize they have teeth. A friend of mine used to load up his tray in the cafeteria line—and by the time he got to the cashier it was empty. He would then report on what he'd eaten and pay for it on the honor system. His idea of a "leisurely" lunch was when there was a long lineup and it took him several minutes to reach the cash register. Other people consume hamburgers, french fries, Cokes and milkshakes several times a week. Or they eat nothing till supper time, then gorge themselves before plopping down on a sofa for the evening. You don't have to be a student of nutrition to eat a healthy, balanced diet. Someone I know simplified all the guidelines for her mother with this sage and practical advice: "Ma, just make sure there's a lot of color on your plate!"

The changes I advocate are to eat three meals a day, have a well-balanced diet (eating from all the food groups each day—dairy, meat/poultry/fish, vegetables, fruit and grains/cereals), eat slowly, and avoid junk foods and fried foods. Nothing fancy or difficult here—just the basics. Although this may require a lot of discipline and planning for some folks, most can make these changes easily and virtually all report feeling better for it.

Exercise Regularly

The next area I explore with people is physical exercise. I once heard the statement that "exercise is the closest thing to the fountain of youth that we know of." Exercise has numerous benefits. It increases energy, promotes cardiovascular fitness, builds strength and endurance, drains off stress energy, burns calories (so it helps lower weight and control diabetes), lowers total blood cholesterol, raises HDL cholesterol ("the good cholesterol"), helps lower blood pressure, strengthens bones (thus helping to prevent osteoporosis and fractures), enhances bowel function (preventing constipation), improves mental function and makes people feel better about themselves psychologically. It also stimulates secretion of beta-endorphins (natural hormones produced by the brain that are similar to morphine but much stronger), which are excellent painkillers and give a sense of euphoria and well-being—often called the "runner's high." Last, exercise can be a social activity, allowing people to meet others, develop camaraderie (teammates, golf buddies, tennis partners, etc.) and get together with friends and family. If you could put all these benefits in pill form, you would make billions of dollars, win a Nobel Prize and revolutionize society all at once.

Human beings were not intended to be sedentary. We were built to be physically active, and our ancestors (from cave-dwelling hunters and gatherers to later generations of farmers and laborers) would be appalled by the degree of inactivity in our "advanced" society. The good news is that as little as half an hour of exercise every day or two is enough to produce a good level of physical fitness.

I urge people to get into a regular exercise routine. It can be as simple as a daily walk or as ambitious as learning a new sport. The key is that it should be regular, enjoyable and of mild to moderate exertion. Most individuals can identify activities they've enjoyed in the past so it's just a matter of getting back to them. Only a small number of people have trouble choosing an outlet that pleases them.

General Principles of Healthy Exercise

1. Exercise a minimum of three times per week, preferably four or five. The fitness benefit starts to wear off after forty-eight hours.

2. Exercise a minimum of half an hour each time.

3. Do aerobic exercises (walking, jogging, bicycling, swimming, racket sports, skiing, etc.), which build endurance and cardiovascular fitness.

4. Do strenuous exercise before meals or two hours after consuming food.

5. Pace yourself. Avoid overexertion. Don't ignore pain.

6. See a doctor before starting an exercise program if you're over forty, have been inactive for several years or have had health problems.

7. Do a proper warm-up before exercise and a cool-off after you finish.

8. Use proper equipment and dress appropriately.

9. Choose proper places and conditions to exercise. The main issue is safety.

10. Pick an activity you enjoy. Otherwise you'll find every excuse to avoid it.

"Lifestyle" Exercise Versus "Structured" Exercise

People often tell me they don't need exercise—they get enough doing housework, running after little kids or walking all day at work. They have a point. There are two kinds of exercise, and both are beneficial. *Structured* or *planned* exercise is the training or workout program described above wherein you say, "I'm going to exercise now." *Lifestyle* exercise is the kind you do in the course of your day, a few minutes here and there, with no special equipment or preparation. Walking or bicycling to the store instead of driving, taking stairs instead of elevators, parking a few blocks from your destination and walking the rest of the way, getting off a bus one or two stops early and walking the remainder, and taking a walk with a friend instead of sitting down to visit are ways of building exercise into your daily routine. None of these measures is major in itself, but the cumulative effect in a day or a week can be significant. Some studies show these increments of physical activity may do more for general fitness and weight control than an exercise program done a few times per week. Of course, combining the two makes the most sense: regular workouts plus general exercise during the day gives the best results. It's a pretty painless way of getting fit.

Once people are off caffeine, getting adequate sleep, eating properly and exercising regularly, they feel better physically and psychologically and feel more in control of their lives. The next area to explore is also the most pleasurable—leisure. This will be dealt with in the next chapter about "taking breaks from the game."

Avoid or Moderate "Vices"

Only after patients have adjusted their caffeine, sleep, nutrition, exercise and leisure habits do I invite them to deal with their vices. I'm referring here to tobacco, alcohol and drugs. Often there is a strong dependence or addiction, so these changes are the hardest to make—which is why I leave them till last. The best way to deal with these habits is to never start. But for those who are already hooked, the goal is to stop smoking and using recreational drugs, to modify alcohol intake and to use prescription drugs only under a doctor's advice and supervision.

Guidelines for Responsible Alcohol Use

With regard to alcohol, one glass of wine (4 to 5 ounces), one beer or 1.5 ounces of liquor are counted as one drink each, the alcohol contents being roughly equal. With this in mind, I advise the following:

- Maximum of two drinks per day.

- Maximum of one drink per hour.

- Alternate one glass of water, juice or pop with every drink of alcohol.

- Don't drink on an empty stomach.

- Don't use alcohol as a tranquilizer or relaxant.

- Don't make a habit of drinking alone.

- Don't drink early in the day.

- **Don't drive after drinking.**

A Case History

Let me conclude this section with a brief case history of a man in his forties who made a dramatic overhaul of his previously self-destructive lifestyle. He came to see me having just quit smoking (from sixty to seventy per day). However, he was still having eight to twelve caffeine drinks a day and five liters of wine a week, eating a poorly balanced diet and getting minimal exercise. Within months he was off all caffeine and alcohol, still wasn't smoking and was eating breakfast for the first time in his adult life. He said: "It's been years since I knew what my natural rhythms are" (referring to his high and low energy times which he had been masking with caffeine and alcohol). "I'm having a whale of a time with it all. It's fun!"

Where Is the Gap?

When I talk to people about lifestyle, they often say that none of the information is new. Or that it's just common sense anyway. I agree. But that just raises the question: if most of this "lifestyle stuff" is so obvious, why don't people take better care of themselves? The gap is not between what you know and what you don't know; the gap is between what you *know* and what you *do*. Even if you're not an expert, you know most of the basics already. So if you know the information, why are you *ignoring* it?

Two paradoxes highlight this gap. I often ask patients whether they would accept *their* lifestyle habits from their *children*. I ask them what they teach their kids about nutrition, sleep, exercise, smoking, alcohol and drug use. It's an important question to reflect on. People tell me they are vigilant about their children's wearing seat belts—but admit they often don't buckle up themselves. They're unrelenting in getting their offspring to bed on time—but they don't hit the sack till after midnight. I often hear: "I don't eat breakfast—but I damn well make sure my *kids* do!" This is the "Do as I say, not as I do" school of parenting. What a credibility gap between what they know (and teach others) and what they do themselves.

The other striking irony is that many patients take better care of things than they do of themselves. A woman told me she spends most of the day taking care of her home. She took great pride in telling me how immaculate the house was, how beautiful the lawns and gardens were and how many compliments she received as a result. There was a glaring paradox though. She never had time for herself. I said: "It sounds to me as though you take better care of your house than you do of yourself." She went suddenly quiet. My comment caught her off guard and had a profound impact on her. She decided her priorities needed reassessment. Over the years, I've found many people who look after their possessions better than themselves. With men, it can be the house, but it's often their car or garden that receives the attention and loving care that they never lavish on themselves.

Where and Why People Get Stuck

Let me return to the perplexing question of why people don't take better care of themselves. As I've noted, there is a large gap between what most people know and what they do. I ask patients *why* they do the things they do, and why they avoid changes they know would be in their interest. The question has two purposes. One is to smoke out the alibis, excuses and stories people have been hiding behind for so long. The other is to uncover the genuine obstacles to a more constructive lifestyle. The smokescreens are challenged and dismissed. Then the real problems are dealt with. Progress begins when people decide not to let barriers stand in their way.

My friend and mentor, Dr. Matthew Budd, taught me a concept that has been very useful to me and my patients. "In life, there are either results or there are reasons." To which someone added: "And reasons are the booby prize of life." The message is that you have two choices. You can do or get what you want in life, which is satisfying and rewarding. Or you can live with your excuses and cop-outs about why you haven't gotten what you want.

Here is an exercise I do in my seminars. List the lifestyle changes you'd like to make or know would be beneficial to you. Next, note the benefits of these changes. Then list your "reasons" for not doing them. Study the lists and consider whether you would accept those excuses from your employees or children. Ask yourself whether you'd prefer to live with those "reasons" or whether you'd rather have the results. Finally, brainstorm ways to overcome your barriers. In some cases it will be simple to correct things. In others it will require some problem solving and creativity. But all the lifestyle suggestions made in this chapter are within everyone's reach. It's time to stop telling yourself stories and start to make things happen.

Here are some of the excuses I hear from people about why their lifestyle is the way it is. I'll list these in categories, but you'll notice a lot of overlap.

List Five Lifestyle Changes You Would Like to Make

1. _____

2. _____

3. _____

4. _____

5. _____

Why Haven't You Made These Changes Before?
(Reasons, Problems, Barriers)

_____

_____

_____

_____

_____

What Payoffs Would You Expect from These Changes?

1. _____

2. _____

3. _____

4. _____

5. _____

How Can You Overcome These Barriers?

_____

_____

_____

_____

_____

Nutrition

The most common excuse is "I don't have time"—to shop for food, to prepare meals and/or to eat. Other favorites on the alibi hit parade include: "I hate cooking," "I can't afford healthy food" (this is no disrespect to those who truly can't afford to eat well, but there are people with money for beer and cigarettes who are suddenly broke when it comes to food), "My wife never buys what I like," "There are no restaurants near my office," "I'm watching my weight," "I'm not hungry in the morning," "Eating in the morning makes me gag," "I get up too late," etc.

There is another obstacle to good eating: the belief that it's not important. If you believe that all the hype about nutrition is overblown, your eating habits will match your mind-set. You have to be convinced that all this theory is valid. For that to happen, you need an open mind. Either talk to knowledgeable people or read reputable books on the subject. The evidence is overwhelming if you seek it out. Better yet, prove it to yourself by eating properly for a few weeks and see how you feel.

Sleep

It's fascinating how many people don't get the sleep they need. Many have trouble sleeping (insomnia), but most are not the victims of their sleep problem. They are the authors of it. They go to bed too late, get up too early or interfere with the quality of their sleep in other ways. It's not that they can't sleep, it's that they *won't* sleep.

One man told me he was going to bed at 2:00 a.m. and waking up tired at 7:00 a.m. His energy had been "pathetically low for years." He explained his late bedtime by saying: "I'm a night person." Many people stay up late because "that's my alone time." Things like reading, TV or knitting are saved for this window of time in the mid-to-late evening when things are quiet. People would rather stagger in to work feeling wasted and bleary-eyed than to miss the late-night talk shows.

Another group sacrifice sleep to meet the needs of others. One scenario involves couples in which one or both work late. They stay up because "That's the only time I get to see Kristen" or "It's our only chance to be together." A woman told me she stays up unwillingly to spend time with her late-working husband. "He wants me to stay up till he gets home. If I don't, he gets angry." Then there are people who wake up early to make breakfast for their mates and teenage children, all of whom are quite capable of feeding themselves.

All these people are making choices that deprive them of much-needed sleep. While the desire for more leisure or together time is understandable, the trade-off these folks are making is not serving them well. They continue to choose the losing game of sleep deprivation and fatigue.

Another place that people get hung up is in their beliefs about sleep. Some feel it's an option they can pass up; a luxury they can no longer afford as life gets more hectic and complicated; a nuisance that gets in the way of an already overloaded schedule; or even a waste of time, something frivolous with no intrinsic value. I know people who think "sleep is for sissies" or "it's just a cop-out for people who can't face the challenge of life." These beliefs become slogans to justify their chronic lack of sleep. The truth is that everyone needs sleep, usually seven to eight hours a night, and those who don't get enough suffer as a result.

Then there are folks who sabotage their sleep—with caffeine, late-evening meals, mid-evening naps or exercise too close to bedtime. Upsetting TV images (from horror movies to the late-night news) can also block people's drift into slumber.

Exercise

Resistance to exercise often results from misconceptions like "If it doesn't hurt, it doesn't help" (or "no pain, no gain"). It doesn't have to be unpleasant to be beneficial. The guiding motto should be: "Train, don't strain."

When it comes to resistance, exercise brings out some of the fiercest opposition (and most persuasive excuses) I encounter in my work. The "reasons" I hear for not exercising include:

No time. An interesting excuse, considering that the average North American watches television three or four hours a day. Better management of your schedule can usually free up some exercise time. Otherwise, reorganizing your priorities is required. A busy businessman told me: "*Finding* time doesn't work—you have to *make* time."

No energy. There is a paradox here—exercise actually generates energy.

No babysitter. This can be a real problem for some, especially single parents with small children, but solutions can be found—from taking the child with you to swapping babysitting chores with a neighbor.

Unfriendly weather. Skip the terrible days and bundle up on the others. Thermal clothes or indoor exercise can overcome this problem.

No exercise facilities. Most communities provide recreational opportunities through local parks (public tennis courts, swimming pools, jogging trails and bicycle paths) or gymnasia in local schools, Ys and colleges. Racket, fitness and aerobics clubs abound.

No place to change or shower after daytime exercise. Some companies provide facilities but other resources may be found (a local gym, club, Y or even hotel that might accept some arrangement).

No one to exercise with. The solution is taking the initiative. One woman canvassed her neighbors and found a different walking partner for every day of the week. Another put an ad in the local paper and formed her own walking club. Some people won't exercise without their spouse but feel it's improper to seek other exercise partners. This stems from the belief that couples should do everything together. One woman stopped bicycling because her husband wouldn't go with her. Negotiation with your partner and reassessing your limiting belief will overcome this problem.

Economic limitations. Money may be a problem for some exercise options but should not be a barrier to exercise, per se. Many public facilities exist, and activities like walking, jogging and swimming require minimal equipment.

"Exercise is boring." To these skeptics, I offer about twenty sports or activities and invite them to choose at least one and do it regularly for three weeks. If they're still bored, pick another. I've never met anyone who couldn't find their niche. Other boredom-beaters include exercising with a partner, using a personal music device for company or turning your exercise into a game. Varying your activity also helps. Walk some days, bicycle on others and add the odd tennis game or swim for variety. Another option is dancing.

Lack of ability. Don't let that ruin your fun. The worst thing you can do is *not* participate. To quote G.K. Chesterton: "Anything worth doing is worth doing badly" (as opposed to not doing it at all).

Fear of injury. Pick activities you feel comfortable with. Exercise should be a part of life for everyone, no matter how old or frail. It should simply be suited to the person's health and ability. A proper warm-up is essential to protect against injury.

Laziness. This is the bottom line for a lot of people. Exercise feels too strenuous. Or it's inconvenient, a hassle. Interestingly, these same folks admit that when they exercised in the past, they felt considerably better. It's worth getting back to.

"Exercise is not beneficial." Some individuals believe the claims for exercise are greatly exaggerated. However, I've never heard this from anyone who has exercised regularly. I urge them to get involved for a month or two before they deny the value of exercise.

In summary, self-care should be the most logical thing in the world. Choosing a healthy lifestyle has many inherent benefits, like improving your energy and reducing your stress. But there are also symbolic benefits, especially as a metaphor for taking control of your life. Usually lifestyle problems consist of overload or self-neglect—trying to do too much or not doing nearly enough. The goal is to make choices that feature balance and moderation. Keep in mind that in making lifestyle choices, trade-offs are inevitable. As a friend of mine put it: "You can have anything you want. You just can't have *everything* you want!" Decide what you *really* need for a good quality of life. Then slow down enough to enjoy it.

CHAPTER FIFTEEN

Taking Breaks from the Game—Leisure and Time-Outs

AVE YOU EVER SAT THROUGH A SIXTEEN-INNING baseball game? I did a few years back. It was long. About five *hours* long. By the twelfth inning I was hoping the game would end, no matter who won. I got the feeling the players felt the same way (and I *know* the umpires did). Whether it's a marathon tennis match or an overtime hockey game, people get to the point where enough is enough and they need a recess. Fortunately, in most sports players can take a break from the action. Phrases like "intermission," "half-time," "pit stop" and "time-out" reflect this need for intervals of rest. Players perform better with these breaks. In addition, the time between games helps athletes unwind and restore their energy and concentration for the next challenge.

Time off and time-outs are not the only way to relieve tension in sports. Diversion and distraction have an important role to play too. During a baseball game two or three players may have a short meeting on the pitcher's mound—and talk about something other than strategy. Garth Woolsey recounted a wonderful story told by sports psychologist Dr. Peter Jensen. In a tense moment of a ball game, the catcher called time and trotted out to talk to ace relief pitcher Tug McGraw. Instead of giving McGraw some piece of instruction or wisdom, he just leaned in and said: "Isn't this great!" gave Tug a big grin and headed back to home plate. By combining a quick time-out with a bit of distraction, he settled down his pitcher and the game resumed.

From Sports to Real Life

Diversion and time-outs are essential in the world of sports. They are just as important in other forms of sustained activity or pressure. Long meetings, seminars, labor negotiations and courtroom trials would be brutal without periodic recesses. Even entertainments like concerts and plays feature an intermission, as much for the audience as for the participants.

In the workplace people perform better when they have periodic breaks built into the day. Studies have shown that productivity and safety are substantially improved when workers have a pause in their routine. Let's explore this often neglected world of leisure and time-outs.

Leisure

There is no sound more beautiful than the spontaneous laugh of a child. It ranks right up there with Beethoven and Mozart! As children, most of us spent our days in laughter and play. I once heard a humor expert say that the average four-year-old laughs once every four minutes. However, as adults, many of us have stopped laughing and playing—or, even worse, have forgotten *how* to play and have fun. Why? Where did so many adults go off the track and become so serious?

Leisure should be the easiest thing in the world to sell to people. Rest, relaxation, having fun—what can be bad? Yet, in my work, I struggle to convince people to be good to themselves. The work ethic, guilt, and a belief that leisure is selfish or hedonistic conspire to keep people from enjoying themselves. This attitude is costly in two ways. Since it removes a major antidote to stress, it is short-sighted and dangerous. Second, it eliminates much of the joy of life, which is its own tragedy. At the very time when relaxation and diversion are most needed to neutralize the pressure of everyday life, people are getting *less* of it. And the effects of this increasing imbalance are visible everywhere—in the frantic pace of life, in people's rude and angry behavior, in relationship and family breakdown and in substance abuse.

What Is "Leisure"?

I always thought the word meant rest and relaxation. I was surprised and delighted to learn from the dictionary that it means "permission." It comes from the Latin root "licere," which is the root of the word "license" (which means "to be permitted"). The dictionary defines leisure with such words as "freedom, opportunity, unoccupied time, spare time, with no hurry." Anything done out of freedom and choice, anything done without pressure or haste, is a leisure activity.

What activities does leisure include? The list is as long as your imagination, but I have divided it into a number of categories: Relaxation, Recreation, Exercise, Hobbies, Entertainment, Socializing, Personal Development, and Fun and Play.

Relaxation includes reading, sitting by a lake, meditation, daydreaming, listening to music.

Recreation includes gardening, taking a leisurely stroll, playing catch, playing bridge, playing the piano or guitar.

Exercise includes walking, running, bicycling, swimming, racket sports, skiing, hockey, baseball, aerobics, jazzercise.

Hobbies include woodworking, knitting, painting, collecting things, doing crossword or jigsaw puzzles.

Entertainment includes movies, theater, concerts, television, spectator sports.

Socializing includes visiting or entertaining neighbors, going out with family or friends.

Personal Development includes taking courses, learning a new skill, reading about certain subjects.

Fun and Play include social games like volleyball, charades, and board games; costume or theme parties; exploring new towns; playing with children.

If you picked one activity from each of these groups, you would have a rich and varied leisure life that would bring you hours of rest, diversion, pleasure, stimulation and the company of others.

Work-Leisure Balance

In the book *Rusting Out, Burning Out, Bowing Out* Dr. John Howard, Dr. David Cunningham and Dr. Peter Rechnitzer discuss a helpful way to monitor how much of your time you allow for leisure. I adapted this into the inventory on page 201 that I complete with each new patient. It is very instructive and I urge you to take a moment to fill it out. Begin by answering the questions about your work hours at the top of the page.

Now, think of your life as if you live in four compartments or boxes: Work, Family, Community and Yourself. Note that "Work" includes your paid job plus home chores; "Family" encompasses your nuclear family plus parents, siblings, etc.; "Community" refers to volunteer work of various kinds and "Self" involves leisure activities, exercise and things you do for yourself. What percentage of your life goes to each of these four boxes? To determine the percentages, first, count your waking hours in an average week (including the weekend). There are 168 hours in a week. Subtract the number of hours you spend in bed sleeping (from the first lifestyle inventory on pae 180). Subtract another 10 hours for day-to-day routines like getting washed, dressed, etc. The remainder is your available time.

Now estimate how much of this available time you spend in each of these four boxes. Don't just consider *time*; think also of the *effort, energy, involvement* and *intensity* that go into each of them. In other words, how much of yourself do you put into these activities? For example, I knew a secretary who said that her work felt like 75% of her life, even though she worked only 45 hours per week. In this exercise, ask yourself: "What does it *feel* like?" and take the first number that comes to your mind. What it *feels* like is more significant than what it actually *is*. Don't worry if the numbers don't add up to 100%—they probably won't. It's the relative proportions you're interested in. Also, don't fill out any of the chart by subtraction, that is, by asking "How much have I got left?" Do each column separately as if it were the first.

After filling out this chart, take a moment to reflect on the numbers. Does work consume most of your life? Is there very little under "Self"? What do you think of the balance in your numbers? How do you feel looking at your chart (surprise, frustration, sadness)?

I asked a very successful self-employed business executive to do this exercise. He said that 90% of his life was work, 5% went to family and 5% to himself. When I turned to look at him (I'd been writing on a presentation board), tears were rolling down his face. He said: "I never realized it was this bad." Only by seeing the stark numbers written down

PERSONAL LIFESTYLE INVENTORY PART II
(WHERE ARE YOU NOW?)

WORK

Regular work hours (including lunch) From _____ To_____

How much extra time do you work?

Going in early or staying late _____

Evenings at office _____

Weekends at office _____

At home (including professional reading) _____

Commuting: Hours per day _____ Method _____ Stressful?_____

Total hours per week: Regular + Overtime + Commuting _____

VACATIONS

Permitted _____ weeks per year. Taken _____ How divided? _____

Last vacation: When?_____ How long? _____

Where? _____ Restful?_____

WORK-LEISURE BALANCE

	WORK	FAMILY	COMMUNITY	SELF
ACTUAL				
Job	%	%	%	%
Home chores	%			
DESIRED				
Job	%	%	%	%
Home chores	%			

did he realize what had become of his life and how he had lost himself and his family in the process. At his last visit, five months later, he was "feeling great"—and his Work-Leisure Balance chart showed: Work 45 to 50%, Family 30% and Self 20%.

Now that you have filled out the "Actual" numbers for your life at the moment, move on to the next line and fill out the "Desired" numbers. How would you *like* it to be? Short of winning a lottery and not having to work, how would you *like* to distribute your time and energy? Don't be too practical here. Let yourself picture the best of all possible worlds. Unlike the first set of numbers, these numbers should add up to 100%. What percentage of your life would you like to devote to work? To home chores? Would you *like* to be involved in community activities? Once you've written down those three numbers, how much is left (to bring it to 100%)? Now decide how you would *like* to divide the remainder between Family and Self.

Once you've filled in the second set of numbers, you have a recipe or blueprint to follow. It provides direction for change. You'll have to do some reorganizing and make some trade-offs—but the key is to give yourself *permission* to make the changes you say you'd like. Some folks resist part two of this exercise, saying that they *have* to work, they have to take care of the house, etc. They see no element of choice. The fact is you *do* have a choice. I'm not saying you will automatically achieve your fantasy. But your life will be better balanced if you envision what you'd like, then start to make it happen. The payoff for such changes is enormous. Notice that even small shifts in the percentages can make a significant difference. For example, if your self-directed time is only 5% now, adding another 5% *doubles* your previous leisure time.

Looking Back and Looking Ahead

What are your current leisure activities? Is your list long or short? Is there a good variety? Do you have a mix of sedentary and active pursuits? Is there a balance between things you do alone and those you do with other people? Are some of the activities relaxing while others are stimulating? It's important not only to make time for leisure but to have a wide range of activities. Variety increases your flexibility and prevents you from getting bored or single-minded.

One woman listed reading, listening to music and socializing with a few friends as her only leisure activities. She concluded by saying: "I don't feel I'm doing much with my life. It's blah." Then she told me all the things she used to do. It was a great list, including painting, ceramics, playing bridge, going to concerts and theater and playing golf. She became wistful as she recalled these "forgotten pleasures" from years gone by. I didn't have to say much to encourage her to pick up some of those activities again.

Now think back to your own youth—your teens and early twenties. What did you do for fun? for relaxation? for stimulation? for diversion? How many of those things do you still do? "I call these neglected pleasures." How long is your list? Would you like to retrieve some of them? It's never too late. And the key is *permission*.

It's sad to see how many people sabotage their leisure. I always ask folks what they read. A significant number (especially the Type As) list newspapers and work-related books, hastening to add that they don't "waste" their time with fiction or other frivolous subjects. Many admit to watching television but immediately note that they watch only news programs and documentaries. In other words, their leisure pursuits have to have some "redeeming" feature to them. What a loss for these folks! They don't give themselves permission to do things for relaxation or pleasure. It all has to be "worthwhile" or "productive" according to some strict set of criteria (developed somewhere in their lives since the days they played hopscotch or traded baseball cards, and when reading comic books and movie magazines made a perfectly splendid Saturday afternoon).

It's *okay* to read, watch TV, go to movies, just for fun, entertainment and pleasure. Not every activity has to have some lofty purpose to justify it. Need a role model? Just watch kids laugh and play. They know something most "mature people" have long forgotten!

Three final comments: Make leisure a priority, not a luxury. Do something for yourself every day—preferably without guilt. And pace your leisure time. Don't overload it or make it hectic.

Where Is the Gap?

What could possibly explain the lack of leisure time in so many people's lives? Okay, maybe nutrition isn't sexy and exercise requires effort. But pleasure? Relaxation? Enjoyment? Why would folks be reluctant to embrace something so obviously pleasing?

Most people blame their lack of leisure on a lack of time or money. I think there's a more fundamental issue involved. It has to do with belief systems about leisure and the effect of two powerful words: *guilt* and *selfish*. I don't dispute that finding time for leisure is challenging in this increasingly busy world. And I don't deny that lack of money is a bleak reality for vast numbers of people. But those two barriers can be overcome or worked around if there is a will to do so. Again the operative word becomes permission.

Beliefs That Oppose Leisure

There are many limiting beliefs about leisure, but the top two are: "Work should come before pleasure" and "Other people's needs should come before my own." Both of these principles are laudable and worthy. The world would be a better place if more people shared them. I am not opposed to these philosophies per se, and I subscribe to the work ethic. However, when taken to extremes, these two premises lead to problems. It is better to aim for moderation and balance.

Another belief that limits leisure time relates to self-esteem. Some people don't make time for themselves because they believe "I'm not worth it" or "I don't deserve to have fun." My reply is that if you treat yourself as if you are a worthwhile person, you will start to feel like a worthwhile person. Making time for leisure and being good to yourself (even if done mechanically at first) are excellent ways of improving self-esteem.

Other limiting beliefs include the following quotes from patients: "Work is the only thing that counts. Everything else is irresponsible or goofing off"; "All spare time has to be used *productively*"; "Leisure is a waste of time"; "Leisure is for people with money"; "You must always be busy"; "I feel like I'm avoiding my responsibilities if I just do what I want for myself"; "If I have too much leisure, how do I justify my existence?"; and two extreme examples: "Having fun is bad" and "It's not okay to have fun."

Pressure from Others

One woman is told constantly by her mother that reading is "doing nothing" and she should be using her time more "productively." A man told me he can't relax when he wants because his wife nags and undermines him. Her message is: "Everything has to be done for a purpose, a meaning; sitting around or watching TV is a total waste of time." He says she is equally hard on herself and their children. The antidote to pressure from other people is twofold: (1) Resist, hold your ground and assert your right to control the use of your own time. (2) Raise their consciousness about the importance of leisure and the benefits *they* would get from it.

Time-Outs

Leisure offers a great respite from the treadmill. I often tell people that "if you don't sit down, you're going to *fall* down." Nobody can go on interminably. You're going to have to take a rest one way or another, whether it's a *break* (that you choose) or a *breakdown*.

> *The time to relax is when you don't have time for it.*
> SYDNEY J. HARRIS

As the Human Function Curve in Chapter 3 illustrates, after a certain point (beyond "The Hump") increased effort becomes counterproductive and is often the wrong thing to do. Much better to take a break, recharge your batteries and come back to the task feeling fresh and with a clear mind.

Three Kinds of "Time-Outs"

I define three kinds of "time-outs" based on their duration:

> *I don't care if you're loafing. Everybody gets tired. If you feel stale, get some fresh air. But don't let me catch you jumping back to your desks.*
> WALT DISNEY'S INSTRUCTIONS TO HIS ANIMATORS

Maximum (Maxi) time-outs, called "holidays" or "vacations," usually last a week or more (but at least four or five days).

Intermediate (Midi) time-outs can be anywhere from a few hours to a whole day.

Minimum (Mini) time-outs last from a few minutes to an hour or two.

Maxi Time-Outs (Holidays and Vacations)

When I was a kid, my father ran a large dental lab. It was an extremely stressful job, yet he took only two weeks' vacation every year (and he was the boss). Now a days no one would blink if he had taken off four to six weeks each year. I don't know how he kept going, spending fifty weeks a year in that pressure cooker. I know it cost him dearly in physical and emotional terms.

I am astonished when people tell me they don't take their full allotment of paid holidays each year. As a self-employed professional, I don't get paid vacation time. But it would never occur to me to stop taking holidays. I function well with regular breaks. I couldn't function at all without them.

A false sense of economy dominates some people's thinking. Anyone who works fee for service (mostly professionals) or on commission might feel they can't afford to go away because of the lost income. A financial adviser, Fred Meredith, gave an interesting presentation to a group of doctors years ago. He began by noting that business owners have to invest in their business assets. If you are self-employed, your most important asset is *yourself* and you'd be foolish not to invest accordingly. After all, if anything happens to you, who is going to generate revenue in your absence? Regular holidays are one of the best investments you can make in yourself and they pay big dividends.

Meredith noted another way in which cutting back on holiday time is a false economy. He described a 1970s study of doctors who were taking fewer vacations because of financial pressures from runaway inflation. Physicians were matched up according to practice size, average patient load, income, etc. Then they were divided into two groups: those taking four weeks off per year and those taking only two weeks off. Surprisingly, the doctors working fifty weeks a year didn't see any more patients or make any more money than their colleagues who worked only forty-eight weeks per year. To make sense of this, refer back to the Human Function Curve. Those who took more holidays came back to work fresh and rested (on the "Good Stress" side of the curve, probably in the "Comfort Zone"). Then they worked more efficiently and saw more patients, thus earning back the money lost while they were on holiday. The doctors who worked fifty weeks spent more of those weeks on the "Distress" side of the curve, where they had less energy, had poorer concentration and were less decisive. As a result, they worked slower and were less productive than they realized. This led one doctor to declare: "I could never accomplish in twelve months what I can get done in eleven!"

My first rule about holidays is: *take them.* Take all you're given. And if you're self-employed, give them to yourself. Some enlightened companies *make* their workers take holidays because they know it's better for the employees *and* the company to do so. When baseball managers give their pitchers three or four days' rest between games, they're not being benevolent. They just know from experience how long it takes the human arm to recover after pitching a game. I believe that holidays are necessities and that the more hectic your life is, the more you need them to function well and stay healthy.

My second rule about holidays is: *take them on a regular basis.* In other words, spread them out. If you get two weeks a year, don't take them consecutively. I can only imagine how my father felt after his two wonderful August weeks at the cottage, only to return to fifty weeks of work before his next vacation. By spacing them out, you get shorter but more frequent breaks. I take off four weeks a year, one week every three months. On my return from a vacation, I book the next one. As a result, I always feel there's another holiday coming up just over the next horizon and the three months seem to zip by.

My third vacation rule is: *take your holidays before you need them. Then you'll never need them*—you'll just *enjoy* them. A lady once described an expensive holiday to me. She and her husband both had stressful jobs and they hadn't had any time off in eight months. Finally near exhaustion, they booked a week on a Caribbean island. Arriving at their posh hotel, they collapsed into bed and virtually stayed there for five days while they caught up on their sleep. (I tried to detect a twinkle in her eye but apparently sex was not part of their recovery.) On the sixth day they emerged into the sunlight, saw what great scenery and activities they were missing and spent two days lapping up some rays and enjoying the cuisine. They were just getting into things when it was time to fly home and rejoin the rat race.

You could call this a "recuperation" or "convalescence," but it certainly isn't my idea of a vacation. It's also an expensive way to get some sleep! If you wait until you *need* a vacation, you're waiting too long. You'll spend most of the time just recovering from your distress and exhaustion. Whereas if you space your holidays and take them before you need them, you'll use only a day or two to wind down and then you'll have the rest of the time to enjoy yourself.

Midi Time-Outs

In baseball, when pitchers start to get tired, you expect the manager to take them out of the game. But when business executives, professionals and other workers get tired, they think nothing of pushing on anyway, toiling into the evening and weekend even though their energy and efficiency are low. What makes sense in a ball game makes equally good sense in the workplace. Pace yourself and take the time-outs you need.

What can you do when you're working ineffectively or feeling distressed but can't get away for a full-fledged holiday? The "intermediate" time-out might be just the thing. A mental health day, knocking off work at noon, going away for a weekend or even taking a long weekend can do wonders when things are piling up on you.

Mini Time-Outs

As important as holidays and intermediate diversions are in your life, the significance of very short time-outs should not be overlooked. A friend of mine calls them "snap-shot vacations." These are the breaks you can take several times during a busy day that enhance your performance and sense of well-being, yet cost virtually nothing. These breaks can be as short as five or ten minutes, or as long as two or three hours. They can involve a physical diversion (where you actually get up and go somewhere else) or just a mental distraction (where you shift your attention or put your mind into "neutral" without ever leaving your office or home).

Whether it's a hot bath, lunch with a friend, a walk by the lake or a few minutes of laughter with a co-worker, mini time-outs can lift you momentarily out of a stressful situation and give you a much-needed respite from tension. They can be described as "quiet time," "alone time," "decompression time" or "winding-down time." You can also use short "time-outs" as part of a reward system between units of work. When I was studying, I'd treat myself to a refrigerator break or a half-hour of playing baseball whenever I'd finish a chapter. A homemaker might read for half an hour or take a short walk. A busy executive could put earphones on and listen to music or chat with a friend on the phone.

Playing the piano or doing a crossword puzzle can provide a similar benefit.

In summary, the need for breaks and time-outs is well understood in sports, and no one questions their validity. But in everyday life, far too many people ignore this basic principle and somehow think they can perform effectively on a non-stop basis. Leisure is an essential part of a balanced and healthy life. It's also an obvious source of pleasure. Whether your leisure is in short, intermediate or long durations, it's time to make the time! And a mix of all three time frames is best. Remember that leisure literally means permission—and giving yourself that license is the key to inviting leisure back into your life.

CHAPTER SIXTEEN

Choosing Your Behavior

WORKAHOLICS, OVERACHIEVERS, PERFECTIONISTS, Type As, Pleasers, Caretakers and Victims have one thing in common: their behavior often doesn't bring them what they want, or at best it does so with negative trade-offs that make the game not worth playing. What makes people push themselves so hard, often hurting others as well? Why do folks let others walk all over them or take them for granted? It may be that they are unconsciously copying their parents' behavior. I often ask patients who they take after in their family and they can usually tell me. Or they might be perpetuating learned behavior that was once appropriate but isn't working anymore.

But there is another thread that links all these self-defeating, counterproductive ways of behaving. I think all these behavior patterns (except the Victim role, which produces different benefits) are attempts people make to feel better about themselves. To explain this premise, and why I think these measures are usually futile, I'd like to briefly explore the concept of self-esteem.

Self-esteem refers to how good you feel about yourself. It includes things like self-confidence, self-respect, security and feeling worthwhile as a person. Surprisingly few people have a consistently high level of self-esteem. And they are frequently not the ones you'd expect. They're often unassuming and modest, having no need to impress others or to be the center of attention.

Self-esteem fluctuates. It isn't fixed or static. Even the most self-assured person will feel insecure in certain circumstances. Similarly, low self-esteem people will sometimes feel quite pleased with themselves.

Sources of Self-Esteem

There are many sources of self-esteem. I am going to focus on five.

Feedback from Others: From infancy, every person sees a reflection of himself or herself in other people. What they tell you about yourself and how they treat you serve as a mirror of your worth as a person. If you were told that you were "a bad girl" or "a selfish little boy," you didn't argue with that assessment. You accepted it as the truth about yourself. If someone told you (at age three or four) that "you always get in the way" or "you never do anything right," you didn't disagree. Instead, the message became part of the internal picture you were building about yourself. Conversely, if the messages were positive they were also taken to be accurate. Phrases like "You're so pretty" or "Aren't you helpful" made you feel worthwhile and helped build a positive self-image.

Non-verbal messages also had an impact. How you were treated conveyed information about yourself. If you were handled gently, cuddled and spoken to softly, you felt loved, cared for and secure—in other words, valued. But if you were treated roughly, spoken to harshly—or neglected and ignored—you began to feel there was something wrong with you.

Such childhood experiences as being picked on in the school-yard, complimented by a teacher, chosen last for basketball, invited to a party, put down by a friend, asked to dance or refused for a date have an impact on the way you look at yourself and whether you like yourself or not. But major or traumatic *early* events have a more profound effect. Abuse from parents (physical and/or emotional) not only leaves bitter memories and emotional scars, it also devastates self-esteem. Sexual abuse in childhood leaves people feeling humiliated, guilty and ashamed. Growing up in a dysfunctional family can make children feel different from others, embarrassed and not as good as their friends.

The early messages have the greatest impact because they come at the most impressionable age when there is no ego strength to refute the information. But the process continues throughout life. The people who influence you include parents, siblings, family, teachers, friends, peers, colleagues, employers, supervisors, lovers, spouses, etc. It's a never-ending phenomenon. Messages from the past mix in your subconscious computer with recent and current bits of information and influence how you feel about yourself.

Messages from Yourself: Negative "self-talk" has an adverse impact on self-esteem. Especially when the messages are cruel or vicious, self-esteem can be brutally affected. A dramatic example comes from a woman who would say to herself: "You're fat and ugly and worthless" whenever anything went wrong in her life.

Achievements: Your accomplishments and successes also influence how you feel about yourself. Doing well in school, sports, business or other endeavors boosts self-esteem not just if others compliment you, but because *you* are pleased with what you've done. In early years, successes included learning to tell time, tying your shoelaces and riding a bicycle. Later it was having the biggest paper route or mastering the latest dance step. Then top marks in school, proficiency in music or winning an award made you feel good about yourself. In adult years, college degrees, job promotions or organizing community events might be the things you value.

Body Image and Appearance: An important source of self-worth is how you feel about your physical self. This includes height, weight, complexion, hair (amount, color, style), glasses, muscles, bust size, shape and size of ears and nose, scars, etc. All have a bearing on your feeling of attractiveness—which in turn affects your self-esteem.

Possessions: Notice the pride a child has in showing off his new toy or spiffy wristwatch and you realize that things people *own* can make them feel good about themselves. For kids, it's things like a new bicycle or a designer sweatshirt that can set them aglow. Later, the emphasis expands to include clothes, cars, houses, jewelry, art work, adult "toys" (for example, a sailboat or a home entertainment system) and even money. People enjoy their material belongings—not only to show off to others but to admire themselves. A woman told me that when she was a child and felt upset or not good about herself, she would list every possession she owned in order to feel more worthwhile. This is a classic example of the connection between possessions and self-esteem.

Where Are the Traps?

All these factors influence your self-esteem. No matter who you are, feedback from others and your achievements, body image and possessions affect how you feel about yourself. However, it is up to you whether they do so in a balanced, healthy way or in an excessive, problematic way. It is entirely reasonable to enjoy stroking and compliments from others. Similarly, it is understandable to be hurt by criticism or insults. However, if you place a disproportionate value on feedback from others, you set yourself up for trouble. By giving power and control to other people you become vulnerable to them. They can even learn to manipulate you by playing on this ("If you don't do this for me, I'll be very disappointed in you"—that is, I won't like you).

A second problem with feedback from others is that it can be inaccurate. I have a friend who was told by his high school principal that he shouldn't even consider applying to university—he wasn't college material. It's a good thing he didn't listen. He graduated from medical school with honors.

Another drawback of excessive desire for approval is that it can turn you into a Pleaser—with all the disadvantages of this behavior. When you're driven by the need for compliments and applause, you do things you don't want to do, put others ahead of yourself, neglect your own needs and so on. If people manipulate and exploit you enough, you might start feeling and behaving like a Victim.

Thus there are several traps in placing too much emphasis on feedback from people. It's like putting all your self-esteem eggs in one basket. You would do better to simply enjoy the compliments and approval of others without trying too hard to curry favor or making them too important to you.

What if your self-esteem is based predominantly on achievements? There is a trap here, too, that leads to problems. For one thing, it puts you on a treadmill of having to keep achieving to feel worthwhile—the Overachiever or Workaholic syndrome. This treadmill leads to overwork and eventual exhaustion. Worse, the glow from achievements doesn't last very long. As tennis champ Chris Evert observed: "The thrill of victory lasts about an hour." It's as if your internal judge keeps asking: "So what have you done for me *lately*?" If the *standards* of achievement are more important than their *number*, perfectionism can result. If the drive to achieve is number-based, Type-A behavior results with its competitiveness and sense of time urgency (to achieve more and more in less time). You keep pushing yourself to score successes that will prove your self-worth.

There is another reason this quest is futile. Meyer Friedman used this formula (from the eminent American philosopher and psychologist William James) in his second book, *Treating Type A Behavior and Your Heart.*

$$\text{Self-Esteem} = \frac{\text{Achievements}}{\text{Expectations}}$$

This equation shows that self-esteem increases as achievements increase, but *decreases* as expectations increase. So self-esteem is influenced by how well you do *relative to* what you expect from yourself. If your accomplishments are considerable, your self-esteem will get a boost. But if your expectations are even greater than your achievements, your self-esteem may actually diminish. Workaholics, Overachievers, Perfectionists and Type As have such lofty expectations that their achievements never meet these idealized standards. They keep piling up more and more successes to make themselves feel good. But they're doomed to frustration and disappointment because they've set the limit (for what would please them) too high. The solution is not to keep trying to achieve more, but to expect less. Again the element of choice can turn a losing game into a winning one.

A variation of this trap is what a patient of mine calls "the ever-moving goal-post." You set realistic goals, but just as you're about to achieve them, you extend the goals or set new ones beyond the first. The result is that you're never satisfied; your performance is never good enough because you set it up that way.

Making self-esteem contingent on your body image leads to many problems. First, there are aspects of your appearance that you can't change (height being the most obvious). Second, you can become obsessed with appearance, which becomes vanity. Third, bodies change with age, whether you like it or not. Fourth, people who place too much stock in their looks become insecure. They fear people will value them only for their appearance and fret over the possible loss of their beauty. In addition, it can lead to dramatic, expensive or unhealthy measures like extreme dieting, sun-tanning, body-building, plastic surgery, implants and other attempts to reverse the cards you were dealt by nature.

The fourth trap is choosing to let your self-esteem depend on your possessions. This puts you on a treadmill of needing to *acquire* things to feel good about yourself (which can get pretty expensive, especially if you've got champagne taste and an apple juice income). Another problem is that possessions are perishable—you could lose them. Economic reversals have toppled even multimillionaires. It's risky to put your self-esteem on such an unstable foundation. Then there's the question of your value system. A lot of people find materialism to be superficial and shallow and wouldn't want to adopt that mind-set in the first place.

And lastly, the ultimate question: How much is enough? As one man put it: "How many successes do you need before you know you're a success?" At what point can you sit back and say: "I've done enough and have enough to feel good about myself"? For many people, judging by their endless struggle for more and more, the answer seems to be "never." It's like a race that has no finish line except when you drop from exhaustion.

The sources of self-esteem discussed here are not damaging in themselves. It's appropriate to enjoy being praised by others. It's fine to set goals and achieve them—and to feel satisfaction when you do. It's healthy to keep fit and attend to your appearance. And it's okay to enjoy your car or take pride in nice clothes. The trap is when your self-esteem becomes tied too closely to these things. Then the quest for approval, achievements, attractiveness and acquisitions becomes a dangerous force in your life.

Financial advisers say the key word in managing investments is "diversify." Don't put all your money in the stock market or real estate or GICs. Spread it around to hedge your bets. The same could be said about self-esteem. Invest your time and energy in several areas—including work, family, friends, community and yourself.

Self-Validation: The Key to Self-Esteem

There is a source of self-esteem that is better than all the others. Self-validation means that *you* value *yourself*. You give *yourself* the positive feedback instead of needing to hear it from others. It refers to liking yourself for who you *are*, not for what you *do* or how you *look* or how much you *own*. You learn to be happy with who you are. There is an inner contentment that says you are a good and worthwhile person, and you don't require a continual struggle to prove it.

Everyone has the capacity to generate this feeling in themselves. Among the many ways to improve your opinion of yourself that can be learned and practiced are the following:

What You Tell Yourself: Since negative self-talk and negative comments from others undermine your self-worth, the natural antidote is positive self-talk. Words of encouragement, like "You can do it" and "Good for you," give a boost to your confidence. Self-compliments such as "Hey, you look great today" or "That was a really nice thing you just did" are self-enhancing ways to talk to yourself. It's not difficult to do, although it might feel awkward at first. After a while it will become a habit. If you're not sure what to say or how to word it, think of what you'd say to someone else—or what you'd like to hear from a friend—and use those words. For some people this whole notion sounds conceited and self-centered. But a few well-placed words of appreciation are nothing more than a courteous gift you give yourself. And as you feel more deserving, the compliments will come more naturally. One man did a very resourceful thing at work. He was getting no appreciation from his supervisor, so before going home each night, he wrote down three things he'd done well that day—"to give myself the pats on the back I *don't* get from my boss."

How You Treat Yourself: This refers mostly to lifestyle habits. If you treat yourself with abuse or neglect, your self-esteem will diminish. But if you treat yourself *as if* you are a worthwhile person, you will start to *feel* like a worthwhile person. This could be called self-care or self-nurturing. Simple things like eating properly, getting enough sleep and regular exercise help you feel better about yourself. Making time for leisure is especially beneficial. Whether it's a hot bath, a visit with a friend or a hobby, self-directed time makes you feel more worthwhile. Getting your hair done, dressing nicely (which does not mean expensively) or giving yourself a treat (like a manicure or a massage) are other ways of respecting yourself. These measures do not have to be extravagant or self-indulgent—just simple acts of kindness and consideration that, over time, have a positive impact on your self-esteem.

How You Behave: Certain kinds of behavior enhance self-esteem. One of these is *assertiveness*. Being assertive means speaking up for yourself in a way that does not attack or offend the person you're talking to. It helps you feel more in control of your life and better about yourself. Another aspect of assertiveness is telling people what you need and expect from them. Many folks find this difficult. But remember, people aren't mind-readers. The only way they'll know what you want is if you tell them.

Self-determination is another way to increase your self-esteem. It means making your own decisions and acting on them. It also includes taking the initiative, as expressed by a woman who said: "I'm not sitting around waiting for things to happen anymore." She started to contact people she wanted to socialize with, inviting them to share activities with her. She also applied for a job she wanted even though it hadn't been advertised. Another woman started telling her husband when she was going out rather than asking his permission (which she had been doing for years). This simple act of autonomy gave her self-esteem a huge boost. Someone else was delighted to realize: "I can *make* things happen. I don't have to *react* all the time." Giving yourself permission to do what you want is a cornerstone of healthy self-esteem. It means *you* are in control of your life. For Pleasers and Caretakers, this includes doing more "want to's" and fewer "shoulds" so your life has a balance between pleasure and duty. Once you get past the initial guilt, you'll feel wonderful about your newly claimed freedom.

Developing *self-reliance* also improves self-esteem. Some folks never buy clothes without asking other people's opinion. They might ask their spouse, a friend or even a stranger in the store—"Do you think I should buy this?"; "How does this look?"; etc. They just don't trust their own taste. The message they give themselves is: "Your opinion doesn't count for much. I don't trust your judgment." These are hardly messages to enhance self-esteem. Self-reliance is developed when you learn to trust yourself or, at least, when you're prepared to take measured risks and live with the consequences. Start to develop your confidence in areas like shopping or choosing a holiday spot. Obviously, big expenditures like buying a car or house still warrant getting expert advice. Another place to learn self-reliance is minor home repairs. Taking on small challenges and learning to do things for yourself increase both competence and self-trust.

An aspect of self-reliance that I consider crucial is having your own bank account. Even if it doesn't mean you're financially independent (who is these days?), having some money that is yours alone and for which you are accountable to no one else is a symbolic act of autonomy. I encounter many couples in which one spouse controls the family funds. Some of them dole out an "allowance" or money for specific items to their partner, monitoring their expenditures and editorializing about certain purchases. I know adults who even have to ask for money to buy a ten-dollar item. This puts them in a one-down position that demeans their self-worth. They feel dependent and incompetent to make their own choices. This is an unsupportable position to put yourself in. Some measure of fiscal autonomy is vital in building self-esteem.

Self-reliance includes responsibility for your own happiness— not depending on other people to *make* you happy. Here is the story of the wife of a Workaholic. For years, she resented his long absences and lack of involvement when he was home. She felt angry and cheated. He was a charismatic guy whom she loved being around. He took the lead in all their activities. In fact, he had become her entertainment committee, the guy who pulled her out of her shyness, made things happen and kept her amused. She relied on him to bring color and vitality to her life. In discussing this, she realized she had depended on people to make her happy all her life. She'd never learned to generate her own enjoyment and, in fact, didn't like her own company very much.

This woman decided she had to do something. She initiated pleasurable activities for herself—gardening, aerobics, guitar lessons. She visited a friend in another town and arranged for a sunporch to be built for her reading and sewing. She started taking responsibility for her own satisfaction and fun. Not only did this increase her enjoyment but it did wonders for her self-esteem.

When people emerge from a lifetime of dependence and low self-esteem, a glow develops in them that is almost palpable. They look different, they talk differently, they radiate an air of confidence that is wonderful to observe. Rarely does this come across as conceit or arrogance. It is a quiet, modest feeling. Anyone who is afraid that building her self-esteem will make her "too full of herself" or "hard to live with" has nothing to fear. Comments from people who emerged butterfly-like from their cocoons include: "I *like* this person I've become," "I'm getting happier with myself and who I am—I'm not trying to emulate others anymore," "I think I can go wherever I want now. I'm getting control of my life" and "I'm more comfortable with myself."

Choosing Behavior That Leads to a Winning Game

After years of talking to Workaholics, Type As, Pleasers, et al., I believe that their patterns of behaving are actually strategies (conscious or unconscious) to increase self-esteem—and as such, they're usually futile and costly. At one time these behavior styles probably made them feel better about themselves. But the benefits didn't last and the negative consequences increased. Now I'd like to suggest some specific behavior changes to turn these losing games around.

For Workaholics, Type As and Overachievers, the first step to meaningful change is to recognize the futility of your present behavior. Stop and ask yourself *why* are you pushing yourself so hard? What goal or reward are you seeking? When do you think you will achieve it? (And if you do, will you stop and get out of the rat race?) Who are you doing this for? Whose agenda are you following? Are you getting much joy out of your struggle?

The second step is to ask yourself what you need for a good quality of life. So many people pursue *quantity* (of money, achievements, possessions, etc.) without asking whether these things will really enhance the *quality* of their lives. More is *not* better. When it comes to money, remember that *there's no sense making a good living if it doesn't result in your having a good life.*

I know a self-made millionaire who lost his fortune and had to sell his magnificent home. He told me with great sadness that, in the years he lived in that house, he was so busy working he never once swam in his own swimming pool—even though the pool had been one of his main reasons for buying the house. Rabbi Harold Kushner wrote an excellent book called *When All You've Ever Wanted Isn't Enough*, noting the futility of seeking happiness in the wrong places and exploring the ingredients of "a life that matters."

The third step is to cut back on your work time. Some people can do this in a quantum leap. I have seen several Workaholics break their overwork-fatigue-inefficiency cycle in one step. One woman was putting in sixty hours a week, many of which were in the evening and not even paid as overtime. She felt no one else in the office could do her job. During one of her visits with me, I looked out the window at a beautiful summer afternoon—knowing that she was planning to work that evening. I gave her a conspiratorial smile and said: "I've got an idea. For the next two weeks, why don't you just work nine to five and see what it's like? The weather's beautiful, the days are long. Why don't you just enjoy yourself?" Her knee-jerk reaction was resistance. She had too much work to do. And yet the idea appealed to her. After wavering half-heartedly, she agreed.

Two weeks later she bounced into my office with a tan, a spring in her step and a smile the room could barely contain. She reported that the two weeks had been wonderful—liberating, relaxing and fun. She'd cut her weekly hours from sixty to forty and felt like she was on vacation. But the clincher came when she noted that, contrary to her expectation, the work had not piled up around her. She had *not* fallen behind as she'd feared. I used the Human Function Curve in Chapter 3 to show her why. By working in the "Comfort Zone" instead of being close to exhaustion, she markedly improved her productivity and she performed her chores in considerably less time. She became a convert after that, staying only the odd evening to attend a meeting or deal with a crisis. Most days she left at a reasonable time, reclaiming the leisure time she had sacrificed for so many years.

Emboldened by her success, I suggested this experiment to several other people (usually in the summer, when the idea was most appealing). They all had the same result and couldn't quite believe it at first. One professional man, who was working evenings and weekends, agreed to cut ten hours from his work week. He reported, with some amazement, that he was not only getting all his work done in fewer hours, but was actually getting *more* done than before. He was also rediscovering forgotten pleasures like reading, going for walks and being with his family and friends.

You may not feel you can reduce your work hours this quickly. A gradual approach might be easier to implement. Decrease your work week by five hours at first (an hour a day). Go in later and/or leave earlier. If you usually take work home with you, that might be the best place to start. Leave both your briefcase and your thoughts about work at the office. After a few weeks, reassess your situation and shave another five hours from your weekly schedule. Continue until you have found a balance that feels good for you. There is no correct number of work hours that suits everyone. It's a process of trial and error. My own philosophy is that work should not exceed fifty hours in an average week. But there is room for flexibility during peak times (accountants at tax season, teachers marking exams, retailers at Christmas, etc.), and nothing has to be carved in stone.

As you free up more of your work time, the next step is to develop interests and pursuits that give you pleasure, relaxation and satisfaction. In addition to leisure activities, rediscover the people in your life you've been neglecting. Start with your family. Get to know your kids, their interests and their friends. Linger by their bedside at night and watch them sleep for a moment or two. Let a soft feeling come over you, and realize how lucky you are to have these children. Allow that feeling to remind you of what you were missing on the job. Get reacquainted with your partner. Plan time together, outings, weekends away or moments to just chat in the evening. Remind yourself of why you chose to be with this person in the first place. Expand your rediscovery to your parents, siblings and extended family.

Make time also for friends you haven't seen in a while. Several times a year I have dinner with a group of men I grew up with, guys I've been friends with since age twelve. Not only do we laugh a lot, but there is a warmth and camaraderie that makes time stand still. We usually don't talk about our present activities or achievements. Most of the chatter is about the old days, our teachers, our exploits, our memories. We have no need to impress each other. We know one another too well for that. We just enjoy being together. It reminds us of our roots and what was important when we were kids: companionship, being accepted for who we are, trust, shared laughter. Not bad things to cherish. Friendship is one of the most valuable yet neglected aspects of our modern, fast-paced lifestyle. It is a value worth restoring to your life.

Overcoming Type-A behavior can be a complex task but here are some suggestions that I have found helpful. The main message is to *slow down.*

- Avoid trying to do too many things in a given time frame (shorten your "To Do" lists).

- Leave realistic time frames for doing things (especially for travel between activities or errands).

- Carry a book or magazine so that, if you arrive early, the extra time will feel like a bonus (for reading) rather than a frustration. It also decreases your impatience when there's a delay or you have to wait for someone.

- If you're standing in a lineup, occasionally force yourself to do nothing but observe people, relax or chat with someone—just to practice being patient without having steam come out of your ears.

- Take your watch off on weekends and vacations. It's hard to indulge your sense of urgency when you have no way to measure the time.

- Use cruise control on highways—set at the prevailing speed limit. It helps you relax (instead of driving aggressively to save time).

- Practice driving in the middle or even right-hand lane instead of the passing lane. Don't switch lanes to gain a few seconds.

- At stop lights, resist the temptation to look at the cross signal. Do some relaxation breathing or look around rather than impatiently waiting for the light to turn green.

- Take up walking to increase your patience. You might find it tame at first, but gradually you will learn to enjoy the slower pace.

- Resist the temptation to do two things at once. Pick the activity you prefer and concentrate on it exclusively.

- Keep reminding yourself that faster and more are not necessarily better.

- Go through your books, magazines, music albums and CDs and other collectibles. Admit to yourself that you aren't reading, listening to or looking at all the stuff you've collected.

- Ask yourself why you are gathering artifacts you don't make time to enjoy. Then acquire only things you plan to use. Recognize that your life is not greatly enhanced by having cartons and bookshelves full of neglected "treasures" all over the house.

- Get rid of some of the accumulated items you are currently warehousing.

- Start doing things for enjoyment, not just for their "redeeming" value. Give yourself permission to read for pleasure (especially fiction) and to watch TV programs other than news and documentaries.

- Play games/sports without keeping score (e.g., rallying in tennis).

Time Management

Type A people struggle constantly with time management. Using time effectively is a powerful way to turn losing games into winning ones. Note that this does not mean cramming more into your busy day. It can be as simple as getting up earlier to avoid the mad dash for work (flying out the door with a coffee cup and a half-eaten muffin). It can be as logical as leaving earlier for appointments so you don't have to speed or arrive late, puffing and sweaty. Or it can be as practical as scheduling your day with a few empty spaces—buffer zones for catch-up or relaxation. It's astonishing that in an age of high-tech labor-saving devices, people seem to have less leisure time than ever before. The race against time seems to be a national pastime, with more and more people losing. It's time to stop and take stock.

Pacing is one of the buzzwords of time management. A hardworking businessman told me: "I don't know my limits. I believe you can always do a little more. All my life, I've extended myself to the point of exhaustion." People who try to go all out all the time learn something very quickly: they can't sustain the pace (although many don't want to admit that, so they just forge on). It's a self-punishing and grueling way to live. It reminds me of a runner starting a race without asking how long the course is. He zooms along as if it's a 100-yard dash, only to find out that it's a marathon and he's been sprinting. Some people live as if their lifespan is measured in months. They run out of juice long before they run out of time. (A few exceptional individuals live long in spite of their habits. On his 100th birthday, jazz pianist Eubie Blake said: "If I had known I was going to live this long, I would have taken better care of myself!")

Another key phrase in time management is *goals and priorities*. It is an inescapable fact that you can't do everything. So you have to decide which things are important to you and which are not. Then you should devote your time and energy to what matters most and not spend your efforts on things of lesser significance.

Given that you can't do it all, every decision to do something usually involves a decision *not* to do something else. Making such choices is an inescapable part of taking control of your time. Trade-offs are inevitable. For example, if you've decided to learn a new computer program at work, you should concentrate on that. Taking special courses, practicing and seeking advice from experts would be appropriate. This would not be the time to write an article for the in-house newsletter or volunteer to organize the next golf day. If you decide to take your kids to the museum, you tacitly elect to give up other activities that day, such as shopping or playing tennis. A good trade-off simply means you gain more than you lose. As a reformed Type A, I don't do as many things as I used to—but my stress level has never been better.

A different kind of trade-off is *exchanging money for time*. A hard-working businessman set out to paint and wallpaper several rooms in his house. He made the mistake of stripping all the wallpaper first, an onerous job that also committed him to finishing the task because now the walls looked a mess. Months went by. The walls continued to be an eyesore. He did everything possible to avoid the drudgery that awaited him. Then he rededicated himself to the project, spending several evenings a week and all weekend at it. That lasted about ten days and he quit in exhaustion and despair. I made a timid suggestion that he simply hire someone to finish the job and be done with it. Which he did. He considered the cost to be an excellent investment. What he bought for himself was time, relaxation and peace of mind. What are those things worth on the open market?

Some people drive to Florida to save money. I fly to Florida to save time. One of my patients tried to sell his house on his own ("Why should I pay a real estate agent 6%?" he asked). After several weeks of hassle and lost time—including staying home on a summer Sunday to meet a client who never showed up—he decided life was too short and hired an agent. Labor-saving devices like dishwashers are another way of trading money for time. The appliance costs several hundred dollars, but the time it saves can't even be measured. Hiring someone to cut your grass or shovel your snow is another reasonable trade-off. Obviously a line has to be drawn somewhere or you'd end up like comedian Jack Benny, whose household was run by a staff of six.

Another byword of time management is *delegate*. This is hard for some people (especially Perfectionists), but it's a skill worth learning. A colleague told me his office nurse wanted to give allergy shots to his patients. She had given thousands of injections and was totally reliable. He still found it difficult to delegate this task—even though *she* had asked *him*. He finally agreed. Within a week, he was wondering why it had taken him so long.

One thing about delegating is that you have to give up some control. For certain people that's a tough thing to do. One man told me how he delegated. He assigned jobs to his staff and then hovered endlessly, checking to see that things were done properly and on time. He lost more time than he saved—and he fretted a lot more too.

Here are some guidelines for delegating:

- Pick the right people.

- Give clear instructions.

- Confirm understanding (of the assignment, time for completion, etc.)

- Stand back. Give them room to maneuver.

- Supervise periodically.

- Be available to advise or give feedback.

- Hold the delegates accountable for their work (quality and timeliness).

- Modify your expectations as required. Avoid perfectionism.

- Give praise often—and always say thank you.

Perfectionism

Perfectionism is another area in which people are hard on themselves and others. There are several elements involved here: the need for control, taking yourself too seriously and all-or-nothing thinking (where things are either perfect or terrible with no in-between). One of my patients was a neatness freak. He made Felix Unger (from *The Odd Couple*) look like a slob. Everything had to sit symmetrically on tables; nothing could be left lying around. One day his wife was reading the newspaper and got up to go to the bathroom. By the time she returned, he'd scooped up the paper and pitched it in the garbage. Anything left unattended was grist for his mill. Pictures were hung with a plumb line, clothes placed meticulously in drawers and cupboards. His desk was a model of order and neatness. All this compulsiveness was fine except for one thing: he was driving himself and his wife crazy.

I drew a line on my presentation board, labeling the ends as noted:

Utter Chaos ◄──────────────────────────────► Perfect Order

We then explored the range of choices between these two extremes, including states like "messy, sloppy, disorganized, lived-in, organized, orderly and neat." This was intended to break up his thinking only in extremes.

Utter ◄── Messy ── Disorganized ── Orderly ── Extremely ──► Perfect
Chaos   Neat   Order

Then I asked him "How much imperfection can you live with and still be comfortable?" He wasn't sure. To test this I asked him to leave a few things lying around the house (to break into his rigid need for control). I also suggested that he intentionally wear two different socks to work one day (to help him take himself less seriously). In both cases, he was simply to notice what happened.

He returned feeling very well and reported on his two experiments. He wore the mismatched socks and "Nothing happened." This led him to observe: "I worry too much about what I'm doing and what people think." He left some things undone at home, and again "Nothing happened." There was no guilt, anxiety, distress or even discomfort. Later, when he drifted back to some of his old habits, I suggested he use the different socks again as a metaphor for lightening up on himself. I also asked him to wear the goofiest tie he could find for the same reason. (Of course he had to borrow one. Perfectionists do not *own* goofy ties.) Again I suggested he leave a few things lying around the house. There is an interesting paradox here. People use perfectionism to exert maximal control over their environment. Yet if they *choose* to leave some things undone or in disarray, technically they're still in control and therefore relatively at ease. I asked him to keep experimenting to discover how much "imperfection" he could live with and still be comfortable. He will never be accused of being easy-going or laid-back, but at least he's no longer a fussbudget, driving himself and his wife to distraction.

Here is a rather innocuous story that turned into a pivotal experience for one of my patients. She was a self-confessed Perfectionist who prided herself on being a gourmet cook. Unfortunately, her standards were so high she was making herself nuts. Every dish had to be prepared from scratch, using basic ingredients. The soup came from stock and marrow, the salad dressing was her own mix and so on. I suspect she went personally to Brazil to pick her own coffee beans. Entertaining had become onerous and she started to dread dinner parties. Her perfectionism had taken all the joy out of feeding her guests.

Finally she said to me, eyes narrowed in a look of conspiracy, "One of these days I'd just like to serve a Sara Lee cake for dessert."

I said: "Really? When is your next dinner party?"

"A week from Saturday."

"Do you have any Sara Lee cakes at home?"

"Sure, I always keep a couple in the freezer."

"Good! Why don't you serve a Sara Lee cake next week? Without any apology, explanation or comment."

After a moment of hesitation, she smiled and said: "Okay, I will."

Two weeks later she proudly reported that she'd served the Sara Lee cake—and no one complained or commented. They all dug in and enjoyed themselves. That incident was a watershed experience. It broke through her need to be perfect and became a touchstone for her. She realized she had a *choice*, and that gave her a sense of relief and freedom. I still run into her occasionally, and every so often she leans over and whispers, with a mischievous grin: "I'm still serving Sara Lee cakes!"

This woman chose to do something less than perfectly—and it was still okay. I learned some phrases that are helpful to Perfectionists. One is "Dare to be average." Not every dinner party has to be exquisite. Another is: "When all else fails, lower your standards." Don't lower them to zero; just bring them down a notch or two so you ease up on yourself. A woman who supervised several people revised her expectations in overload situations: "People will have to get used to not finishing their work by the end of each day." A young, perfectionistic business executive kept everything in order. When he overcame his perfectionism, he noted: "It wasn't worth it anymore. It's meaningless to have everything (like the shoes in my closet) all lined up." At work, he used to be very exacting in every piece of correspondence. "Now I just say, 'That's good enough' or 'That'll do—send it out,' and I never give it another thought." Another useful maxim came from a computer operator who observed: "Nobody's perfect. We're all built on a faulty program!"

I play three musical instruments, none of them well enough to impress anyone (except my two children, who when they were young, thought I was quite talented; too bad they grew up and saw otherwise). But the important thing is that I play well enough to get great pleasure from my own music. Back in the sixties I used to play guitar and sing folk songs. We had a phrase for people who were too meticulous in tuning their instruments. If they tried to tune each string perfectly, someone would say: "It's close enough for folk-singing." I have often used that expression in other situations, like hanging a picture or lettering a sign for a garage sale: "It's close enough for folk-singing." A friend of mine delights in learning new languages. He's lived in several countries and has picked up a smattering from here and there. He loves trotting out phrases and words in these foreign tongues, even though he's never mastered any of them. He proudly proclaims: "I'm illiterate in four different languages" and he's getting a kick out of every one of them.

Pleasers/Caretakers/Victims

The 1976 movie *Network* became famous for the line "I'm mad as hell and I'm not going to take it anymore!" My advice to people who let others dominate their lives is this: "You don't have to take it anymore.

And you can change it *before* you get mad as hell." The main ways to achieve this are through assertiveness, self-reliance, self-determination and self-care. A separated woman, back in the dating game, met a man who interested her. Her previous relationships were characterized by her giving in to narcissistic men and feeling lonely and unhappy. Aware of that past record, she took a new tack. "I'm not shaping myself to please him. I'm just being myself. I know I can make people love me by doing whatever it takes and bending myself into a pretzel. But I don't want to do that anymore."

Assertiveness is an important skill for Pleasers to learn. It is especially beneficial for people who feel abused, exploited or taken for granted. Being assertive means speaking up for yourself, telling people how you feel, telling them what you want and learning to say no. It is very different from being aggressive. Let me put this on a line diagram.

Passive ←——————————————————————→ Aggressive

"Passive" connotes being a Victim, letting things happen and giving in. "Aggressive" indicates being pushy, bullying or attacking and leaving the other person feeling hurt and angry. "Assertive" is a concept that bridges the gap between these two extremes. It means speaking up for yourself without attacking others or putting them on the defensive. It is a communication that is open, honest and direct. It is polite and respectful but firm and persuasive. Now the spectrum looks like this:

Passive ←——————— Assertive ———————→ Aggressive

There are three main principles in being assertive. First, *use "I" statements* so you are talking about yourself, not the other person. If your partner doesn't share in chores around the house, instead of calling him a lazy slug or a selfish oaf you might say something like: "I don't appreciate having to do all the housework myself." That is a statement about you and one he can hardly take offense at. The second principle is to *tell the other person what you want* (or at least negotiate an arrangement agreeable to you both). Don't make him guess or read your mind. In the above example, you might say, "I'd like it if you would clean up after meals and take care of the garbage," which makes it clear that you want some specific cooperation from him. The third principle is to *tell the person how it will benefit them.* Everyone wants to know "What's in it for me?" So tell them. In addition to the fact that it's more equitable and fair, you might say: "If you share the work load with me, I'll have more time and energy for us to do things together in the evening." Now he can see a payoff and is more likely to respond favorably. Saying nothing (passive behavior) will get you nothing. Insulting him (aggressiveness) will probably alienate him or start a fight. But being assertive will get your message across and probably result in a positive outcome.

Negotiation is another important skill for Pleasers to learn. This involves finding a compromise that satisfies (or is at least acceptable to) all parties—known as the win/win solution. It requires patience, flexibility, creativity and a willingness to listen.

A lot of Pleasers and Caretakers feel guilty when they start meeting their own needs. It's helpful to put things in perspective. It's not necessary to choose between yourself and others. You can take care of yourself *as well as* other people. It's not a question of who comes first so much as making sure that everyone is attended to and no one is neglected. It's not "Me first" or "Me only," but "Me too."

There is a trap in being a Caretaker that should be noted here. Some well-meaning folks take on other people's problems. The real trouble starts when they fall into the role of rescuer and protector. This role leads to several undesirable consequences. An obvious one is the extra work and hassle they create for themselves. But another more subtle result is that the person they're helping doesn't learn to fend for himself. So helpers actually disempower the recipient, perpetuating his state of helplessness and turning him into a Victim. They end up hurting the person they want to help. As the old saying goes: "Give a man a fish and he can eat for a day. But teach him how to fish and he can feed himself for a lifetime."

Victims regularly blame others for how they feel. Their overpowering boss, their intimidating spouse, their guilt-tripping parent is responsible for them feeling wretched, angry, frightened, etc. This is not to suggest that there aren't some pretty nasty and overbearing folks out there. But Victims might ponder this message: in some way, the Victim is often in collusion with the perpetrator. The Victim in some way allows the victimization to continue—especially if it occurs over a long period of time. In fact, the abuse or exploitation can continue only with the cooperation or tacit agreement of the Victim. Every abuser needs an abusee; all dominating people need someone to be submissive. In abusive relationships (be they spousal, partner or employer-employee) there is an unspoken message that gets passed from the Victim that says: "It's okay to keep doing this to me." That message can be stopped at any time the Victim gets tired of his or her role. It is vital to recognize the element of choice.

When I bought Dr. Susan Forward's book called *Men Who Hate Women and the Women Who Love Them*, I wondered why she used such a long title. After all, the book was about misogynists. Why not just call it *Men Who Hate Women?* Upon reading the book I quickly realized that, as the expression goes, it takes two to tango. Men who hate women would all be unpleasant hermits if there weren't a roughly equal number of women who were prepared to love them and put up with their behavior. In tennis, it takes two players on opposite sides of the net to keep the ball in play (see diagram on page 232). But it takes only one player to break up the game—by simply deciding not to hit the ball back. I've used this simple analogy to encourage dozens of my patients to take control of their lives and end dominant-submissive relationships. It's not always necessary to leave the other person in a relationship, job or friendship. You just have to put an end to the offensive dynamics. This can be done with assertiveness, detachment or a simple declaration that "I don't want to do this anymore."

One woman told me how she ended the feud between her and her spouse: "I just don't return the serve anymore." In other words, when he says or does something to provoke her, she simply lets it pass without comment. When he tries to bait her, she ignores him. He can't lure her into the game anymore. Most abusive people get tired of playing the game alone. After all, you can't be a master if no one's prepared to be your servant. Another woman told me that she gathered all her courage and stood up to her husband for the first time in their marriage. Instead of backing away, she gave him a disapproving look. He immediately backed down. She did this a few more times and found him malleable, cooperative and even pleasant. She was astonished at the ease with which the power shifted in their relationship. And all without her saying a word. She simply acted differently. The non-verbal message her husband received was clear: "The jig's up. The rules have changed. Don't mess with me anymore. I don't want to dominate *you*. I just want you to stop dominating *me*." This is the goal for Victims—to take control of their own lives without trying to take control of anyone else's. To gain autonomy, not dominance.

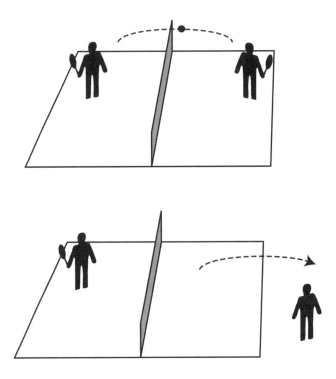

Here is a metaphor I have found helpful for Victims. Many people live as if they are locked in a room, trapped, without options. Then one day they turn the doorknob—and the door falls opens. They then realize the door wasn't locked at all. In fact, it was never locked. They just lived as if it was and wasted all the time in that room unnecessarily. They could have emerged any time they wanted. I challenge my patients who are living lives of dependency and helplessness to realize the door to autonomy and independence is not locked and *never* was locked. The only thing needed to open it is their willingness to take the initiative and to accept responsibility for the outcome. If you don't like what's happening, it doesn't help to blame others. *You* have to change it. It's not as easy as playing it safe, but the prospects are considerably better.

In summary, there are several kinds of behavior that can be called losing games. Most of these are probably subconscious attempts to enhance self-esteem but they usually don't achieve that goal. In addition, they have negative side effects. The solution here is to change the losing game by choosing behavior that works better. But keep the principle of *balance* in mind. Overachievers don't have to become underachievers or sloths—just "achievers." To stop being a Pleaser doesn't mean you stop being *pleasant*. Victims need to become assertive, not aggressive. Workaholics don't have to drop out of the work force. They can be conscientious and diligent, but they should stop taking it to extremes. Type As won't become laid-back Type Bs, floating around in the Lotus Land of Life. But they can ease up and slow down, becoming "A minuses" so to speak. All of these adjustments represent a compromise, a balancing out of previously extreme and dysfunctional behavior.

For those who have made the transition, the payoffs are great— a much improved quality of life, a higher feeling of control and self-esteem and an easier day-to-day existence most of them never imagined possible. And all at a price that is quite affordable: the willingness to give up what isn't working and the courage to try something new.

CHAPTER SEVENTEEN

You're Not Alone—The Need for a Support System

A NEW PATIENT CAME TO SEE ME for stress counseling. He was so agitated he could barely sit in his chair. He talked fast, non-stop, for almost an hour. It was as if a dam had ruptured and everything was rushing out at once. This chap had shared so little about himself, had kept so much in for so long, that even his wife didn't know how many siblings he had. Now it was all coming out in a torrent of words and emotions. I just sat and listened. Occasionally he'd say something like "I can't believe I'm saying all this to a total stranger," or "I've never talked this much in my life." At the end of the session he got up smiling, grabbed my hand and thanked me for all my help. I'd said almost nothing.

No man is an island entire of itself.

JOHN DONNE

Here's another story. A patient I'd known for years called me in early December to tell me about her depression. She was waking up in the night, not eating, isolating herself—the same symptoms she'd developed at the same time the previous year. We had an appointment already set up for the next week. At her visit nine days later she said, "I felt better almost immediately after our phone call. Acknowledging it and getting clear about what was happening made it dissipate—like 'Oh, that's what it is, I'll just ride it out.' I started talking to other people and found a lot of people have the same problem this time of year."

No matter what accomplishments you make, somebody helps you.

ALTHEA GIBSON

There are several common themes here. One is our need to express emotions and the benefit we get from doing so. Another is the value of having someone to listen to us in an empathetic way. A third is our ability to do a lot self healing. The overall message is that we all need a support system to help us cope with difficult times. *People who suffer alone suffer a lot.* There's another expression: *A problem shared is a problem halved.*

You're Not Alone

Think of times of rapid or extensive change: after 9/11 or in the aftermath of the economic meltdown of 2008. We can help one another through periods of upheaval. This is a time for people to pull together, not stay separate. We need and benefit from the support of others—at work, at home and in our communities.

When people lose their jobs, they have a tendency to withdraw. They feel embarrassed or even ashamed. And others often avoid them. They feel uncomfortable, don't know what to say. Or maybe the pain is a little too close to home and they don't want to face up to the fact that this could be them sometime soon. A similar dynamic can occur when individuals become sick, especially if the illness is chronic or terminal. Or when people endure a terrible loss, such as the death of a child. The sufferers turn inward and the others turn away from them. This scenario of isolation and mutual discomfort is the last thing any of us needs in an emotional crisis. These are extreme examples, but they make the point: when times are tough, we need to hang together, not split apart.

Sue Johnson is a psychologist at the Ottawa Civic Hospital. She works with trauma survivors. In a radio interview she noted that when certain animals are scared, they band together for mutual protection, support and reassurance. Think of elephants, which are very intelligent animals, or puppies, or muskoxen, forming a circle, each facing outward, when they're threatened. Nature tells us there's safety—and comfort—in numbers.

In the Jewish religion there is a tradition of ritualized mourning for the dead that answers the need for people to be together in a time of grief. After the funeral, which is held as soon as possible, there is a prescribed period of deep mourning that lasts for seven days. It's called "sitting shiva" (from the Hebrew word for seven, sheva). During this time members of the immediate family gather together in one place, dispersing only at night to go to their respective homes to sleep. Extended family and friends come to visit and offer their sympathies. It is a mitzvah (Hebrew for "commandment," which has also come to mean "a good deed") to make a condolence call, to visit the mourners.

So it is built into the religion that people should be with the bereaved at times of loss to pay respects to the deceased and to give support to the mourning family. As a book about Jewish life in nineteenth-century Europe notes in its title, *Life Is with People.*

What Can a Support System Do for You?
The benefits are numerous and often wonderful.

- *Understanding, empathy, compassion and emotional support*
  Caring arms to wrap around you, an ear to listen and a shoulder to lean on—these are all things people need at times of struggle, worry, pain and loss. If you fail your exams, lose your job, go through a separation or divorce, become disabled, the nurturing presence of others helps to cushion the blow by letting you know you are not alone.

- *Encouragement and strength*
  When you face a challenge (a job interview, an important speech, a sporting event), a cheering section can give you a big boost. It builds you up to know that others have confidence in you. When I was writing my first book, I purposely told a wide array of people what I was doing. It made it more of a commitment if I announced it publicly; I knew my friends would hold me accountable by periodically asking how it was going, and keep me on track with their belief that I'd succeed. One friend said, "Good for you. Lots of people talk about writing a book. But you'll do it!" Those words came back to me many times and strengthened my resolve. Other friends sent cards, which I kept right beside my computer throughout the five year writing process. One from a colleague said, "Congratulations, David. You began your book! I hope it is a new beginning in a long line of happy experiences. I'm rooting for you." A Peanuts card from my wife said, "I know you can do it 'cause you've got the stuff, and I'm in your corner when the going gets rough!" followed by a beautiful handwritten note. And my nurse receptionist gave me a framed cartoon of a guy sitting at a word processor. The sign on the door reads, "DAVID'S BEST SELLER." It still sits on my window ledge. No one could have had a better support system.

- *Advice, suggestions, information, problem solving*
  Having a problem with your computer? Need to find a new dentist? Looking for ideas for a surprise party? Who ya gonna call (if the Ghostbusters' line is busy)? We usually ask someone we know. "Didn't Roger have this problem last year?" or "Barbara's a whiz at this stuff," or "Bob built two of those things. He'll know," or "Veronica just got back from there. Give her a call."

- *Logistical support and assistance*
  Friends of mine had their lives thrown into chaos when their son was hospitalized for two weeks after a bad hockey injury. There was upset, fear, pain and long hours at the hospital. But there was also another child to attend to, and somehow the structures of their lives had to continue without too much disruption. Meals, supervision and rides to certain activities had to be arranged. The fortnight was a nightmare as it was, but it would have been a total wipeout without the support of wonderful neighbors and friends who sprang into action and kept the home front going. And the key to activating that network was asking for help. "I called on my support network and told them what I needed. I knew we couldn't do it alone."

- *Validation*
  Family and friends let you know you're OK, that you're normal. Parents who lose their temper with their children and feel guilty feel better when they hear that it happens to everyone on occasion. It's helpful to know that other moms and dads can lose their cool and start yelling, and that it doesn't mean you're a bad parent. (I'm not talking here about abuse, which is a different matter.)

Your support system can show you that you're not the only one struggling. People who get panic attacks are often reluctant to admit it, but once they get past their embarrassment and actually talk about their experience, there's a payoff: invariably, my patients describe the relief they felt when they learned that many others have gone through the same thing. Close friends tell them, "Me too!" or "I used to get those," or "My brother-in-law went through that," and they feel an immediate sense of reassurance and affirmation, knowing that they're not weird or crazy or even that unusual. They're also very encouraged to know that it's a self-limited condition that people recover from. Sometimes hearing this from friends is more beneficial than if I (as a physician) give them the same information.

Another form of personal validation comes from knowing that even if you fail at something or behave badly, your family and friends love you anyway. It's wonderful to know that people care about you, faults and all, and that overall, you're a good and worthwhile person. To feel loved and valued in that way is a huge boost to your self-esteem. In its purest form it's called "unconditional love," and it's an amazing support to be able to lean on when you feel lousy about yourself.

- *Feedback and reality checks*
  There are times when we benefit from information we don't want to hear, and who better to give you this feedback than someone you love and trust and who loves and trusts you? This is the "even your best friends won't tell you" stuff—except that your very best friends *will* tell you. This isn't just about the need for deodorant or toothpaste. It's about how you may be putting down your kids or spouse without realizing it. Or about your drinking problem that you don't want to acknowledge and think no one else has noticed. I learned about feminism in the sixties from female relatives and friends who told me when I was being chauvinistic or obtuse. Once, when I was preoccupied about some mundane issues in my bachelor life, a friend said, "What you need is to get married and have children. Then you'd have *real* problems to worry about!" (Ouch— but I sensed she was right.)

  The fact that these messages are delivered with a smile by our dearest friends is very important. Another friend asked my permission before she gave me a blunt opinion. Her words were, "Can I be brutal?" Aside from my immediate curiosity, I knew I was safe with her. I said, "Yes, *you* can be brutal" (because I knew what she had to say would be important, and given with love and caring).

- *Social framework and interaction*
  You move to a new town or neighborhood. You don't know a soul. You're starting from scratch. You're not looking for someone to pour your heart out to, but it would be nice to have some company— someone to chat with, have over for tea or join you for a walk. As society becomes more fragmented and mobile, groups are forming to welcome strangers, and we need more of them. It might be the Newcomers' Club, an alumni chapter of your university, the brotherhood/sisterhood of your local church or synagogue, a parents' group at your child's new school, a neighborhood tennis club. If a group isn't available, you might be just the person to start one.

To Whom Do You Turn?

Most support systems start in the most fundamental unit of our society—the family. Parents, siblings, grandparents, aunts, uncles and cousins. When I was growing up, my father's brother and his family lived two houses away, and my mother's sister lived with her family across the road. It was nourishing to have so many relatives on the same block— and when tragedy struck, as it unfortunately did, the proximity of family was crucial for all of us. But changing times bring changing customs. Geographically close families are far less common, but nuclear and extended-family ties still provide the earliest and most immediate support system for most people.

Not that you can tell everything to your relatives. I heard this story of a guy in his early twenties who started staying out at night, sometimes all night. His mother inquired about his whereabouts but he dodged her questions.

"Tell me where you go at night," she said.

"I'd rather not."

"Tell me. I'm your parent. I want to know."

"You don't want to know."

"Yes, I do. Tell me."

"OK, Ma, I sleep with women."

"This you would tell your *mother*??!!"

Next come friends. Often closer than family, friends can become soul mates with whom you can share anything. And mutual trust is established because they share everything with you. Over time, a trusted teacher, older family friend, family doctor or neighbor may form part of your support system. Later, lovers and spouses are the ones we feel able to open up to. In the workplace, colleagues and co-workers can also fill the role of pal and confidant. And finally, on occasion, we may need to seek out professional help — a therapist of some sort, what a colleague of mine calls "renting a friend." This is when you find a trained counselor to confide in and with whom to work out problems.

Sometimes the support comes not from individuals but from groups. Fraternities and sororities in your student days, book clubs or study groups later on. It might be a chapter of the university women's club or a baseball league. Religious institutions provide a feeling of community and common interest. So do service clubs like Rotary or the local Chamber of Commerce. If you're a musician, inquire about the town band or community choir.

For particular needs, there are specific groups. Alcoholics Anonymous not only provides invaluable support to people who want to stop drinking, but also generates friendship, giving and trust among its members. Al Anon does the same for families of alcoholics. There are breast cancer support groups that people can turn to for emotional help and comfort, and these seem to have a health benefit, as well. Some studies show that women in these support groups live twice as long as breast cancer patients who are not in such groups.

Recent research shows a strong connection between resilience and a strong support system, especially during a difficult time in one's life. When we're alone and in crisis, it's easy to feel overwhelmed. If there's someone we can turn to, even a single important individual, we can draw tremendous strength—and learn important coping skills from them. Studies done on at-risk children show that those who did well and developed into competent and confident adults shared several characteristics, one of which was the ability to find and develop a relationship with at least one caring grown-up outside their immediate families.

A sign of the times, in this post-recession period, is the emergence of networking groups for out-of-work business executives. These organizations help their members with special skills and job-seeking strategies, but they also provide a valuable forum for giving and receiving emotional and moral support: the all-important knowledge that they're not alone. People who are widowed, separated or divorced can get the same benefit from bereavement groups and support organizations.

Build Your Support System Before You Need It

When should you develop a support system? Now. It's not just of value when you're dealing with a crisis, it also enriches your day-to-day life. It's wonderful to have people to share good news with (your promotion, your child's exceptional report card, your hole-in one). Develop a network of people you like and trust and who value and care for you. Then, if you need to draw on their support, they're there for you. Don't wait until something miserable happens and then run up to a total stranger on the street, saying, "Let me tell you about my day!" (Bartenders and taxi drivers are often recruited to fill this role, but friends are better.) As Harvey Mackay says in the title of his excellent book on networking, *Dig Your Well Before You're Thirsty.*

What should you be looking for? Surround yourself (or seek out) people who like and care about you, whom you feel good being around and with whom you feel safe. You don't need a gallery. A few close family members or friends will more than suffice. You want people you feel comfortable with and can trust. Folks that you know you can confide in and the information goes no further. Find individuals who are positive, upbeat, encouraging and fun to be around.

Don't expect a support system to come to you (unless you're incredibly charismatic). You'll probably have to take the first steps and be the initiator. This may require you to leave your comfort zone, especially if you're not naturally gregarious. But you must be willing to put yourself out there. My sister has lived in Edmonton, London (England), Boston, Calgary and Minneapolis in her adult life. And in every city she developed a marvelous network of friends. She told me one of her secrets. "When I arrived in Minneapolis, I joined every group I could find. It wasn't my preferred style and it wasn't always easy, but I made myself do it."

Her other secret was probably even more important: she is one of the most giving, warm and cheerful people you could hope to meet. She exemplifies the teaching we received from our father. His motto was *"Just keep giving and the taking will look after itself."* He not only verbalized that message but he modeled it in his everyday behavior. Simply put, *the best way to get support is to give it.* And to keep giving it. And not keep score. What goes around comes around, and not always from the original source. You might do something kind and helpful for someone and then receive the same treatment at an important time from a totally different person. It's like spinning good vibes into the cosmos. If enough of us do it often enough, the ether's going to be brimming with positive energy, from which we'll all benefit.

A friend described what happened to his sister after she became ill and what had preceded her illness: "From the time of her diagnosis she received an outpouring of support (from friends and acquaintances) that overwhelmed her, and it never stopped. It's like everything she ever did for people was coming back to her. Every day of her life, before she got sick, she did something for somebody else. It was part of her regular daily agenda."

We can give support to others in many ways. A phone call when someone's ill or having a tough time. A card to say, "I'm thinking of you," means a lot to people. A thoughtful gesture, such as buying them a book or CD for no particular occasion. We can offer to take care of their kids, bring over a casserole or take them for a walk.

Here's a beautiful story I heard on the radio several years ago, showing the range of creative ways we can do things for others. It's about a ten-year-old boy in Burbank, California, who developed leukemia. Now, childhood leukemia is one of the most curable forms of cancer, but it still involves going through chemotherapy, which is not a pleasant experience. His doctors told him what to expect from the treatments: that he'd be very tired, lose his appetite, nausea and vomiting—and that his hair would fall out. They suggested he might want to consider having all his hair shaved off at the start, instead of waiting for it to fall out bit by bit. He could get some funky hats to wear and ride out the chemo that way. He discussed it with his family and decided to take the physicians' advice. So he went to the barbershop to have his head shaved.

But he didn't go alone. His brother went with him. His teacher went with him. And thirteen of his classmates went with him. And they all had their heads shaved. And that's how they gave support to their friend at a difficult time in his young life. The teacher said, in a later interview, that he started to call his class "my bald eagles" because half the kids—and he himself—were bald. When it comes to ways of giving support to others, you can be very creative.

What Goes Around Comes Around

Ian Charleson was an aspiring actor from a working class family in Edinburgh, Scotland when he enrolled in the London Academy of Music and Dramatic Art (LAMDA) in the early 1970's. He later became famous in the 1981 Oscar-winning film *Chariots of Fire*, playing the role of Eric Liddell, the Scottish runner who refused to run on the Sabbath at the 1924 London Olympics. The next year he appeared in the movie *Gandhi* that also won the Academy Award for best picture. Most of his career, however, was on the stage in England. I heard him on the radio in the mid-1980's doing an interview I will never forget.

He told the story of enrolling at the theatre school in London and how he had had to drop out after his first term for financial reasons. Between terms, the academy's director called him in and said that the famous actor, Alec Guinness, had heard about his talent and his plight and had put up money to help him through his second term. He'd been tremendously touched by this generosity and was happy to continue at the school. However, at the end of the year he had to withdraw again because of a lack of funds.

The director again called him in, this time to tell him of an unusual offer. I'm paraphrasing from memory, but this is how I remember Ian telling his story. The director said that an anonymous benefactor had come forward with money to pay for his final term but there were two conditions. One: that he not be told who the benefactor was. Two: that he not try to find out who it was. If he agreed to those conditions, they would be happy to have him stay to complete his studies. He felt both humbled and grateful for the offer and eagerly accepted. He finished his final year and went out into the world.

His talent was apparent and he became quite successful. Years later, after a stage performance, he was sitting in his dressing room with a group of friends and told them the story of how he was able to stay in acting school. One of the people in the room asked,

"Did you ever find out who the benefactor was that put up the money?"

"No, I never did. That was the condition of the offer."

"Do you want to know who it was?"

"Certainly. Do you know who it was?"

"Yes, I do."

"I'd love to know. I've always wondered about it."

And here's the answer that left me stunned: "Ian, it was your classmates."

I wondered then, as I have many times since: what must Ian have done to endear himself to his classmates such that they would contribute their own money, a sacrifice most of them could probably ill afford (as students who likely didn't have two shillings to rub together themselves?) And then to do it anonymously so as to protect Ian's self-respect and dignity? This is a profound story about what a support system meant to Ian Charleson, but it could not have happened by accident. To me, it resonated the wisdom of my father's philosophy, **just keep giving and the taking will look after itself**.

Mentors, Coaches and Teachers

Jerry White lectured and wrote on issues related to money management. Many years ago I attended one of his presentations, entitled "What the Rich Do." It was entertaining and instructive, but for me, the big take-home of the night was that rich people all have a financial adviser. They don't try to manage their money themselves, unless that's what they do for a living. I researched and found someone to manage my assets. But that's not all he does. He has become my teacher. We meet quarterly to review my investments, discuss other options and have my questions answered. That's how I'm learning about this important and complex field.

This is another dimension to my support system. It's not just about emotional or logistical support. It's about education and personal growth. I also have a health adviser: my family doctor. And even though I'm a physician, when I get sick or injured, I seek his counsel and heed his advice. Lawyers do the same when they need legal counsel. They hire another legal eagle. They follow the adage that "a lawyer who takes his own case has a fool for a client."

Mentors and coaches are part of our support system. And not all of our teachers need to be paid professionals. When I got interested in the field of stress management in the early 1980s, I had the good luck to meet Dr. Matthew Budd, a gastroenterologist who works in Cambridge, Massachusetts, and teaches at Harvard. He offered to direct my learning; I watched him work, met his colleagues in the stress field and was even invited to stay in his home. It was a remarkable gift, for which I will be forever in his debt. He did it with enthusiasm, generosity and grace, asking nothing in return, except that I apply myself, follow through on his suggestions and use the knowledge and wisdom I was acquiring to help others. This was true, altruistic mentoring. And I, in turn, have shared what I know with others in my profession.

The best advice I received before I left to do my internship was this: "Make sure you get along with the nurses and let them teach you things. They know a lot more than you do about day-to-day patient care. If you're respectful and receptive, they'll help you enormously." Truer words were never spoken. Nurses enriched my learning throughout that year and the seventeen years that followed in my general practice career. Unofficial coaches can make a huge contribution to our work, as they can in areas like music, sports, or parenting. We all need to be lifelong learners, and it helps to seek out people who can guide and advise us.

Sam Telford taught me ninth grade English and history and directed our junior high play in which I had a small role. Mr. Telford was a gifted teacher and one of the most remarkable individuals I met in all my years in school. He was articulate, outspoken, funny, kind and charismatic. He loved kids and treated them with respect. In return, his students adored him. I kept in touch with Mr. Telford through high school and university. I'd go to visit him periodically, and later we'd meet for lunch a few times a year. I don't remember our specific conversations as much as the general tone of the relationship. He was interested in my development academically, socially and personally. And I was fascinated by his view of the world and the way he thought about things. He was a strong influence in my life—my mentor, ongoing teacher and cherished friend.

In med school, I learned more about the art of medicine from Dr. Tait McPhedran than from anyone else. He was a surgeon at the Toronto General Hospital and a superb teacher. I developed a warm relationship with him and would hang around with him, enjoying his company and watching how he interacted with patients. He was kind and down-to-earth with them, and had a great sense of humor—which they all appreciated. Dr. McPhedran had a profound effect on me as a doctor and as a person, and I kept in touch with him for decades after I graduated.

Whether it's a teacher or a boss you like and admire, a favorite aunt or a wise and funny neighbor, mentors are all around us if we care to find them. You don't need a contract or formal agreement ("Excuse me, will you be my mentor?"). You just need to be open to what's possible. Develop a friendship. Ask questions. Solicit advice. Let them know you value them as individuals and respect their opinion. And give something in return if you can. Depending on your age and stage, it might be mowing their lawn, helping them with their groceries, baby sitting their kids, dropping them a line when you're away, inviting them over at Christmas, remembering their birthday. It's about relationship and friendship, as well as teaching and learning. The rewards for both parties are tremendous. And if you have a chance to mentor others, take it. It's another way of giving back—and you will receive a lot by giving.

Building a Network

Networking is a way of developing a support system of strategic contacts and allies. These are not necessarily folks you confide in, nor are they teachers per se. They are co-workers and acquaintances with whom you share common interests or pursuits, who can often supply information or advice on an ad hoc basis, and through whom you can meet other people and learn of new opportunities.

It's easy to be cynical about the idea of networking and dismiss it as a self-seeking pursuit in which people put on phony smiles, chat up others or frankly hustle them for personal gain. I used to think that way, and I'm still turned off by opportunistic or gratuitous associations, but I've changed my mind somewhat about the general concept. In his book, *How the Best Get Better*, Dan Sullivan says that successful entrepreneurs need to make a paradigm shift from "rugged individualism" to "unique teamwork." Strategic relationships are more productive than trying to do everything yourself. In this rapidly changing and increasingly complex world, we need each other more than ever. No one can be expert in everything, and if we can create constructive alliances with people who have the skills (and interests) we lack, and vice versa, why should we waste valuable energy trying to do things we're not good at, or searching for information that others can give us in five minutes? In the workplace, networking also shows up in the concept of team building. Employees leverage off one another's knowledge and skills, work collaboratively and create much greater results through synergy.

Networking can also provide business opportunities. Eighty percent of jobs are never advertised. They're filled by word of mouth. That's how I found an assistant for my office when my nurse receptionist retired after twelve years. I drew up a job description listing skills and qualities I was looking for, and circulated it to a small group of trusted friends and associates. One day I answered my phone and received the following welcome news: "I have found you the perfect office assistant." That's a real networking success story. I've also been introduced to speaking agents and my literary agent by friendly intermediaries. And I've returned the favor whenever possible.

So I've changed my mind about networking. I now understand its considerable value. But I have two personal rules that I live by:

- I don't network with anyone I don't genuinely like. There are too many nice and agreeable people around to bother with those who aren't. No matter how well connected or knowledgeable the person is, if it feels phony or unpleasant, I pass.

- I don't ask for anything without offering something first. Any good networker will tell you to give before you expect to get. In fact, giving without expecting to get is the basis of the whole structure, so just make it a part of how you function. If someone asks about something you know, share your knowledge. If someone expresses a need in your area of expertise, offer to help them. If you see an article that you know a person would find useful or interesting, send them a copy. If you know two people you think would enjoy meeting each other, introduce them. (I'm not talking about matchmaking here—unless your name happens to be Yentl!) As my dad used to say, "Just keep giving..." If the networking is not a two way street, my guilt meter rings loudly and I back off.

Networking's value shows up in a hundred different ways. You may draw on the wisdom and experience of relatives in matters of child rearing or gardening. You might ask a neighbor's advice about building a deck, writing a resume or designing a Web site. When I first decided to write a book, I called a Toronto publisher and longtime family friend to find out how to get started. When it was time to buy a new car, I consulted a friend who reads *Consumer Reports* religiously. Same with researching new stereo speakers. If I don't know who's an expert on a given topic, my network can help me there too, guiding me to the local maven. In return I happily field calls about who's a good cardiologist, how to change careers, where to learn relaxation skills or how to find an agent. If I hear of an opportunity that will benefit someone, I'll call them or give their name to the person offering the opening. When networking is done with balance and integrity, everyone wins.

In summary, remember that you're not alone in these stressful times. Everyone's trying to manage and adjust. We can all help one another. Building a support system provides four major areas of benefit: emotional support, logistical help, mentoring and networking. It involves taking initiative to build relationships. Don't isolate yourself, and don't wait for people to come to you. Share yourself with others in order to build trust. Sometimes that means allowing yourself to be vulnerable. Even admitting the need for help can be difficult for some folks. But in today's turbulent world, we're all feeling the strain. It's OK to say, "This is tough. I'm struggling," or "I'm frustrated, angry, tired, frightened." It doesn't mean you're weak. It only means you're human.

So seek and accept the support of others. But give support to them in return. One of the added benefits of doing for others is that it takes our attention off ourselves and helps us see we're not the only ones having difficulty. It also tends to make us feel better about ourselves.

One More Story

A woman who had very low self-esteem told me this simple but powerful story. It's about the value of a support system, and also about how little it takes to make a profound difference to someone — sometimes just the right words at the right time. This woman bought a new and very becoming dress to cheer herself up and tried it on for some friends, saying, "This is the new me!" One of her friends, who valued her much more than she did herself, said, "No, Cynthia, that's not the new you. That's the *real* you!"

CHAPTER EIGHTEEN

If It's Not Working, Stop Doing It— Why People Don't Solve Problems

I F YOU'VE EVER HAD BACK TROUBLE YOU KNOW how frustrating the treatments can be for these ailments. Sometimes one kind of therapy will work—and other times the exact opposite will produce relief. So if one approach doesn't work, you have nothing to lose and everything to gain by trying something else (within the limits of safety). If heat doesn't work, try cold. Some symptoms respond to rest; in other cases, keeping active is the answer. I know someone who went to a specialist and was told to do flexion exercises. His back got worse. He returned to the consultant, who said: "Well then, we'll try you on extension exercises." They worked dramatically and he's been using them ever since. The wisdom in back care is to change what isn't working—sometimes by doing the opposite of the initial treatment.

This example illustrates the benefits of an open mind, flexibility and willingness to take chances. It also makes the process sound pretty simple. Unfortunately some problems aren't so straightforward. They may be more complex or may involve things you don't have control over. Then the process gets more challenging—and interesting.

An organized approach to problem solving includes some of the following steps:

1. Clearly define the problem. Be as specific as possible.

2. List all the options, alternatives and solutions you can think of. Don't eliminate anything at this stage. Brainstorm without editing.

Be as creative as possible. Explore every possibility.

3. Evaluate the pros and cons of each option.

4. Eliminate any options that are deemed unworkable or impractical. Then list your choices in order of preference.

5. Select one option and develop a plan of action.

6. Begin implementing your plan.

7. Follow through.

8. Evaluate the results and adjust accordingly.

Although it seems eminently sensible to solve problems when they arise, this often doesn't happen. I've been fascinated for years by the reasons people *don't* solve problems.

Looking for Solutions in the Wrong Places

To introduce this concept, I invite you to do the following exercise: the nine-dot problem (from Dr. Paul Watzlawick's book *Change*, which he co-authored with John Weakland and Richard Fisch). The rules of this puzzle are simple. You are to join all nine dots in the diagram below by drawing four straight lines without lifting your pencil from the page. Take a moment to do this puzzle before you proceed. I'll get back to it shortly.

Problem

There's an old joke about a drunk looking for something at night under a streetlamp. A passerby asks him what he's searching for.

"I'm looking for my keys."

"Where did you lose them?" asks the stranger.

"Down the street about a block."

"Why are you looking here if you lost them over there?"

"The light's much better here."

Looking for solutions in the wrong place is surprisingly common. Have you ever been asked for directions by a stranger who doesn't speak English? You give your answer slowly and carefully, right? If he doesn't understand, do you repeat yourself—only *louder*? As if *volume* is going to get the message through. It's like kids doing jigsaw puzzles. If a piece doesn't fit, but looks like it *should* fit, kids are likely to push harder, as if they can *force* it to fit. But they can push all they want—if it's the wrong piece, no amount of pressure is going to turn it into the *right* piece. If you're looking in the wrong place, you'll never find the solution to your problem.

Call it blinkered thinking, tunnel vision or barking up the wrong tree, people limit themselves unnecessarily. The nine-dot puzzle illustrates this point graphically. As you can see from the diagram below, the solving of this puzzle requires you to step "outside the box" for the solution. Most people don't see this as an option because they assume a rule that is not stated: that you have to stay within the confines of the square. But this limitation is self-imposed—it is not contained in the instructions. If you begin with this assumption, you cannot solve the problem. The lesson of the nine-dot puzzle is that if you look for answers only in conventional or "logical" places, you will fail to find solutions to many of life's problems.

When obvious or logical solutions don't work, try something else—even the opposite. Like the sore-back example, there are times when a 180-degree turn works out very well. I learned this twenty years ago

Solution

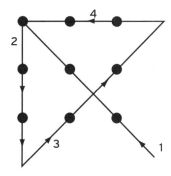

when a woman came to see me with her twelve-year-old daughter. The daughter was a real behavior problem at home; she also resented being lugged off to my office to see me. From the outset, I couldn't get a word out of her. Just a sullen look and the occasional grunt. I was pleasant and friendly, I asked questions, I kidded with her, I even got a little annoyed. Nothing worked. She had no intention of talking to me. Recognizing the futility of the situation, I ended the visit and called a child psychologist friend of mine to discuss strategy. He volunteered to sit in on the next session.

He began by asking the child some questions, which she again ignored. He then said: "Well, okay, if you don't want to speak to me, I'll talk to your mother." He proceeded to do so for about fifteen minutes and they had a nice conversation about the girl's behavior. As he continued to ignore the daughter, she became uneasy and tried to interject. The psychologist, feigning annoyance, said: "I wasn't talking to you" and continued to chat with the mother. The child interrupted again. He said: "Look, you didn't want to talk to me and we're doing fine without you, so please let us continue." By now the girl was literally rising out of her seat. Finally the psychologist, with mock irritation, said: "All right. What do you want to tell us that's so important?" The girl spoke up. He responded. Then the mother made a comment and the girl replied. Pretty soon, the session had become the three-way conversation that the psychologist had been engineering all along. And the girl was participating without realizing that she had given up her show of defiance. My strategy of entreating the girl to talk didn't work. The more I beseeched her, the more power she had by resisting. The psychologist's strategy was to exclude the girl (thus taking away her power), which provoked her to respond. This is an example of paradox. He got her to talk by not letting her talk.

Creativity and innovation are important elements of problem solving. They lead people to look for solutions in improbable places. A great example came from a 7-Eleven store, which was plagued by loitering teenagers. The owners tried the usual measures of asking them to leave and seeking help from the police. But nothing worked. Then they came up with an imaginative idea that did the trick. They began playing orchestral music by Mantovani inside and outside the store. No self-respecting hip teenager was going to be caught hanging around a place where elevator music was played, so the loiterers vanished. The proprietors had solved a problem using ingenuity rather than threats.

Repeating Strategies That Didn't Work

Some of the worst losing games are actually misguided attempts to resolve problems. Dr. Paul Watzlawick, a therapist in California, called this: "When the Solution Is the Problem." Whenever you face a problem, you usually try to solve it with some plan of action. This attempted solution (or strategy) will result in one of two outcomes: it either works or it doesn't. If it succeeds, all well and good. But if it fails, you have three options to choose from. You can try a new strategy; you can give up and accept things as they are; or you can employ the same strategy again. A new strategy may or may not solve your problem. But if you repeat the strategy that *didn't* work, it probably won't work the second time either. If you persist in trying it a third (and a fourth time), it will likely fail again. What's worse, it will often lead to additional problems that weren't there before. This is illustrated in the following diagram (adapted from Dr. Watzlawick's book *Change*).

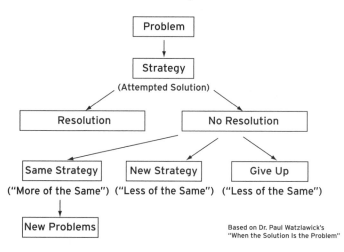

Problem-Solving Model

What, you may ask, would make someone use a strategy that has failed? You might even think I'm talking hypothetically about some rare occurrence. I assure you this phenomenon is remarkably common. And even though it's hard to fathom why people engage in this futile exercise, they do—and it's a losing game every time.

Take a typical winter problem: a car stuck in snow. What's the first thing you do when your car won't move? You probably rock it back and forth to get loose. If this strategy works, you are relieved and drive off. However, if it doesn't work, you often try it again to see if rocking the car more forcefully will get you out. It might work on the second try, but often it doesn't. Now it's logical to get out and assess the situation. But a lot of people keep rocking that sucker until it damn well gets unstuck, right? You hear those tires whining and engines roaring every winter. As frustration increases, some people just keep flogging their cars, adding profanity for emphasis. If you've ever been in this position, you'll know there is a point beyond which you realize it's futile—but you keep doing it anyway.

How does this situation fit the diagram? The problem is the car stuck in snow. The attempted solution is rocking the car back and forth. When it fails, continuing to rock the car is repeating the same strategy that didn't work. Dr. Watzlawick calls this "More of the Same" and the result is also the same—futility. If you persist in rocking the car, not only do you not solve your problem, but you actually make it worse by adding new problems—you create ice under the wheels, your car sinks deeper into the snow and you get more upset. If you decide to do something else ("Less of the Same"), you could choose among shoveling, using sand or salt, putting a board under the wheels, getting someone to push you or calling a tow truck. Even if you did *nothing*, you'd be better off because at least you wouldn't be making matters worse.

Not only in snowdrifts do people spin their wheels uselessly. *Nagging* is another strategy that not only doesn't work but makes things worse. Take the common scenario of a parent trying to get her teenager to take out the garbage, pick up his laundry or come to the dinner table on time (pick your favorite example). The parent makes a request. The verbal reply is anything from silence to a muttered complaint to a reluctant "okay." However, the active response is nil. The kid doesn't move, the garbage remains and the parent repeats the request. Still nothing. After a while, the parent asks again (with some annoyance) and yet again the result is inaction. By now, frustration and anger are setting in and the exchange is getting testy. As the request becomes more insistent, the response gets more intransigent. Phrases like "Get off my case" may be heard.

This has now become a battle of wills—and nobody is backing down. Paul Watzlawick calls this a "symmetrical escalation" where each side keeps upping the ante. It demonstrates his formula: **persistence produces resistance** (and vice versa), creating a cycle of behavior that is as damaging as it is pointless. By the end, the garbage is still there— but worse than that, there is a lot of tension and two angry people. The fact is that nagging is a losing game, a strategy that repeatedly fails. And yet many people persist in its use long after they see it's a waste of time.

As Dr. Watzlawick points out, "more of the same" maintains the very behavior it's intended to stop. The problem persists not *in spite of* your strategy but *because* of it. Your solution has, in fact, become the problem.

There are other losing games based on repeating previous mistakes. *Dieting* is a classic example of spinning your wheels uselessly. In most instances, diets either don't succeed at all or they work for a while but then the lost pounds are regained. It's a cycle of frustration and failure because the premise is faulty. The body resists the effects of dieting by lowering the metabolism rate to preserve weight. It literally misinter- prets the diet as famine and goes into a self-protective mode to conserve calories, thus sabotaging the diet's effects. Furthermore, after the dieting stops, the metabolism rate does not return to normal and people often gain back more weight than they lost in the first place. This rebound obesity is well known to most dieters as the cruel aftermath of their highly disciplined efforts. The healthy way to lose weight is to eat sen- sibly and exercise regularly. Aim at losing no more than two pounds a week. And be patient. The process may be slow when it's done properly, but the results are much more likely to last.

Prohibitions also yield negative results. Make something off limits and you immediately give it added appeal. Underage drinking is an ex- ample. So is drug use. When alcohol was legalized (after the failure of Prohibition), alcohol consumption actually decreased. Tell a child that a part of the house is out of bounds and where do you think she'll go at the first opportunity? This phenomenon also shows up in relationships. Parents who object too strongly to their children's friends often drive those kids straight toward the censured individuals. It's even worse when the parents forbid the relationship. Ever since Adam and Eve ate the apple in the Garden of Eden, the forbidden fruit has been the most desirable.

Punishing (especially physical punishment) usually doesn't achieve its intended goal of modifying behavior. It may seem to work initially, but mostly it breeds resentment that fuels further rebellion. A man in his forties told me about his relationship with his father when he was growing up. There was a cycle of violence and defiance when his father physically abused him. "I learned to pretend it didn't hurt. I wouldn't give him the satisfaction. The more and the harder he tried to control me, the harder I resisted." The boy became more rebellious after each punishment in what turned into a power struggle. He suffered the beatings from his father, but they never changed his behavior. The only effect of the punishment was to alienate the boy from his father forever.

Rewards and positive reinforcement work much better than punishment and negative incentive. And not just in children. Companies that manage by intimidation get much less out of their employees (in productivity, loyalty and goodwill) than those that treat their employees with respect, promote enthusiasm and show appreciation for good work.

Lecturing is another strategy that rarely proves beneficial. It may help the lecturer feel he's in control or providing discipline, but usually the payoff is more illusory than real. Watch the eyes of the person being lectured (child or adult) and you'll realize they tune out very quickly. Some will be brazen enough to ask: "Is this going to take long?" before plastering a look of bored impatience on their faces. Keep your message short and simple if you want it to get through.

Threats and ultimatums are real losing games, often leaving you with egg on your face. You expect your threat to produce obedience and compliance. When, instead, your warning is met with disregard or defiance, you're faced with a no-win dilemma. You can back down (and lose face) or you can make good on your threat and feel sorry, silly or guilty. Why put yourself in this position in the first place?

Retaliation (sometimes known as tit-for-tat) isn't much of a strategy either. Look at the crisis in Northern Ireland that went on for decades or the situation in the Middle East to see what happens when retaliation becomes the game plan. Each side increases the stakes to avenge previous attacks in a cycle of violence that is as destructive as it is futile. Everyone tries to get the last word, but nobody ever does.

Sometimes people repeat mistakes and do "more of the same" because they get locked into *scripted responses*. A classic example of an automatic response is when someone asks "How are you?" and you say "Fine" or "Great"—even when you feel lousy. You reply without thinking about it. "Nice to meet you" is another one of those knee-jerk statements.

Scripted responses come up in other ways, as illustrated by this story. Bernie was a macho guy who had scratched his cornea at work. He came to the emergency room where I examined him, explained the problem, outlined the treatment (rest, antibiotic ointment and an eyepatch) and assured him it would heal within twenty-four hours. His immediate reply was: "I'm not wearing no sissy eyepatch." I explained the need for it (to keep the eyelid from rubbing over the scratch every time he blinked), but he was unimpressed. Just then his girlfriend appeared. She was quite dramatic as she flew to his side, mothering him as if he had a major illness. She asked "Will he be all right, doctor?" in a voice full of melodramatic concern. When she heard he wouldn't accept the eyepatch, she asked what would happen without it. I said it would take longer to heal, would hurt a lot and could even get worse. Now she was beside herself. She prevailed upon him with great anguish, begging Bernie to accept the treatment. "You could go blind, Bernie. Please, do this for me. It's only until tomorrow."

Through the entire episode, Bernie remained adamant. His girlfriend's behavior just made matters worse. The more she pleaded, the more tough and heroic he felt. Now his honor seemed to be at stake. He was doing his Gary Cooper routine out of *High Noon* (a man's gotta do what a man's gotta do), while she was following the Grace Kelly script (beseeching him not to risk danger by "being a man"). Finally, I saw this was going nowhere and asked her to step outside. I then quietly explained his options, asked him to think it over and excused myself. Without anyone in the room, he had no audience to impress with his "tough guy" act. Within minutes by himself (and with no fawning female to give him a payoff), he agreed to the eyepatch. The game was over and Bernie rode off into the sunset.

This story illustrates a pattern I saw countless times as a family physician: women taking responsibility for the health and medical care of stubborn men. What is behind this scenario? It is about scripted roles in which men aren't supposed to be sick (weakness) and certainly aren't supposed to ask for help (double weakness). Women are supposed to be caretakers, and it's okay for them to offer the help (which the men can reluctantly accept after putting up some initial resistance). Everyone plays their part, but it sure can get tiresome.

Pride and False Pride

Another reason people repeat mistakes rather than choose a new strategy is *pride*. Or, more accurately, *false pride*. I learned about this important distinction from my uncle, the late Dr. Gordon Yudashkin, who was a psychiatrist in Upstate New York. Years ago we went to a pops concert featuring Arthur Fiedler and the Rochester Philharmonic. It was held in a sports arena that was set up cabaret style, with people sitting around tables. The people at the table next to ours were a cheerful crew who had arrived under the influence of alcohol and seemed to get happier as the evening wore on. That was fine except I found their boisterous behavior very distracting. At various times I looked over at them pointedly only to have them leer back at me. My requests that they please keep the noise down were met with sneers of derision. At one point I walked over to ask for some cooperation, which only brought rolls of laughter from them. I asked an usher to intervene, but they ignored him. I was stymied, frustrated and very irritated by the whole thing. I certainly didn't enjoy the concert.

On our way out of the arena, my uncle said to me: "I think you handled that very well." I grumbled some answer like "How do you figure that? They didn't shut up for one minute." With patient understanding he explained: "I'm not saying you got the result you wanted. I'm saying you handled yourself with restraint and behaved like a gentleman. You did as much as you could in the circumstances without behaving as badly as they were." I told him that it didn't feel very satisfying. I would have preferred to get them to smarten up. He replied: "You could have been obnoxious or bullied them into keeping quiet. That would have satisfied your false pride. But the way you chose to behave was a reflection of your true pride."

"What's the difference between pride and false pride?" I asked.

"Pride is when you behave in a dignified, self-respecting manner. You don't give up your principles and integrity just to make your point. False pride is about winning; when you do anything to get what you want—even if it means compromising your own behavior and throwing tantrums, making threats or whatever."

This distinction has profound implications when it comes to problem solving. Call it ego, stubbornness, the need to be right—people often get locked into losing behavior because of false pride. This pattern is especially common in the classic confrontation called "the power struggle" or "the battle for control." Consider the scene where a parent tells her two-year-old child to come upstairs for bed—and the kid says no. Mother says yes, and the child repeats no. The Yes/No game is now on. The insistent mother is determined to have her way, the child equally committed to prevail. This game will continue—resulting in anger, crying or exhaustion—unless someone changes strategy. One day I caught myself in this futile exercise with my son (then aged two) and decided to fake him out. He kept saying no every time I said yes. Suddenly I said no, and he stopped dead in his tracks, totally confused. After a long pause in which he tried to figure out what had happened, he laughed and did what I asked. Some months later, after re-enacting this routine a few times, he smiled and said, "You got me." After that it was a playful joke and not a battle of wills anymore.

I don't tell this story to be smug. After all, how much credit can you take for outwitting a two-year-old? But the principle of this little exchange is instructive. Children will usually stop playing a game as soon as there ceases to be a payoff. If they can engage you in a power struggle, they'll wear you down because they have more patience for that sort of thing than most adults. Just getting your attention is a payoff for them. If they can get your goat, they're really winning. But if there's no benefit at all, they'll usually lose interest and stop.

Adults (and nations) aren't as smart as kids. They will often get locked into situations where backing down is considered unpalatable and compromise is viewed as weakness. Men have fought duels to the death and countries have gone to war rather than lose face. The results of such stubbornness can be catastrophic. I heard the story of a pilot who boasted that he never turned back his plane because of bad weather. This heroism cost him his life two weeks later when his plane went down in a storm that he should not have risked flying through. He and his passengers died because of his false pride and his belief that confronting danger is a macho thing to do and that turning back is cowardly.

When I counsel couples, I find that false pride and ego are often barriers to resolving conflicts. Frequently I ask these people "Would you rather be right (and win) or do you want to solve your problems?" Worse than needing to win and be right is the need to make others lose and be wrong. This need leads people to do things like blame throwing, fault finding, and saying "I told you so," as if rubbing the other person's nose in it is going to prove something. There is a price to be paid for this kind of behavior—antagonizing people and thwarting cooperation. On the other hand (to quote a sports saying), "It's amazing what can be achieved when no one cares who gets the credit." Trying to be right by making others wrong is counterproductive and offensive—a real losing game.

Rigidity

Another barrier to problem solving is when people are rigid and won't entertain new ideas or try new strategies. Folks with fixed beliefs keep doing things the same way, regardless of the results. For years there was a method of high-jumping that was universally accepted. It was the front roll (or "barrel roll") in which the athlete cleared the bar with chest and face down. Everyone knew this was the "right" way to high-jump. Then, in 1968, along came a guy named Dick Fosbury whose style was totally unorthodox. He went over the bar chest and face up. His detractors disdainfully labeled his technique the Fosbury Flop. It was obviously the "wrong" way to high-jump. Except for one thing: it worked better than the conventional style, and eventually it became the "right" way to do it, revolutionizing the whole sport.

Many physicians have an uneasy relationship with chiropractors. I practiced medicine for twenty years without ever utilizing the chiropractic skills available in my community. Then, in 1990, my back seized up on me (for the umpteenth time since my teen years) and none of my usual remedies helped. One morning a patient noted my struggle to get around and suggested I see a chiropractor. My first reaction was resistance, my stereotypic response. But I was so desperate, I said: "If I knew a good one, I'd go. I'll try anything at this point." She said: "I'll tell you a good one. Go to see mine." I did. Within four days I was on the road to recovery. I saw her for fourteen years, and my back was much better. I only regret the years I had a rigid mind-set against using this form of healing.

Lack of Persistence

Have you ever known someone who quit a sport after two or three lessons because they "just couldn't get the hang of it"? Some people give up quickly if they don't get immediate gratification. They lack the three Ps required to learn a skill or change a behavior: Patience, Persistence and Perseverance. This bodes ill for solving problems.

More and more, people are changing jobs, houses and relationships when things don't work out. Rather than stay and address problems, folks often take the easy way out. I'm not saying people shouldn't leave an untenable situation. But I generally advise them to explore ways of improving the present circumstance before bailing out.

Denial

As obvious as it sounds, some people don't solve problems for the simplest of reasons: they don't admit there is a problem. And obviously, if it ain't broke, there's nothing to fix. However, burying your head in the sand is not the key to success. Some of the things these ostrich types fail to acknowledge include burnout, alcoholism, an unhappy child, a failing business, a disintegrating marriage. Usually this denial is subconscious and therefore hard to overcome. It may require a relative, friend or co-worker to see the obvious and label it. But as long as a problem is not recognized, it cannot be solved.

The Road to Romance Isn't Always Smooth

Being creatures of habit, people generally do what is familiar and comfortable, even when they see it's not working. Sometimes it's because they think the strategy is logical and *should* work. Sometimes they just can't think of an alternative.

Here is a success story to illustrate the principle that when "more of the same" isn't working, "less of the same" is always a better bet. Man meets woman. He dates her a few times and starts to show some physical affection. Then he hits a roadblock. She doesn't reciprocate. He's in love, she's in "like."

In this true story, the man dealt with his problem by employing a common strategy: he tried to charm her. He called her more often, was more entertaining and bought her little gifts. Nothing changed. She kept accepting his invitations and enjoying his company—but it was still platonic. So he charmed on, using all his best moves—a classic case of doing "more of the same." Only now it was starting to get uncomfortable for both of them. He was feeling anxious and insecure; she was feeling pressured and defensive. More tension appeared in their relationship. The harder he tried, the more she retreated.

When he told me the story, I explained what I saw happening using the diagram on problem solving. Clearly his strategy wasn't working. And it was creating new problems: anxiety on his part, alienation on hers. I suggested he stop doing what wasn't working. He'd never thought of his behavior as a strategy but admitted he had indeed launched a campaign to win her over. He felt he had two choices: give up completely or back off but continue to see her. He opted for the latter, inviting her out but acting low-key. He didn't work so hard at being charming and funny. He relaxed and stopped trying to hold her hand.

Something wonderful happened. He had a nice time again and so did she. There was less tension and more laughter. Even more important, she became more chatty and showed the odd gesture of affection. In other words, when he stopped persisting, she stopped resisting. That didn't mean she threw herself into his arms. But she did stop pulling back. And several months later his patience paid off. She had become very fond of him and was now ready to enter an intimate relationship. It's now years later and they're still together. By recognizing his losing game, this man was able to replace it with a more effective strategy. There was no guarantee of success, but at least his new approach had a possibility of working—whereas his previous strategy was doomed to keep failing.

What Does Work?

If nagging, punishing, lecturing, threatening and retaliation don't work, what are the alternatives? Here are some suggestions for a constructive approach to problem solving:

- Communication (which includes listening), negotiation and assertiveness
- Conciliation and compromise
- Flexibility, creativity and keeping an open mind
- Staying calm, sensitivity and empathy
- Suitable consequences, consistency and fairness
- Willingness to acknowledge when you're wrong

- Taking responsibility for your behavior and for the outcomes that result (rather than defending yourself and blaming others)

There are no guarantees that these guidelines will work, but they have a much better record for success than the losing games previously discussed.

Even No Idea Is Better Than a Bad Idea

When you can't think of an alternative to a losing game, you're still better off to *stop doing what isn't working*. A couple were upset because their teenage son left his school bag by the front door every evening. No amount of telling him to move it, nagging or threatening had any impact on him. The school bag was thrown down like a gauntlet and became the focal point of arguing and family tension. Clearly the parents' strategies weren't working. But even worse, the fallout from this small issue was contaminating the atmosphere in their home. In discussing this matter with them, I learned that the father was leaving his briefcase at the door too (the old double standard). I advised them to stop playing their "losing game" (of nagging and threatening) and urged the father to stop leaving his briefcase at the door. We had no time to discuss an alternative strategy, but we agreed to devise a new plan at our next visit. On their return, I raised the issue of the school bag and they started to laugh. It was no longer a problem. Their son, without a further word from them, had started taking his bag up to his room. This story illustrates two points. First, even if you can't think of another approach, it still pays to stop using the strategy that doesn't work. (Doing nothing is a form of "Less of the Same." It often works because when you stop persisting, the other person usually stops resisting.) Second, non-verbal communication can be very powerful. The parents didn't announce what change they were making. They did it quietly, which made it more effective.

In summary, a lot of losing games are sincere attempts to solve a problem. Unfortunately many of these strategies not only don't work but actually make things worse. Whenever your approach isn't working or you're repeating past mistakes, stop yourself. Find another strategy to solve the problem. This often requires understanding, patience, flexibility, open-mindedness, creativity, risk taking and perseverance. But even if no alternatives come to mind, resist going back to the losing game you were playing before. Either way, if it's not working, stop doing it!

PERMISSION

CHAPTER NINETEEN
Giving Yourself Permission to Change

W HEN KIDS PLAY FOOTBALL AND THE QUARTERBACK throws the ball to someone, one of three things will occur. The receiver will drop the ball, or he will catch it and just stand there, or he will catch the ball and run with it. This is an analogy I use in my work. In a sense, I throw my patients a football when I offer them information, ideas and suggestions. And as with football, one of three things usually happens. Some folks never catch it. They either don't understand or ignore what I'm saying. Others catch it but just stand there. They do nothing with the information. They're not much farther ahead of the people who never catch it in the first place. The third group not only catches the ball but runs with it. They take the ideas and use them. They apply them to their daily lives. Some even modify or expand on them. This is the group that gets the benefit. And the key is *follow-through*. In the realm of personal change, nothing happens until you take action. In the model that I use, I call this final stage *permission*. It makes things happen. Until then, it's just words and ideas.

If I am not for myself, who will be for me? But if I am for myself alone, what am I? And if not now, when?

RABBI HILLEL, 1ST CENTURY

This book is filled with stories about people who applied this principle: the woman who gave herself permission to serve a Sara Lee cake, thus overcoming her perfectionism; the lady who gave herself permission to leave her bed unmade for two weeks and found a freedom she hadn't known in forty years; the guy who allowed himself to go on a weekend camping trip with the commitment not to drink, even though everyone else was, and uncovered a discipline and courage in himself he didn't know he had; the teacher who gave herself permission to stop worrying in June about her new job—and not to start fretting until three days before Labor Day; the many people who gave themselves permission to cut their work hours from sixty to forty a week and were rewarded with a double payoff: twenty hours of leisure time and the realization that they could complete their work in much less time if they paced themselves and stayed fresh; and the innumerable folks who have given up caffeine, gone to bed earlier or started to exercise regularly—and felt immeasurably better as a result.

These stories have several things in common. They happened to people no different from you and me—people who began with an awareness of a problem or something in their lives that wasn't working out. They all showed a willingness to try something different. And they all got a payoff—not just in feeling and performing better, but symbolically as well. All of them took control of a part of their lives they had not controlled before. And for each it opened a door to other possibilities. When people catch the ball and run with it, wonderful things start to happen.

The power of permission is impressive. But it's not always easy to grant yourself, as many people have discovered. It should be a simple thing, especially if it involves something you really want to do. But for some reason a lot of us get stuck when we try it. I learned about permission in the following way.

The problem I was addressing concerned my work hours and my efforts to restructure them. From 1971 to 1986 I worked from eight in the morning until seven at night—which included a mid-day break for exercise and lunch. That was fine for seeing patients and doing paperwork. But by 1986, I was also presenting lectures and seminars. I ended up doing speech preparation in the evenings and on weekends. This routine pleased neither me nor my family. But I was struggling to find an alternative.

I was visiting a friend in Baltimore and told him of my dilemma. He said: "Why don't you stop seeing patients earlier and leave yourself a few hours to read and write?" It sounded nice, but there were several problems. In wrestling with this, I realized where I was stuck. I had an *awareness* of what I'd been doing and that it was costing me family and leisure time. I knew I had a *choice*, especially because I am self-employed and can set my own schedule. But I was having trouble giving myself *permission* to make a change.

There were several factors behind my resistance. First, it would mean seeing fewer patients, and I had a long waiting list. Second, I would no longer be able to see people after their work. I had always believed I should be available to patients before and after their work hours. My 8:00 a.m. and 5:00 p.m. appointments were always very popular. Third, I wondered what my colleagues would think, given that they ran their office hours until suppertime. Fourth, I had always worked long hours, and it felt self-indulgent to do discretionary things during the work day. Last, I wondered how my late father would have felt about such a decision. He had always worked very hard and had a strong work ethic. His office hours had been 8:00 a.m. to 6:00 p.m. (with minimal time for lunch) and it felt like a betrayal to shorten mine.

So here was this appealing, sensible idea and I was marshaling all my arguments against it. I admitted I was having trouble giving myself permission. My friend said: "I'll tell you what. *I'll* give you permission to do it. It's not like you're going to be goofing off. You'll be staying in your office and doing things that are a part of your work—in fact, they will actually *improve* the quality of your work. And it will allow you to be with your family when you're at home. I think it's a reasonable trade-off." The persuasiveness of his reframing and the sanction he was giving combined to convince me. I returned home and revised my schedule. It worked out well and felt fine.

Eighteen months later, I called my friend and told him I'd made another decision. I still had insufficient time and was too tired at the end of the day to do all my reading and seminar preparation. So I'd hatched a new plan. I would start earlier in the morning and see all my patients before lunch, leaving the whole afternoon for reading, writing and prep-work. To compensate for the reduction of patient hours, I would see five people on Saturday mornings. "I'm going to try this for just a month, as an experiment, and see how it goes. What do you think?" (I was obviously seeking his permission or at least his agreement.)

He started to laugh. "If you have to frame it as a temporary experiment before you can give yourself permission, that's okay. But both of us know it's a great idea and I'm sure it'll work out wonderfully." It went as well as he predicted. And ten months later I decided to stop the Saturday-morning appointments. That decision was made with ease and without a call to my friend.

This story illustrates the difficulty people can have giving themselves permission. We all have barriers or old baggage that can make self-permission difficult. But don't let that block you from proceeding. My struggle went through three stages. First, someone else gave me permission when I couldn't do it for myself. Then I generated the permission, but tentatively—and seeking external support. Finally, I was able to give myself permission comfortably, quickly and with no outside blessing. And it keeps getting easier the more I do it.

Who Gives You Permission?

As I have illustrated, permission can come from within or without. Preferably you should grant it to yourself. But if for some reason you are unable or unwilling to do that, let someone else give it to you. I frequently do this for my patients, parents do it for their children, employers do it for their employees, friends do it for each other. Most commonly it is called "encouragement." Sometimes it feels like a kick in the pants. But whether others encourage or push you, they are actually giving you permission.

I often give my patients permission to choose a new way of doing things. After they've experienced the resulting benefits, they start to give themselves permission. They've proven to themselves that it's a good idea. Then the habit becomes self-perpetuating. In other words, the payoff reinforces the behavior.

Permission —————————→ Action —————————→ Payoff

If you feel okay giving yourself permission to do things that serve you well, jump in and enjoy it. If you're struggling with self-permission, find someone to encourage you to get started. But don't depend on them for long. The goal is to become self-reliant and self-determining, to develop an internal locus of control where you initiate your own decisions and behavior. Letting someone else give you permission is only an interim step to developing your own autonomy.

Two Kinds of Permission

There are two different circumstances in which permission is needed: to do things you *want* to do and to do those you *don't* want to do (but know are either necessary or will probably be helpful). The first group includes taking time to relax and have fun, saying no to people who lean on you for favors and hiring someone to shovel your snow. The second group contains such disciplines as losing weight, quitting smoking, being on time and asking your boss for a raise.

It's understandable that folks resist doing things that are unappealing. Giving up things you like (ice cream or alcohol) or doing things that require discipline (school assignments and home chores) can be downright unpleasant. In this case, self-permission feels more like giving yourself a shove or biting a bullet. My most vivid memory of this kind of task is writing essays in high school. What a drag! But inevitably, such jobs had to be done. Mind you, once I sat down with pen and paper, it was usually less onerous than I feared. That's a good thing to remember. With chores you dislike but have to do, it's helpful to break the task into small pieces and build in lots of breaks and rewards. Giving yourself permission is not always easy. But you can do it.

As easy as it is to comprehend why people avoid the "have to do's," it's hard to fathom why they have trouble with the "want to do's." Are there this many masochists in our midst? Not likely. But there *are* barriers that hold folks back. And the biggest of these is guilt. So many people feel it is wrong to meet their own needs; that it's bad to have too much fun; that they don't deserve to enjoy themselves or to ease the burden of their lives. For these individuals, I believe the following discussion will be relevant and helpful.

Self-Interest Versus Selfish

Many people neglect themselves, have no leisure time and even wear themselves out because they feel that anything they do for themselves is an act of selfishness. Some deprive themselves of sleep to do household chores. Others don't play a favorite sport or read because they feel they should be playing with their kids or helping a friend build a deck. When confronted about these choices, they identify a feeling deep inside that it's wrong to do things for themselves. When pressed to explain this, the word *selfish* usually comes up, followed almost immediately by the word *guilt*. A lot of lives are being run (and ruined) by these two words. Years ago I began making a distinction for my patients that most found not just helpful but liberating. The distinction introduces the term "self-interest."

"Selfish" is defined as "caring unduly for oneself in disregard, or at the expense, of others." The opposite word is "selfless," which I define as "caring for others to the exclusion of yourself." I don't endorse either of these positions. Picture a line with these words at either end.

Selfless ◄────────────────────────────► Selfish

People who condemn leisure or self-directed activity often think in extremes (all-or-nothing thinking). Things are either all good or all bad, all right or all wrong. It's important to explore the gray area in between. "Selfless" people do for others but overlook themselves. They are the Givers, the Pleasers, the Helpers, the Caretakers and, in extreme cases, the Martyrs. There is great merit in serving others, but not to the extent of ignoring their own needs. "Selfish" people are those who think *only* about themselves and couldn't care less about anyone else (if they even notice others at all). I call the selfless end of the spectrum "Self-neglect" and the selfish end "Self-indulgence." There is no virtue in either extreme.

Now let me explore the middle ground. I use Alexi de Tocqueville's phrase "enlightened self-interest." *Enlightened* because it is an enlightened concept and *self-interest* because it implies being concerned about, and taking care of, yourself. I call this "Self-care" and recommend it to everyone. I base my support of self-care on four principles:

1. You have needs just like everybody else.

2. Your needs are just as valid as everyone else's.

3. It's just as appropriate for you to meet your own needs as it is for you to meet the needs of others.

4. And—you can do *both*.

The spectrum now looks like this:

Selfless ◄────────── Self-Interest ──────────► Selfish
(Self-Neglect)   (Self-Care)   (Self-Indulgence)

It is now clear that there is a middle ground, and that taking care of yourself is reasonable and healthy, but it does not prevent you from looking out for others as well. In fact, a balance between the two is the best mix. One of my patients put it beautifully when he said: "I'm still doing things for people. But I've added one more name to the list—mine."

For people who struggle with self-permission I cite the Bible for a useful precedent. One of the Ten Commandments is to honor the Sabbath Day. Even thousands of years ago it was prescribed that people rest from their labor every seventh day. This rest was not just to give homage to God but for physical restoration as well. Another biblical injunction is even more instructive. Fields were to be planted for six consecutive years, but during the seventh year they were to lie fallow. Why? Because the soil needed a rest, an opportunity to replenish its nutrients and restore itself. Otherwise it would soon become arid desert, unable to sustain crops. Even in biblical times the concept of self-nurturing and self-regeneration was understood and sanctioned. How strange that in our advanced technological world we have lost sight of such a fundamental principle. It is basic to the survival of all living things, plant and animal. Should it not apply equally to us?

A colleague of mine developed a metaphor that makes the same point. She calls it "The Empty Teapot Syndrome." If you fill a pot with tea and start pouring it into teacups, you will eventually run out of tea. At some point the pot will be empty. If it is not refilled with tea it will be unable to fill any more cups. Similarly, if you keep pouring out your energy and do nothing to replenish it, you will eventually have none left—to give to others *or* to use for yourself.

We are all like fields and teapots: we can only give out what we put in. If we don't nurture ourselves, we dry up and are of no use to anyone, including ourselves. I have seen hundreds of people do this to themselves. Whether they give to their co-workers, children, parents, neighbors or friends, they save nothing for themselves and *allow* nothing for themselves. They are running on empty. And many of them don't even know it. All they know is that they are exhausted, stressed, confused, hurting and often angry. What they need is self-care and self-interest. This self-nurturing includes good nutrition, adequate sleep, regular exercise and sufficient leisure time for activities, relationships and fun. It is the very essence of health. And there is nothing selfish about it.

Can't Versus Won't

Another important distinction relating to permission is the difference between can't and won't. Patients often tell me they want to do something but can't. "I'd love to take more holidays but I can't get away" and "I want to tell my father off when he behaves like that, but I just can't hurt his feelings" are some examples. Earlier in this book I cited beliefs that had the same tone, such as "I can't have fun without alcohol" and "I can't sleep without sleeping pills." The word *can't* is like a brick wall for these people, the ultimate barrier to what otherwise might be possible. It disempowers them because it instills a belief that something is impossible or at least unavailable to them.

When I consider what can't be done, I think of three things: I can't change my age, I can't change the color of my eyes and I can't be in Pittsburgh and Cleveland at the same time. Just about everything else is "I won't" or "I'd rather not." In a world where renowned Canadian Paralympic athlete Arnie Boldt was able to high-jump with one leg and a quadriplegic friend of mine can drive a van, the word *can't* rings pretty hollow from most people, especially when folks say things like "I can't hold my temper," "I can't resist chocolate donuts" or the famous "I just couldn't help it."

Simply because you've never done something before doesn't mean you can't learn to do it now. When people tell me they can't quit smoking, I remind them of the thousands of heavy smokers who are admitted to Intensive Care Units every year. In the ICU no one is allowed to smoke. All these patients have to stop smoking, cold turkey, and they all do it. Mainly because they have no option. I'm not saying it's easy or that they enjoy it. And many of them resume smoking the first chance they get. But they *can* stop.

I explained this distinction to an alcoholic who said he couldn't get through the Christmas season without a drink. I asked: "Do you mean 'can't' or 'won't'?"

"Can't," he replied.

"Not even if I gave you a thousand dollars for every day you abstain over the holidays?" That stopped him for a minute. "Seriously, if it meant a thousand dollars a day, do you think you could tough it out?"

"Well, if you put it that way, I could probably hold out."

I said: "I agree. In fact I'm sure you could. And that's the difference between what you *can* do and what you're *willing* to do."

He got the message clearly. When he returned in January (he stayed dry *and* had a fine time), he told me: "Whenever I was tempted to drink, I thought about your offer of a thousand dollars a day and laughed. I sure understand the difference now between can't and *won't*." Can't is the excuse—won't is the truth.

The Problem with "Trying"

Another disempowering word is *try*. When you're looking for initiative, commitment or determination, saying "I'll try" doesn't cut it. At best it sounds half-hearted; at worst it's a cop-out. For example, I know people who "try" to go to bed by 10:00 p.m. but never make it before midnight; or "try" to exercise three times a week and end up doing it twice a month. Using the word *try* often misleads or obscures the truth. Aside from deceiving others, the greatest damage is when you fool yourself. It's a way of making things look better than they are. When people say "I tried," they equate effort with results. Or they suggest a concerted attempt when only a token gesture was made. Think of a time when someone said she'd call you and didn't. Later you noted that she never called, only to hear: "Oh, I tried to phone you but there was no answer." She doesn't mention that she called only once and hung up after two rings. It's as if everything is fine and all's forgiven as long as she "tried."

Another way people hide behind the word *try* is when they don't intend to do something but would rather not say so. Have you ever asked someone to do something and, instead of a firm "Sure," he says "I'll try"? You just know he isn't going to do it. I've often suggested a lifestyle change to a patient and instead of a determined "I'll do it," I hear a half-hearted "I'll try," which tells me not to hold my breath. In these cases, "I'll try" is almost a code word for "I probably won't do it but I don't want an argument by telling you so." Lack of commitment or responsibility is a barrier to changing a losing game and making your life work out better. This point was made beautifully in one of my favorite "Herman" cartoons: it shows a couple getting married. They're standing at the altar and the clergyman says to the groom: "You're supposed to say 'I do,' not 'I'll try.'"

How Can People Learn to Give Themselves Permission?

The simple answer would be "Do it." Or, "Get on with it, you'll like it." But for many folks it's not that easy. One way to get unstuck is to remind yourself of the drawbacks of your present behavior, of all the ways your game is costing you. Write down the negatives on a sheet of paper: how you're feeling, what you're not accomplishing, etc. Then write down all the benefits that would result from the change you are contemplating. Studying the two lists will often motivate you to action. This is a way in which *awareness* can be used to initiate or reinforce *permission*. Reminding yourself that what you're doing now isn't working will increase the appeal of a positive change.

Another approach is to identify what's holding you back. Fear? Guilt? Limiting beliefs? The opinions of others? List these factors and then explore arguments to refute or neutralize them.

In the business world, sales people are told to sell benefits, not products. You don't say "Buy this widget"; you say: "I've got something here that will relieve your headaches, unclog your drains and lower your heating bill 30%." That's the approach that sells. Similarly, when contemplating change and giving yourself permission, present the benefits to yourself, not the change itself. For example, if I were to tell you to give up caffeine for three weeks you might be turned off. But if I were to say: "Here's something that will improve your sleep, increase your energy, reduce your stress and lessen your heartburn," you'd likely sit up and take notice. Highlight the payoffs when you're stuck. And keep reminding yourself of them if your resolve starts to slip.

Another approach is to view the change as an experiment. If self-permission seems daunting, set it up as a trial period in order to get started. Tell yourself that if it doesn't work, you can always stop. (But, of course, if it does work, the payoff will reinforce the change and it'll be easy to continue.) In addition, set short time frames. Alcoholics Anonymous uses the phrase "One day at a time." Rather than saying, "I'll never drink again," alcoholics say, "I'm not going to have a drink today." Anyone can do something for a day. Then you make the same resolve the next day. When I urge people to go off caffeine, I present it as a three-week project, not a lifetime ban. Giving yourself permission for a limited time is easier to accept. And it helps get you over the initial hump.

When patients really struggle, I appeal to their curiosity. "Aren't you curious to know if this can work? Don't you wonder if there's a better way to do things than the losing game you're playing?"

Another suggestion is to step outside yourself. Years ago I was tussling with something and my sister asked me: "What would you tell a patient who came to you with that problem?" As soon as I looked at it objectively, the answer was obvious. So if self-permission is difficult, ask yourself what you would tell your child or a friend to do, and see if the change looks clearer and more compelling.

Last, if necessary, enlist the support of a relative or friend to get you started. This reminds me of the California psychiatrist whose business card simply stated: You have my permission. When you turned it over it read: You don't *need* my permission.

In summary, permission is the final key to changing a losing game. You can be *aware* that your game isn't working and see preferable *choices* to your current situation, but until you take *action*, nothing will change. You will continue to suffer or get less out of life than you could. The permission can come from you (preferably) or from someone else. It can be welcoming like the opening of a door, or it can be like a shove to do something you'd rather avoid. Both kinds of permission are needed at different times. If the fear of selfishness blocks you, the concept of enlightened self-interest can neutralize your discomfort. If you're hiding behind words like *can't* and *try*, stop letting yourself off the hook with these cop-outs. Nothing short of positive results should be acceptable to you. Many people have trouble giving themselves permission, but you can overcome your barriers. And it gets easier the more you do it. Finally, the payoffs of permission are considerable and will reinforce both your resolve and your comfort.

There is an old saying that there are three kinds of people:

Those who make things happen.

Those who watch things happen.

And those who ask, "What happened?"

Which of the three are you? What type would you like to be?

CHAPTER TWENTY

Making It Happen

OW DOES ONE CHANGE? SOME SPORTS TEAMS tinker with their lineups to find the best combination of players. Others do a thorough house-cleaning and bring in a totally new roster. Depending on the circumstances, each of these strategies has its merits and drawbacks. Sometimes goal setting is required, followed by careful planning. Conversely, "winging it" may be perfectly acceptable. There are many ways of embarking on the process of change. There's no right way to do it. Just pick a formula you like and go with it.

rpe diem—Seize the day.
ACE, 23 BCE

When someone says: "I'd like to change but I don't know where to start," I offer the following selection of models and formulas from which to choose. It is less important *where* you start than that you *make* a start.

Decide What You Want, Then Make It Happen

The most direct approach is to determine what change you want to make and then take action. Thousands of smokers have stopped by declaring they're going to quit and then doing so. Cold turkey. No muss, no fuss. Some found it easy, others had to fight cravings and temptation, but they all succeeded. No strategy, no pronouncements, no game plan. I've watched people start to exercise, get more sleep, stop eating junk food, spend more time with family, quit jobs and change careers, just by deciding to do so and then following through. This is the simplest model for change, and if it works, there's nothing more to it. Some people tell me that's too simple, it can't be that easy. I always ask them why they assume it has to

e world belongs to
se who dare and do.
MAN WOUK

be difficult. Or whether they have a vested interest in its being complex and complicated. And I often tell them the following story.

When I was in general practice, I asked one of my non-smoking patients if he had ever smoked. He had. How long ago had he given it up? Five years. Had it been difficult? No. How had he done it? His family doctor at the time told him he should quit smoking, so he did. It was no big deal. Then he laughed and told me the sequel. "When I went back to my GP the next year, I told him I'd quit. He said: 'How come?' I reminded him that he had told me to. He said: 'You mean you did it just because I told you to? It was that simple?' I said, 'I guess it was.' Then my doctor, a smoker himself, smiled and said to me: 'Look if it's that easy and it really works, do me a favor. Tell *me* to quit smoking! Nothing else has worked so far!'"

Set a Goal, Make a Plan and Then Act on It

Sometimes deciding on a change isn't enough. You have to be more organized and draw up a plan. The steps in this formula are as follows:

1. Decide what you want (goal).

2. Devise a plan for achieving it (strategy). List the steps involved and give a time frame for each.

3. Determine what you'll need (resources, tools)—for example, equipment, money, special skills or training, help from others, emotional support and encouragement. Then obtain and assemble those resources.

4. Put your plan into action, one step at a time.

To see how this works, let's take a common losing game: a job you dislike and have decided to do something about. One of my patients was working in a retail store and not enjoying it. He had always wanted to be a school teacher, so that became his *goal*. A career counselor told him the procedure for becoming a teacher and he worked out a *strategy*. The steps included applying to teachers' college and getting some experience as a classroom assistant. After teachers' college, he'd have to apply to various school boards to get a job. Depending on where the job was located, he might have to move to another town. Then he listed the *resources* he'd need. First, he required one subject he hadn't taken in university. Money was another requirement—for tuition and living expenses while attending teachers' college full time. Psychological support would also be helpful. Finally, with his plan mapped out, he put it into *action*. He enrolled in the course he missed at university. He got a part-time job, approached his parents for financial help and signed for a student loan. Then he found a summer job working with children in a playground (to give him credentials for getting a classroom assistant's job). In addition, he sought encouragement from his family and friends. Finally, he applied for a classroom position and was on his way.

Goal Setting

Setting goals is a whole subject of its own, but a few words would be helpful here. There are different time frames to consider in goal setting: long term (ten to twenty years), intermediate (three to five years), short term (one to three years) and immediate (six to twelve months). Experts in this field suggest deciding on long-term goals first, then working toward the present, because your short-term goals will depend on your long-term ones. If your goals are not congruent, they need to be revised. For example, if you intend to retire at age sixty, your intermediate goals (to travel the world, build an expensive house and send three children to college) will not be consistent with your long-term aims.

Goals should be specific. Instead of saying "I'd like to get more exercise," you would say: "I want to start jogging three times a week." One man told me: "I want to be in control of myself," which was too vague. So he clarified this by listing specifics: renovating his den, playing tennis one night a week, making a "To Do" list every day, organizing his personal papers at home and throwing out his old clothes. His goals were now tangible and concrete. Then he put a time frame for completion on each.

Goals should be objective so you know when you've reached them. "Improving my relationship with my children" is subjective and hard to verify. "Spending time with them every weekend" is observable and can be measured.

Goals need to be action-oriented but worded so that your behavior is what matters. Rather than saying "I'm going to make some friends in this new community" (which involves the response of others to fulfill), you could say: "I'm going to invite one of my neighbors to lunch each week for the next month." That is a goal over which you have total control, even if they decline your invitation.

Goals as Directions

What about people who don't *know* what they want? Many folks have trouble setting specific goals. They can't think years ahead or articulate exactly what they want to happen. Or the exercise sounds too organized and formal—like you're planning your whole life and removing the element of spontaneity. There is a way around this dilemma. Think of goals as *directions*, not destinations. In this context, goals are like a general guide rather than a precise blueprint, giving you a sense of where you're heading without specifying the final target.

A young Workaholic knew his overwork was a losing game. But he found it "very difficult to calm down. This work ethic is hard to change." He started to notice people who had cut back their work hours and said, "I'd like to get closer and closer to that." In other words, he decided the direction he'd like to go (to work fewer hours and have more leisure) but had no idea what the final result or destination would be. Would he end up working nine to five, five days a week? Or eight to six, four days a week? He disliked the idea of a goal that was so specific that "you haven't reached the goal until you've hit it exactly." However, by having a general direction, he was able to evolve toward this non-specific goal without needing to know what the end-point would be. He began by not going to the office on weekends. Then he gave up working at home in the evening. He started to exercise, read and even putter in the garden. Soon things started to fall into place without a clear plan.

Envision What You Want, Then Identify and Overcome Barriers

If you're unclear about what to do next but know that your present situation is a losing game, here are some questions to help you. I call this exercise "visioning," a form of fantasizing or daydreaming about the future that can be very instructive. Let your mind go and see what pops up. Write down your ideas. Don't hold back or edit anything, no matter how crazy or grandiose it might sound.

You see things that are and say, "Why?" But I dream things that never were and say, "Why not?"
GEORGE BERNARD SHAW

How would you like your life to be? What would it look like? Where would you be living? What would you be doing?

What are your dreams? Marriage? Family? Career? Wealth? Travel?

What would your ideal job consist of? Whose job would you like to have?

Whom do you admire or envy? Why?

Whose behavior would you like to emulate? Who are your mentors? Whose example do you want to follow?

If you had all the money you wanted, what would you like to do with your time?

If you had only one year to live, what would you want to do in that year?

How would you like to be remembered by others (your family, friends, colleagues, etc.)?

Think of a time you were really happy. What was it about that time that made it happy for you? What were the factors and ingredients that contributed to your pleasure? Can you reproduce those ingredients?

From this list of dreams and ideas, pick one that really excites you and that you'd like to explore further. Now picture this idea as a goal (Step One)—but instead of making a plan, ask yourself what stands in the way between you and what you want. (Step Two) What are the barriers or obstacles between where you are now and where you'd like to be? Perhaps it is a lack of time or money, insufficient expertise, outside competition, etc. The third step is to brainstorm ways of overcoming those barriers. Don't let the obstacles block you. Figure out how to get over them. What will have to happen for you to achieve your goal? Do you need to generate revenue, manage your time better, give up certain beliefs, let go of guilt, take responsibility, stand up to someone, solve a logistical problem, etc.? I have found this to be a powerful model for mobilizing people to action. See what it looks like in diagram form on the next page.

This is similar to the exercise on overcoming barriers to lifestyle change in Chapter 14. Only here you might be addressing ideas like starting a business, organizing a community activity, planning a special trip or writing a book.

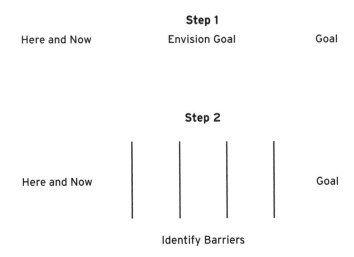

Step 1

Here and Now   Envision Goal   Goal

Step 2

Here and Now   Goal

Identify Barriers

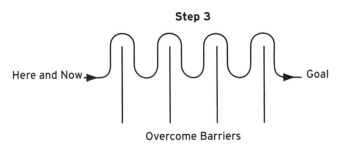

Step 3

Here and Now →   → Goal

Overcome Barriers

The Model of "As If"

Dr. Paul Watzlawick and his colleagues at the Mental Research Institute in Palo Alto, California, use a technique called the "therapy of 'as if.'" They suggest that people behave "as if" the world is different from what they see. They imagine a different reality in which their behavior can change and make sense. The story of Archie Leach (aka Cary Grant) is a classic example of this. He behaved "as if" he were a sophisticated, elegant, worldly person, even though he was none of those things initially. But by pretending to be them, he slowly changed and acquired those qualities. A colleague of mine made a fascinating observation about Lech Walesa (later the president of Poland) when he was leader of the Solidarity Movement. He said that "Walesa accomplished what he did and led Poland to free itself from communism by behaving as if he were already free." His assertive, self-respecting, courageous and at times defiant behavior was that of a free man. No citizen who felt himself enslaved by the system could have acted in this way. The theory of "as if" can be very powerful.

How would this work in a common situation I encounter with patients—namely, the wish to be a more involved, attentive parent? Many people are tired, busy or stressed after work and don't give their children the time and attention they would like to be giving. Or they are irritable and impatient with their kids. I give them the following instructions: picture the kind of parent you want to be. It's helpful to think of someone you admire (or even the image of a nurturing parent from a movie or TV show) and list the qualities they demonstrate: patience, affection, willingness to listen, empathy, humor, etc. Then behave "as if" you have those qualities. Pretend you are giving a demonstration of good parenting to a group of observers—and let yourself be the good parent you envision (but don't fall into the trap of idealized expectations and standards).

If you want to change your behavior, picture yourself having already done so and behave "as if" you are the person you want to become. You will create a positive and constructive self-fulfilling prophesy.

Change by Eliminating What You Don't Want, and Evolve from There

Q. How do you carve an elephant out of marble?
A. You take a big slab of marble, get a hammer and chisel, and chip away everything that doesn't look like an elephant.

A lot of people have trouble saying what they want. But they sure know what they don't want. For these folks, there is an approach to change that doesn't require looking forward (as in the previous goal-setting models). You don't have to articulate your goals, visions, dreams, etc. You just have to identify and eliminate what you *don't* want in your life and, by doing so, you will gradually evolve toward what you *do* want—even if you can't specify ahead of time what that is. Trust that some goal or direction will eventually become clear to you.

This model recognizes that there are two kinds of change:

Change *toward* something (earning money, planning a holiday, striving for a promotion, developing new friendships, etc.)

Change *away* from something (leaving a job, moving out of a noisy neighborhood, ending an unhappy relationship, etc.)

With the first kind of change, you know where you're going. With the second kind, you don't necessarily know where you're heading—but you do know you're getting away from something you dislike. This may sound like change by default or a vague way to proceed, but it actually works quite well.

A good example is cleaning out your clothes closet. When you start, you don't know what your eventual wardrobe will look like, but you start pulling out the obvious throw-aways. Things you never liked or wore, colors you're tired of, stuff that doesn't fit—all get the heave-ho. Now you get a clearer picture of things. When you take a second run-through, clothes that looked marginal are now unacceptable (everything being relative) and you pitch them out. Although you're not finished, the closet is looking better—nicer clothes and more space between the hangers. After a time, you go at it again, pruning even further. Meanwhile, the overall picture is improving. You're making progress even without an organized plan or idea of what the final picture will look like. You're able to make headway despite working toward an ill-defined goal. This is an example of change by elimination and evolution.

The same principle applies to other pruning activities. A young woman was overstressed and overloaded. "I decided to start taking more control by eliminating the things I don't like in my life—like commuting long distances." She was a part-time secretary in three different companies, which involved driving up to two hours a day. She quit her most distant job and found something closer to home. In addition, she cut back on some of the "shoulds" in her life (including some home chores, visiting distant relatives, and one of her volunteer positions). She had no special plan for the free time she was creating. In the first week, "I spent a leisurely day for myself, with no structured activity, which I enjoyed a lot." As her pace of life slowed down and her daily schedule opened up, she decided to take a course at a community college. But that idea hatched *after* she freed up some time—she didn't cut back her hectic schedule with any such plan in mind. As she continued to eliminate what she didn't want, she kept reshaping her life to include more of what she wanted and enjoyed, none of which she planned at the outset.

The Jigsaw-Puzzle Metaphor

The "elimination and evolution" model of change is similar to doing a jigsaw puzzle. One of the satisfying things about jigsaws is that every time you fit a piece, two positive things happen: you see a little more of the picture falling into place; and you have one fewer piece to sort through as you look for the next parts of the puzzle. Similarly, as you sort out your life, take control, solve problems, etc., every negative element you eliminate makes the overall picture a little clearer and also removes a little more of the clutter—which makes the next pieces easier to see and fit into place.

Another variation of this model is what I call the *One and One Approach*. This involves eliminating one thing from your life that you dislike and adding one thing that you'd like to have or do. Many people come to see me for lifestyle counseling. They know their lifestyles are unhealthy, but they don't know where to start changing. I don't ask them what their goal is or what their ideal life looks like. Nor do I know myself what will work best for them. We just begin by eliminating the negatives and substituting positives. They go off caffeine and start drinking juice; they cut down on junk food and add fruit; late evenings of television are phased out and replaced by an extra hour of sleep; extended work hours are shortened and leisure time is made available; and so on. Neither of us knows where this is ultimately leading. We just agree that each step is in the right direction, which they confirm by reporting that they're feeling better and better. It's an evolutionary process—gradual, non-threatening and constructive—and it reaps progressive benefits.

There is a certain amount of experimenting in this model, which leads to another variation on the theme: the *Trial and Error Method*. This is how all inventors and researchers work. It requires a willingness to take risks and keep an open mind. Patience also helps—don't expect instant gratification. In addition, it contains a sense of adventure and challenge. As my wife says, "I'll try anything once and twice if I like it." That's a positive way to look at life. It breaks through the timid mind-set of people who balk at change.

With the trial and error method you have to expect to make mistakes. It goes with the territory. It's not only inevitable, it's okay to make errors—that's how you learn. Just don't keep making the *same* mistakes. The main thing about miscues is to learn from them. They are not signs of failure—they are steps on the road to success.

Creating Context for Change

No matter which formula you choose as your strategy for change, another model will be extremely helpful. This concept (courtesy of Dr. Matthew Budd) involves creating a "context" in which the change can occur: producing conditions that both promote and support the change you want to bring about. It increases the likelihood that change will occur and be maintained, although it doesn't guarantee these results.

Here is an example of creating context. My work is in stress management and lifestyle counseling, so I provide an atmosphere for patients that promotes relaxation and comfort. My office is spacious and decorated in pastel colors, with soft lighting. The furniture is comfortable, and there is minimal noise. There are restful pictures on the wall and several plants. It's set up living-room style, so people don't feel they're in a doctor's office. All this is done to establish a tranquil environment. Most people feel welcome and relaxed in this setting. It's much more restful than if the room were small, noisy, cluttered and decorated in bright, vibrant colors. My office does not ensure people's comfort, but it certainly increases the probability of that outcome.

This principle can be used for any change you want to make in your life. Say you decide to stop smoking. Creating a context to support you is critical. The obvious things would be to stop buying cigarettes, get rid of all your ashtrays, avoid places where people smoke, ask your friends not to smoke around you, seek out non-smokers for company, decrease activities that you associate with smoking (like long telephone conversations, coffee at breakfast, etc.), find cigarette alternatives (such as carrot sticks, lollipops, gum, etc.) and set up a reward system (put the money you would have spent on cigarettes in a jar every night. Watch it add up and then treat yourself to an evening out or a new sweater). All these measures will support you in your resolve to quit smoking. They will remove you from temptation and create an atmosphere that is conducive to giving up the weed for good.

Creating Context for Change in Others

The concept of creating context can be used not only to assist you in changing yourself, but also to promote change in other people and in your relationships with them. While it's true you can't *make* other people change, you can create conditions and circumstances that *favor* a change in their behavior. This is not intended as a manipulation, but only to bring out the best in others and to improve your interaction with them.

To understand how this works, try this simple exercise in "creating" friendly people. Walk along the sidewalk of a busy street and notice the expression on people's faces and how they act. Be circumspect while you do this. Don't look them straight in the eye, and keep a blank expression on your face. Be as natural and unassuming as possible. After a few blocks, cross the road and walk back the same number of blocks on the opposite side of the street. Observe the strangers you pass as before, only this time make eye contact with as many as possible, smile and, if you like, say a quiet "Hello." That's all. At the end of this exercise you are likely to notice an interesting phenomenon. The people on the second side of the street will seem friendlier than those on the first side you walked down. The second group is likelier to smile or say something pleasant whereas the first group will probably ignore you as you pass.

What's the message here? That the only difference in the behavior of the two groups of strangers is *you and your behavior*. So the next time you find people unfriendly or unwelcoming, ask yourself how you acted toward them. Although your behavior is only one factor influencing their actions, your reaction toward people *can* make a difference and that's worth remembering.

If you are having a conflict or misunderstanding with someone, ask yourself: What am *I* doing to perpetuate the problem? What am *I* contributing to the dynamics of the relationship? And what can *I* do to improve the situation?

This concept of creating context is also useful in the workplace. There are many different management styles, from laid-back and hands-off to hovering and critical. However, to get the most out of employees, the leading business consultants advise a fair, caring, nurturing environment in which people are challenged, given responsibility and valued for what they do. They are expected to perform well and are treated with respect and dignity. Management by intimidation, on the other hand, creates the worst possible climate in which people can be asked to give their best effort. If someone's work is falling below standard, if they're making mistakes or being careless, treating them in a threatening way and making sarcastic comments is counterproductive. If you want to show them who has the power, you will make your point. But if you want their work to improve, you have to create a context conducive to that end. Increasing their anxiety level will only increase their inefficiency. Conversely, creating a mood of support and understanding is likely to help them get back on track. Again, there are no guarantees when you create context in this way—but the odds are greatly in your favor that the situation will improve because of the atmosphere you create.

Awareness—Choice—Permission

The formula upon which this book is structured is another useful model for creating change. To illustrate this, take a common scenario—getting your kids upstairs at bedtime. Every parent has struggled with this at one time or another. If you end up with a confrontation (or a war) some nights, be aware that whatever you're doing isn't working—*and* it's producing tension and conflict. This is a losing game, not just because you're not in control of the situation, but because everyone is getting upset. Stop and explore your choices. What are your options? You can start moving the kids upstairs sooner to allow time for the inevitable delays. You can threaten, punish, bribe, reward, yell, give up, give in, physically carry them up the stairs, etc. You could change your beliefs about bedtime and tell yourself it's not important what time they get to sleep (if that's credible for you) or that the odd exception is no big deal and just go with the flow. A lot of parents turn it into a game: "First one upstairs gets to choose the book for tonight" or "I'm the airplane that's going to fly you up the stairs." It's amazing how quickly kids can switch from defiance to cooperation when you make things fun. If you try all your options and none works, come up with a new set of choices. After all, **where availability ends, creativity begins**. You're never beaten unless you quit. Now give yourself *permission* to implement one of your options. The criterion for success isn't just to get them upstairs, but to do so with everyone in a good mood and feeling good about themselves.

Another example of how this model works is the story of a conscientious woman who had just started a business out of her home. The new enterprise was going nicely, but it made her a shut-in because she had to answer the phone when customers called. She was now *aware* that this home-based venture had left her feeling trapped in her own house. We explored the *choices* available to give her some freedom: an answering machine, a portable phone (they were new at the time), an answering service and pocket pager, or someone to relieve her periodically (her husband, children or someone she would hire). This list presented a wide array of options, some of which she ruled out because of her belief systems: "If a customer calls, they don't want to hear an answering machine," "You can't run a business and not be available to answer the phone," and a belief that raised staying home to a status symbol: "If you're stuck in, you must be needed and therefore worthwhile." She surveyed the alternatives and decided on a portable phone that she could answer anywhere, as if she were sitting at her desk. She gave herself *permission* to buy one. By being aware of her dilemma, listing her options and allowing herself to do something different, she solved her problem.

One of the merits of this model is that it not only guides you through the stages of change making, but it helps you identify where the obstacle is if you get stuck. Someone was telling me lately about the bad luck he was having finding competent office staff. What he didn't know—and no one had told him—is that he wasn't paying enough to attract good applicants. He was *stuck at the awareness stage:* he didn't know what was causing his problem. Then he asked the right questions and discovered the answer.

An executive in a small company struggled with her perfectionism. In trying to find something one day, she stumbled across a supply cupboard in the office that was a mess. She set about organizing things— and promptly spent two hours (right in the middle of a busy day) at this self-appointed housekeeping task. When we explored other ways she could have handled this messy closet, she couldn't come up with anything at first. To her there was only one way to do this job: "The *right* way. The *perfect* way. My way!" She was *stuck at the stage of choice*. We discussed this further and she soon discovered several ways to deal with a cupboard in chaos: delegate it, ignore it, do it perfectly, do it serviceably (like "close enough for folk-singing") and in the latter categories, do it now, do it later or do it in stages. Suddenly she saw lots of alternatives.

A consultant was working in two different offices. One of them was off the beaten path between his home and the other office, and it was costing him a lot of time (and money) to keep servicing this client. He knew he could drop this account, but he balked at doing so, even though it made perfect sense to him. "How would they feel?"; "I'd be betraying them,"; "The guilt would be too much." He was *stuck at the permission stage.* We then went back to his list of options. Could he do their work but at his home? Could he have work sent by courier and only go in occasionally? Could he do their work on site but in blocks of time, every few months? The struggle continued because he wouldn't bite the bullet and tell them he was withdrawing his service, nor would he implement any other option. He ended up taking an altogether different job, partly so he wouldn't have to confront this situation.

The Power of Commitment

Whichever formulas for change you use as a guide, there is one more ingredient that is vital to the change process: *commitment.* Commitment means a promise or pledge to do something. Here the person to whom you are making the promise is usually yourself. And promises you make to yourself can be the most compelling of all. Commitment is often the difference between forging on and giving up when the going gets tough. It provides the strength, conviction, persistence and determination to carry you over the rough spots. So many people start things—an exercise program, a weight-loss plan, a basement renovation—but never finish. They don't follow through. Commitment is the beacon that keeps you on course when change is difficult and draining. You don't need it when things are going smoothly. It's when you're stuck and discouraged and want to quit that you need commitment most.

When you plan a change in your life that looks daunting, make yourself a sacred promise that you will finish what you set out to do. But don't make frivolous promises or commitments that you don't fully intend to keep. Such pledges, when not kept, undermine you and program you for giving up. Make commitments with sincerity and conviction—and then see them through.

The best example I ever heard about the power of commitment is the story of John Newton, an eighteenth-century ship's captain who ran slave-carrying boats from Africa to America. One day, his ship was caught in a terrible storm and he feared for his life. He had never been so frightened. In his desperation, he started to pray and made a solemn promise to God that, if he was spared from the storm's devastation, he would give up his work as a slave runner and spend the rest of his life in the service of the Lord. No one knew about this promise but him. The storm lifted and he survived. It would have been very easy for this man to forget about his pledge or renege on it. After all, no one would ever know except him. But he honored the commitment he had made. He eventually gave up slave running and entered the clergy. He spent the rest of his life as a minister and wrote about his transforming experience in a hymn—probably the best known hymn in America: "Amazing Grace." When you make a promise to yourself, keep it. There is great power in commitments that are honored this way.

In summary, there are many different ways to approach change. There is no right formula—all provide a helpful framework depending on the person and the circumstances. Just pick one you like, or combine two or three, and start to make things happen in your life.

Steps/Ingredients in the Process of Change

Start with a desire to change **(Motivation)**.

Decide what you want **(Goal)**.

Devise a plan of action **(Strategy)**.

Develop time frames for your plan **(Schedule)**.

Decide what you'll need to achieve your goal **(Resources)**.

Identify the obstacles that lie in your way **(Barriers)**.

Decide how to overcome those barriers **(Solutions)**.

Create conditions that support the change you are seeking **(Context)**.

Develop a support system—and believe in yourself **(Encouragement)**.

Make a promise to follow through until you succeed **(Commitment)**.

Make a start **(Action)**.

Monitor your progress **(Evaluation)**.

Modify your plan as required **(Adjustment)**.

Persevere when things get difficult **(Persistence)**.

Keep thinking about the end result **(Visualization)**.

Acknowledge your successes **(Celebration)**.

Guidelines

Don't aim for too much at once. Set realistic, reachable goals and schedules.

Start with easier changes. This programs you for success, which builds confidence.

Early change is the hardest because it's new and different. Once you build momentum, it's easier to keep going and feels more comfortable.

Strive for gradual changes (incremental, step-by-step approach), not sudden or radical ones. Pace yourself. This gives you time to adjust to the changes.

Dare to experiment. Try new things.

Dare to risk: the unknown, embarrassment or failure.

Expect and accept setbacks. Some backsliding is inevitable. Be patient. Don't get discouraged.

Change is often like dancing—two steps forward, one step back. That's okay because the overall momentum is forward and that spells progress.

Celebrate your small victories and triumphs with little rewards or self-compliments.

Some changes are real breakthroughs—quantum leaps forward. But most come in small, incremental strides that accumulate over time to produce noticeable results.

Avoid negative self-talk and pessimism ("I'm too old," "It's no use," "I can't").

Anxiety about change is normal and predictable—but shouldn't be allowed to be a barrier.

Never stop trying.

Have fun. Learn to laugh at (and with) yourself. Lighten up. Enjoy yourself.

Post-Game Wrap-Up And Celebration

T HIS BOOK HAS BEEN ABOUT MAKING CHANGES in order to overcome losing games, about where people get stuck and about how to get back on track. We have seen what is possible when you identify problems (Awareness), explore options (Choice) and then take action (Permission).

The idea of change is threatening to many people. Some believe it is impossible or at least very difficult. Yet the world of sports is famous for great recoveries and victories against all odds. These examples provide inspiration for even the most ardent pessimists.

For instance, no baseball team in the twentieth century had ever gone from last place to first place in a single season. Then, in 1991, both the Minnesota Twins and the Atlanta Braves did it in the same year.

Life is full of these stories, too. Who gave freshman junior Senator Barack Obama any chance when he threw his hat in the ring of

God grant me the Serenity to accept the things I cannot change, the Courage to change the things I can and the Wisdom to know the difference.

REINHOLD NIEBUHR

the Democratic Party presidential primaries in 2007? How likely was it that three guys from Niagara Falls would become hugely wealthy when they first dreamed up their game of Trivial Pursuit? Breakthroughs and victories are also made by people who are not famous or exceptional. In fact, they are no different from nor more talented than you or me. People who overcame perfectionism, victimness, self-neglect, negative self-talk; who modified Type-A behavior, stood up for themselves or solved difficult problems; who let go of stressful thoughts, improved their self-esteem and took control of their lives. They showed that ordinary individuals are capable of extraordinary things when they set their minds to it.

Even far-reaching situational changes are possible. Never before have people been so free to change their life circumstances when things aren't working out. Leaving abusive relationships was not much of an option until the last forty to fifty years. Now separation and divorce are common. Changing jobs was once a difficult and risky thing to do. Nowadays, people don't leave just dead-end or stressful jobs, they even switch for variety or a change of pace. In fact, changing *careers* has become acceptable and job retraining is commonplace. Not many decades ago, folks usually grew up and died in the same town, never leaving except for holidays. Now our society is so mobile that people move to new towns like they change cars. However, it's not necessary to make such sweeping changes to improve the quality of your life.

Whether changes are small or all-encompassing, in the final analysis *change is about choices*—and when you make choices that support and serve you well, life is easier, more enjoyable and more fulfilling. Instead of being frightening, change can actually be liberating.

Can people really change? Absolutely! The world is full of rehabilitated alcoholics and drug users, reformed smokers, soldiers who became pacifists, couch potatoes who are now fit, modified Type As, Workaholics who got off the fast track, passive people who learned to be assertive, selfish people who now nurture others, shy people who became more outgoing and self-neglecting folks who now make time for themselves. I have worked with patients who modified all kinds of behavior. Many made profound breakthroughs and some even transformed themselves. It's a myth that only special or gifted people can change. We all have resources within ourselves that we can tap into.

Always Change a Losing Game isn't the answer to all life's difficulties. Some issues are complex or deep-rooted and require a different approach. But for the majority of problems, big and small, it's an effective philosophy and works well. I urge you to start taking inventory. Identify areas in your life that aren't working as well as you'd like. Then change them. Next identify other issues and chip away at them one at a time. In doing so, you will get better at it and the process will feel more comfortable.

Acknowledging Progress

One of the great rewards of my work with patients is to see people take ideas and suggestions from our visits and use them in their daily lives.

At the start of each session I usually ask my patients how they are and what's new. I'm especially interested in reports of progress. What ideas did they follow through on and what benefits did they derive? Often the changes are small, such as eating regular meals or going to bed earlier. Frequently they're larger in scope: resolving a problem at work, speaking up assertively at school, finishing a task that had been put off for months. And sometimes the changes are real breakthroughs—doing something significantly different for the first time. For example, a patient who had trouble holding his temper proudly related an incident that happened with a quarrelsome neighbor. "It's the first time I ever kept my wits about me and thought before I reacted instead of exploding. I thought, 'This isn't going to be worth it'—so I said to her: 'I have no time for you' and walked away."

On rare occasions the changes are nothing short of monumental, like the woman who overcame her fear of heights and walked along a catwalk in an enormous factory. "I had to go to the bathroom and I didn't want to walk all the way around to the stairs. I had always said I was afraid of heights so I never tried it." After that experience, she drove through some high mountain roads that she'd always avoided before. "I was very scared but I did it. It was great." She was exhilarated just telling me. In the same visit she told me about another breakthrough. She bought a house in a new subdivision and asserted herself with the builders who were planning to paint her doors a color she disliked. "I insisted that they not be that color and I won. The other neighbors objected but took no for an answer. I didn't!" This was amazingly forthright behavior for this woman who had always been very timid and submissive.

Another patient made a remarkable breakthrough. She was an avid jigsaw-puzzle fan. She also did crossword puzzles and word-search games. Unfortunately, she was more than an enthusiast. She spent hours at a time on these activities. Realizing these hobbies were monopolizing her life, she decided to deal with her "addiction." I was astonished when she reported two weeks later that she had overcome her life-long obsessive compulsive behavior and rechanneled her energy into other things. She was thrilled. "I feel fantastic about it. I have control over it. Before *it* controlled *me*. Now I have a *choice*." And the change was lasting.

Yet another woman made a *series* of breakthroughs and they all began with small changes like giving up caffeine, improving her eating
habits and exercising regularly. Then she changed jobs, enrolled in a
night school course and got her finances under control. Once a compulsive house cleaner, she let go of her perfectionism and freed up some
time for leisure that she hadn't had in years. She also started to get out of
the house more. She not only overcame her social reticence, she actually
became outgoing. The next major hurdle was to confront her controlling
husband and demanding children. Through her courage, resilience and
perseverance, she transformed herself from the resigned and unhappy
person who first walked into my office the previous year. And through
all these breakthroughs her self-esteem soared.

Celebrating Triumphs

I ask patients to tell me about their victories and triumphs, even the little successes. I encourage them to acknowledge these events and even to
celebrate them. The diagram on the next page is one I drew up to help
them do this in a visual way.

Each circle in the pyramid represents a tangible change the person
has made. I ask them to start at the bottom left and write a word or
phrase in each circle whenever they've done something constructive
for the first time. These can include: earlier bedtime, regular exercise,
less alcohol, quit smoking, patience with kids, organized my desk, essay
in on time, spoke up to boss, kept to highway speed limit, afternoon
off to relax, stayed calm during interview, etc. As the circles get filled
with big and small changes (with the important breakthroughs being
highlighted), the picture is one of momentum and taking control. Once
the bottom row is filled, they continue on the left of the second row.
Sometimes they shade the circles in bright colors to make it more vivid.
The visual image is one of building blocks that are, collectively, erecting
an edifice of progress. This simple exercise provides a personal record
that people take pride in.

You might want to do this for yourself on the diagram. Every change,
large or small, is worth noting and enjoying. It can be a minor lifestyle
change like eating less junk food or a major one such as paying off your
credit card debt. Or you can note a behavioral change like this one by
a patient of mine: "I've stopped biting my nails the past week. I know I

**CELEBRATING
YOUR
TRIUMPHS**

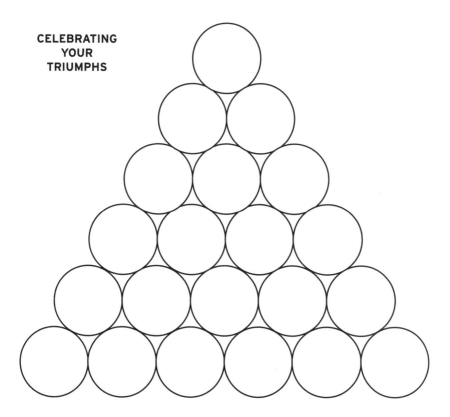

shouldn't—I work with the public. I must have *chosen* to bite my nails before and I've chosen not to bite them the past week. It's so *simple*. Why didn't I see that before?" This moment of victory and insight was summarized as "stopped biting nails." A change in your thinking should certainly be recorded, as with the patient who told me: "I realize I can choose when I want to worry—and I'm doing my worrying at the office, not bringing it home." He summarized it on his chart as "no work worry at home." Situational changes you make should also be noted, such as "moved office" for the man who was commuting two hours a day until he decided to relocate his office ten minutes from home. When it comes to changes:

- make them,
- acknowledge them,
- celebrate them, and
- continue them.

Voices of Success

If change feels intimidating, I suggest people focus not on the change itself but on the payoffs they expect will result. What are the benefits of change? What is possible in your life if you change your losing games into winning ones? Let me share a few quotes from my patients who discovered what can happen:

> "I'm seeing everything differently. Something has changed in me. And I realize it's *better* to think positively—not more right or wrong, just better! I feel high."

> "I'm happier with myself—feeling less push lately to do things . . . I'm going to start satisfying *me*. For the first time in my life I'll be putting *myself* first. I think it's *time!*" (She's sixty-two.)

> "For years I just thought of myself as a hyper person. I didn't *know* there was another way of living my life." (From a reformed Type-A person.)

> "I felt so *good* after I confronted him. I felt *alive* again. I felt so much *better* about myself. I became so aware of how repressed I've been."

This is what is possible in people's lives. It is what's possible in your life. These comments came from ordinary people who were struggling, suffering and didn't know how to get out of their self-defeating patterns. The information in this book made a difference for them. I hope it does the same for you. As another of my patients said: "This isn't food for *thought*—it's food for *action!*"

Index